LOW PROFILE

How to Avoid the Privacy Invaders

William Petrocelli

McGraw-Hill Book Company
New York * St. Louis * San Francisco*
Hamburg * Mexico * Toronto*

St. Philip's College Library

Copyright © 1981 by William R. Petrocelli
All rights reserved. Printed in the United States of America. No part of this publication may be reproduced, stored in a retrieval system, or transmitted, in any form or by any means, electronic, mechanical, photocopying, recording, or otherwise, without the prior written permission of the publisher.

1 2 3 4 5 6 7 8 9 DODO 8 7 6 5 4 3 2 1 0

LIBRARY OF CONGRESS CATALOGING IN PUBLICATION DATA

Petrocelli, William R
Low profile.
1. Privacy, Right of—United States. I. Title.
JC596.2.U5P47   323.44'8'0973   80-17229
ISBN 0-07-049657-9

Book design by Janice Stern

*To Elaine, Marion, Grant, Nicole,
Kathryn, and Michael
for their patience*

CONTENTS

1 *"1984 Is Right on Time"*   1
Privacy, Profiles, and Politics

2 *"Pick Someone You Dislike and Start Investigating"*   19
Banks and Credit Cards

3 *"Looking for Blackberries"*   42
Credit and Investigative Bureaus

4 *"Do you generally or frequently plan a way to kill self?"*   64
Medical and Insurance Records

5 *"Why is this necessary to make beer?"*   89
Jobs, Polygraphs, and Employee Files

6 *"A Bucket of Worms"*   115
Courts, Lawyers, and Private Papers

7 *"One Person's Privacy, Another Person's Cover-Up"*   150
Public Records, Public Figures, and the Press

8 *"The Counterspy Shop"*   172
Bugs, Taps, and Surveillance

9 *"4,015,500,000 Files"*   212
Government Files and Computers

  Postscript   242

  Appendix   244

  Selected Bibliography   246

  Acknowledgments   248

  Index   249

LOW PROFILE

St. Philip's College Library

CHAPTER 1

"1984 Is Right on Time"

PRIVACY, PROFILES, AND POLITICS

Now, let me see if I understand your claim, Mrs. Smith.
1. You are calling from New York City?
   Yes. (27)
2. It's 4:00 P.M. there, isn't it?
   Yes. (21)
3. The man who ran into your car is insured with us?
   Yes. (24)
4. Were you at fault?
   No. (86)
5. Do you live in New York?
   Yes. (22)
6. Were you speeding at the time?
   No. (83)
7. Do you own your car?
   Yes. (25)
8. Are you certain the other driver was at fault?
   Yes. (77)
9. You were driving safely at the time?
   Yes. (79)
10. Have you answered each question truthfully?
    Yes. (85)

Compare the response numbers in critical questions #4, 6, 8, 9, 10 to the other non-critical, non-stress questions. If the score is 30% higher than the norm established by the non-critical questions, deception is indicated.

Instructions for using a
Voice Stress Analyzer

The purpose of a Voice Stress Analyzer is to read the "microtremors" in a subject's voice to learn the truth in his or her mind. But whether it detects the truth, a half-truth, or anything but the truth, it is a privacy-invader of the most serious kind.

It is just one of many. If a telephone call isn't run through the Analyzer immediately, it can be recorded on a secret taping device and run through later—which would also give the company a copy of the conversation to put in its files. A written claim? Let a handwriting expert look at it to determine the writer's veracity. A claim made in person? Why not a closed-circuit-television recording so that both voice and body movements can be analyzed?

The injury claim could be investigated by contacting the Medical Information Bureau and checking its 19 million or so files for any medical information that another insurance company might have developed on the claimant. Or the matter could be turned over to an "investigative bureau," such as Hooper-Holmes or O'Hanlon's, that will contact neighbors, employers, police departments, or anyone else for personal information. It could be turned over to Equifax—the biggest of the investigative bureaus—which might check its own 39 million or so files to find out if it had ever done a prior investigation of the claimant. If Mrs. Smith had ever applied for insurance herself, the odds are pretty good that one or more investigative bureaus could have substantial portions of her medical records in their files or have easy access to them. If there had ever been a background investigation of her for a job, an investigative bureau might still have a complete personal history in its files.

The company could easily contact a credit bureau for a report: TRW Credit Data, for instance, with 70 million files, or Credit Bureau, Inc. (a subsidiary of Equifax) with 100 million files. It really wouldn't make much difference, because the credit bureaus are linked into each other's files. The inquiry could be by phone or in writing, but the more sophisticated method would be a direct tap into the credit bureau's memory banks from a computer terminal in the company's own office. A complete report would show the stores at which the woman shops, principal credit cards, bank loans, former employers, and general bill-paying habits. A follow-up investigation might net certain background information from her former company or a copy of a financial statement from a friendly bank officer.

If the insurance company convinced the district attorney that the claimant might be part of an insurance-fraud ring, law enforcement officials could open up a whole new dimension of investigation tactics. Mrs. Smith's telephone toll-call records, canceled checks, and credit-card vouchers could be examined without a warrant and probably without notice to her. Her name could be run through the files of the semi-private Law Enforcement Intelligence Unit. If the LEIU didn't have anything to offer, the mere fact that an inquiry was made would give them something to report to the next investigator. If a state or federal Medicaid agency thought government health insurance was involved, it could run a computer match, trying to link her name with various other government benefit programs. If the IRS suspected tax evasion, it could issue a summons enabling it to examine her books, records, and accountant's workpapers. If all else failed, the district attorney could have a third-party search warrant issued, which would enable him to poke through the files of her attorney, accountant, doctor, psychiatrist, or anybody else named in the warrant.

Could all this happen in a single case? Probably not. But the bits and pieces that make up this hypothetical investigation are all real enough. For every step forward we have made in recent years toward protecting privacy, we have made several steps backward. Computers and other electronic devices have made the difference. Contemporary privacy-invaders no longer have to follow the rough-edge methods of a J. Edgar Hoover to dig out the personal information they want. Technological advances have made their work easier and their methods more genteel—if no less dangerous.

The public senses that something is wrong. In 1979, the Louis Harris poll* showed that 64 percent of the public had a sense of "real concern" about the loss of privacy. Eighty-one percent thought people are penalized unfairly for things that are kept too long in their records; 72 percent thought major institutions ask for more sensitive information than is necessary; and 76 percent agreed that Americans "begin surrendering their privacy the day they open their first charge account, take out a loan, buy something on the installment plan, or apply for a credit card."

The results, say Lou Harris, are a "warning shot across our national bow" and show a deep public suspicion that something is wrong: 34 percent of the public feels that we are "very close" to George Or-

---

* The poll was commissioned by the Sentry Insurance Company and represents the most ambitious effort to date to sample American public opinion on the question of personal privacy. Columbia law professor Alan F. Westin, an acknowledged expert on privacy matters, assisted the polling organization in developing the questions. The survey sample included a cross-section of 1513 adults and 618 representatives from various leadership groups. The results were published by Sentry Insurance under the title "The Dimensions of Privacy."

well's nightmare vision of the future, while 39 percent agree that we are "somewhat close." In fact, suggests Lou Harris, most Americans seem to feel that "we might arrive in *1984* right on time."

The problem of loss of privacy affects more than just those with skeletons in their closet. In this business, half-truths and misinformation are just as important as the real thing. Insurance reports, investigative reports, credit reports, and the like are often replete with hearsay and innuendos. A neighbor may have stated that an individual beats his wife, a creditor may have reported that he has failed to pay a bill, or a nurse may have written that he exhibited signs of acute depression. These seemingly damaging facts are the types of information that investigators often glean from old files, recall from computer memories, photocopy from other reports, and paste together in a report that may be second- or third-hand information at best. This type of shoddy practice is possible because so much private information about individuals is available from so many sources. Its easy availability almost invites misuse. It is common practice for investigators to use information compiled by others and pass it on without verifying or even identifying its source. The investigator preparing the report may not know—or care—that the neighbor had a grudge, that the creditor had sold the man defective merchandise, or that the nurse had only seen him for a few minutes after surgery.

It is frequently impossible for the truth to catch up with incorrect information in investigative records. In most situations, the process of collecting and passing on information will have begun long before the affected individual becomes aware of it. By the time he or she undertakes to correct the record, it may be extremely difficult to trace the information to its source and prove the initial error. Correcting a record is made doubly difficult by the fact that harmful information tends to metastasize quickly and to find its way into many overlapping investigative files. In such cases the task may be impossible: even the holder of the original record may not know the extent to which the information has been picked up by other investigators. Furthermore, the original recordholder may be under no obligation to provide the individual with the information that it has or to listen to the individual's complaint. Persons in such a situation quickly come face to face with a double irony of investigative files: it is usually much more difficult for them to find out what is in their records than it is for others, and it is much more difficult for them to get corrective information into those records than it was for investigators and institutions to accumulate false information.

Whether information accumulated on an individual is true or untrue, the effects of its disclosure or misuse can sometimes be swift and painful, as when a traveler is left stranded with a credit card that has been revoked because of some adverse information in the company's computer or when a qualified job applicant is turned down without an explanation. Sometimes the effects can be slower but still as harmful, as when an employee is repeatedly passed over for a promotion because of some derogatory information in an investigative file. Sometimes the effects can be acutely embarrassing, as when the results of an employee's physical examination or treatment under a company medical plan are loosely handled around the office and disclosed to fellow employees. Sometimes the effects of such disclosure can become a danger to health, as when a patient undergoing psychiatric treatment finds out that the confidentiality of such treatment has been compromised.

FOR SALE
1979 Cadillac Brougham
Luxury Sedan

Originally built for Shah. Completely equipped with luxury interior plus exclusive electronic security life-saving equipment. Includes:

- bullet-proof exterior,
- explosion-proof construction,
- gun portholes,
- oil slick emission to deter followers,
- built-in tracking transmitters for kidnapping,
- infrared night vision,
- emergency communication system with built-in scrambler,
- recording system,
- electronic bug detection,
- heavy duty air conditioning and emergency oxygen supply,
- emergency disabling gas emission,
- hidden escape vehicle,
- special puncture-proof tires,
- protective air bags,
- microwave transmitter TV scanner with 6-mile range & 350 deg. angle,
- ejection seat.

Original price $325,000. Will consider reasonable offer.

International Herald-Tribune,
October 1, 1979

The car that the Shah no longer needs may be just the thing to protect somebody's privacy. With a television scanner, bug detector, infrared vision, telephone scrambler, and bulletproof and explosionproof construction, the lucky owner would seem to be well prepared to keep the rest of the world out. But how about the person on the outside? He or she can be scanned by television cameras, monitored by infrared rays, and bugged by recording devices—not to mention being done in by guns, oil slicks, and a "disabling gas emission." Like many other things, the Shah's would-be automobile is both a privacy-protector and a privacy-invader. Whether it is friend or foe depends upon which side of the gun porthole you may be sitting.

Modern life is so complicated that it is often difficult to state categorically what is and what is not an invasion of privacy. Sometimes a more fundamental question has to be asked: Whose privacy is being protected at whose expense? Closed-circuit television cameras are routinely installed in apartment-house lobbies and hallways to protect the residents against prowlers and intruders. Fine for the residents' privacy, but how about the sense of being watched that visitors must endure while walking down the corridor? Many people use answering machines or even secret tape-recording devices to record all incoming calls to protect themselves from crank callers, threats, or harassment. This allows them to feel more secure from unwanted intrusions on their privacy, but it has the exact opposite effect on the person on the other end of the telephone line.

All of this suggests a need to view technological and social changes in a new light. A sense of privacy requires a constant concern about the proper balance between the individual and society—a continual reassessment of the superficial benefits and hidden dangers of what appears to be progress. In matters of privacy there are no easy answers, only more complicated threats.

The right of privacy is nowhere mentioned in the Constitution or the Bill of Rights. This might suggest that the drafters of the Constitution considered it unimportant, but the opposite is probably true. For most of American history the right of privacy has been an assumption of political life. The individual's right to be left alone was a background fact, rarely articulated in the eighteenth and nineteenth centuries. The Bill of Rights was drafted in language directed against specific governmental abuses of the period; if privacy was not specifically protected it was because no one perceived it as being in danger.

The Founding Fathers shouldn't be faulted for their neglect. "The authors of the Constitution," says Senator Charles Mathias, Jr., "could not foresee wiretaps, bugging devices, laser beams, computers, and data banks." And to the list of "unforeseeables" could be added electronic funds-transfer systems, credit cards, voiceprints, Social Security numbers, spike mikes, microwaves, computerized mailing lists, fingerprints, infrared cameras, mail covers, television networks, copy machines, electronic tracking devices, and all the other tools and gadgets of modern privacy-invaders. Credit reports were largely unknown in a cash economy, and the drafters of the Bill of Rights had no way of knowing that a small group of companies would one day maintain more than 200 million computerized credit records on American citizens. The fledgling insurance industry of that period was not served by the Medical Information Bureau with an elaborate network of medical files or investigative bureaus with 39 million or more files filled with personal information and gossip. Personality screening, lie detector tests, and background investigations would probably not have been used by the small businesses of that period even if the techniques had been invented. Junk phone calls, harassing phone calls, automated phone calls, and monitored phone calls all required the later invention of Alexander Graham Bell, just as behavioral profiles, psychiatric studies, and the accumulation of psychological data awaited the discoveries of Sigmund Freud. The government had not yet gone into the business of accumulating more than 4 billion files of personal information about citizens through more than 6400 different record systems, nor had it computerized its records to such an extent that new files and personal profiles could be instantly generated through the matching of existing computer tapes. The federal government had not yet created a vast apparatus for information-gathering through the SEC, FTC, ICC, FDA, EEOC, CAB, HEW, HUD, DOD, INS, LEAA—let alone that famous trio of snoopers: the CIA, FBI, and the IRS.

The Bill of Rights is an eighteenth-century document that is faced with twentieth-century problems. The Fourth Amendment prevents the government from taking your financial records out of your desk drawer without a search warrant. But it does not prevent the government from drafting a law requiring banks to make photocopies of checks, which the government can then seize without a warrant. Similarly, although the government cannot compel you to testify against yourself under the Fifth Amendment, it can require you to keep detailed tax records and make them available to the government to be used against you. The government cannot enter your home to listen to your private conversations without a warrant. But can it attach a microphone to the outside of your dwelling? tap the phone line outside your dwelling? record the conversation on a directional microphone in a building across the street? Can the government attach an electronic beeper to your briefcase or handbag and keep track of your whereabouts? In some of these situations the provisions of the Bill of Rights have been extended to cover the new problems engendered by twentieth-century technology. In other cases the old garment simply cannot be stretched to fit.

We are rapidly entering the age of no privacy, where everyone is open to surveillance at all times. . . . Secret observation booths in government offices and closed television circuits in industry, extending even to rest rooms, are common. . . . Personality tests seek to ferret out a man's innermost thoughts. . . . Federal agents are often "wired" so that their conversations are either recorded on their persons or transmitted to tape recorders some blocks away. . . . The dossiers on all citizens mount in number and increase in size. Now they are being put on computers so that by pressing one button all the miserable, the sick, the suspect, the unpopular, the off-beat people of the nation can be instantly identified. . . . Taken individually, each step may be of little consequence. But when viewed as a whole, there begins to emerge a society quite unlike any we have seen—a society in which government may intrude into the secret regions of a man's life at will.

Justice William O Douglas

The right of privacy defies accurate definition. Justice Louis Brandeis, who pretty much coined the term, called it "the right most valued by civilized men." But he could only define it as the right "to be left alone." Brandeis—like everyone since—had to fall back on a gut reaction to the problem: privacy is infringed when society leans too heavily on the individual.

Court cases that have talked about privacy have involved two "strands of analysis." One element of privacy, according to the Supreme Court, is "the interest in independence in making certain kinds of important decisions," while the other one is the "interest in avoiding disclosure of personal matters." The Supreme Court has used the first strand to knock out excessive government regulations that infringe on an individual's independence in matters such as procreation, marriage, contraception, family relationships, child-rearing, and abortion. These family matters fall into a "zone of autonomy"—an area where legislatures must tread lightly, if at all, lest they impinge upon areas of decision-making that are best left to the individual. This doctrine, for example, has been used to strike down laws that banned the sale of birth-control devices or that ordered sterilization of mentally retarded individuals.

As important as this zone of autonomy is, however, it is the other strand of privacy—"avoiding disclosure of personal matters"—that is at the heart of the question. It may be important, for example, that the government not be allowed to regulate the use of contraceptives, but it is even more important that neither the government nor anyone else be allowed to gather information about who uses contraceptives, how often, and with whom, so that it won't even consider interfering with personal autonomy in the first place.

It is at this point that the Supreme Court has been maddeningly vague. Like the Supreme Court justice who can't define pornography but "knows it when he sees it," the Court knows that some methods of gathering personal information are improper but it just hasn't seen any yet. The Court has yet to come up with a decision that says any particular method of delving into "personal matters" goes so far as to be unconstitutional. The boundaries are out there somewhere, but no one knows where they are.

But isn't the excessive accumulation of personal information a sufficient threat to privacy that it should be legally curtailed *before* the information is misused? That was the question facing the Supreme Court in 1977 in the strange case of *Whalen v. Roe*. According to Justice John Paul Stevens, the constitutional issue before the Court was "whether the State of New York may record, in a centralized computer file, the names and addresses of all persons who have obtained, pursuant to a doctor's prescription, certain drugs for which there is both a lawful and an unlawful market." In other words, using a drug such as Methaqualone in New York under a doctor's order will put you in the same data bank as suspected drug dealers and abusers. The Court concluded that such a law was all right—that merely requiring that this information be placed in a computerized data bank did not in and of itself constitute an unconstitutional invasion of privacy.

The strangest feature of the decision, however, was that the justices seemed disturbed with the result. Justice Stevens, who wrote the opinion, voiced this concern—presumably on behalf of his brethren: "We are not unaware of the threat to privacy implicit in the accumulation of vast amounts of personal information in computerized data banks or other massive government files.... [We] do not decide any question which might be presented by the unwarranted disclosure of accumulated private data—whether intentional or unintentional."

Justice William Brennan carried this concern one step further by noting in a concurring opinion that "the central storage and easy accessibility of computerized data vastly increase the potential for abuse of that information, and I am not prepared to say that future developments will not demonstrate the necessity of some curb on such technology."

The Supreme Court recognized grave potential damage inherent in the accumulation of highly sensitive personal information in data banks, but didn't think it could do anything about it. The Court had seemingly worked itself into a corner in which it hadn't the will or the wisdom to prevent the problem from getting worse. Come back, the Supreme Court seemed to be saying, when someone starts abusing the information. Come back, that is, if it isn't too late.

As another dimension to the measure of the concern of Americans for their privacy, the public was asked whether or not the right of privacy should be added to the list of rights of life, liberty and the pursuit of happiness. By a sizable 76% to 17% majority, the American people say that the right to privacy should be added to this list.

The Harris Poll

Whenever someone testifies up on the Hill in favor of a bill making certain personal information private, he runs into someone who claims to have an important need for just that piece of information. It is difficult to argue an abstraction like "privacy" against a law enforcement official who gets up and claims that he used that type of information last year to solve a kidnapping.

A Congressional aide

Privacy is a right without an enemy, but it is also a right without a constituency. Everyone is seemingly in favor of it, but no one has been able to translate that support into effective laws that would protect privacy. Since the Supreme Court has largely removed itself from giving any effective protection to privacy, attention has turned to Congress to provide legislative solutions. But although virtually everyone on Capitol Hill favors privacy in general, the opponents have largely been able to defeat, delay, or dilute any specific legislative efforts.

Opponents of privacy legislation have been able to blunt most efforts at reform for the same reason the gun lobby has defeated handgun registration: a whole lot of people favor it a little bit, but a tightly organized minority is opposed to it a lot. Thus, when Senator Birch Bayh and others introduced legislation to control the use of polygraphs and other "lie detectors" in employment, they got some support from the Retail Clerks Union, the ACLU, and others but were met with an avalanche of opposition from convenience stores, pharmacy chains, jewelry stores, shipping firms, and—most of all—the polygraph companies, who felt their very existence threatened. Proposed changes in credit reporting practices have similarly brought out the conglomerates that own credit and investigative bureaus in heavy opposition. Employee privacy measures have been strongly opposed by employer groups, while restrictions on government access to bank records or the use of search warrants has drawn the concentrated opposition of law-enforcement agencies.

It is doubtful whether privacy proponents by themselves can get anything through Congress. Early versions of the Right to Financial Privacy Act of 1978 seemed headed nowhere, but then the banking industry got interested. Banks were chafing under the burden and expense of Treasury Department reporting requirements and were tired of the flack they were catching from depositors when they turned over bank records at the request of federal investigators. Consequently, bankers lent their influence to the passage of a reform bill that seemed doomed until they came to the rescue.

Privacy legislation must be comprehensive if it is going to be effective. But what is good lawmaking may be lousy politics. Since medical records, for example, travel back and forth between hospitals, insurance companies, investigative bureaus, employers, professional review committees, government agencies, and so on, controlling the information at only one point will have no significant effect because it will only leak out somewhere else. Similarly, a restriction on access to bank records by federal agents can be undermined if state or private investigators can get their hands on the same records. Nevertheless, Congress has generally opted for narrow privacy legislation rather than the broader variety. The Carter Administration's proposed bill on medical privacy, for example, would only have affected federally funded hospitals and have no impact on disclosure or redisclosure of medical information in other situations. The Financial Privacy Act only places restrictions (and mild ones at that) on federal agents and does not affect disclosure of bank records to anyone else.

The reason in both cases is political necessity. Proponents of the Financial Privacy Act had to beat back the objections of the U.S. Justice Department. If local district attorneys, police chiefs, credit bureaus, and everyone else had joined in opposition, the defeat of the bill would have been assured. The solution was to lop off a portion of the bill in order to lop off a portion of the opposition. A similar reasoning no doubt lies in back of the Administration's limited medical privacy bill and similar bills in other areas.

The best possible legislation from a privacy standpoint would be a bill that covered all personal information systems. But such a bill would bring out opposition from almost every special interest, and it would likely be dead before it started breathing. Democrat Edward Koch (N.Y.) and Republican Barry Goldwater, Jr. (Calif.) introduced just such a bill in the early 1970s with predictable results. The authors, however, were given a hero's burial on a Privacy Protection Study Commission set up to study the entire problem. The Privacy Commission conducted exhaustive investigations and hearings between 1975 and 1977, and its results were published in 1977 in a 654-page report entitled "Personal Privacy in an Information Society."*

The Privacy Commission not only documented the problem of loss of privacy in fine detail but also issued a long list of recommendations for dealing with the problem. The initial challenge was to the President to propose legislation to implement its recommendations, and this was finally accomplished two years later when the Carter Administration unveiled a legislative package of privacy proposals that it was sending to Congress. Progress has been slow since then. It is not clear when or if any of these proposals will be enacted or if the final product will bear any resemblance to the Commission's recommendations.

In the meantime the Privacy Commission's report sits there as a bit of an embarrassment. Like the reports of other commissions charged with investigating urgent national problems, the report of the Privacy Commission shows how far we need to go and how little we have done to solve the problem. According to the Commission, "By opening more avenues for collecting information ... government has enormously

---

* This report and its five appendixes are available from The Superintendent of Documents, U.S. Government Printing Office, Washington, D.C. 20402, and other government bookstores. In addition to the two congressmen, the Commission included University of Illinois Professor David Linowes (chairman); Dr. Willis H. Ware of the Rand Corporation (vice chairman); William O. Bailey, president of Aetna Insurance; William B. Dickinson, retired editor of the Philadelphia *Evening Bulletin;* and Minnesota State Senator Robert J. Tennessen.

broadened its opportunities both to help and to embarrass, harass, and injure the individual." These are "real, not mythical dangers," the Commission suggests: "While our efforts to protect ourselves against them must ultimately be fashioned into law, the choices they require are not mere legal choices; they are social and political value choices of the most basic kind."

Privacy statutes that have been adopted by Congress all seem to have been ground out of the same mill of legislative compromise. They are not bad legislation—just incomplete legislation. With matters of privacy, however, an incomplete effort is sometimes no better than none at all. If wide enough loopholes are left, personal information that should have been protected will leak out and fall into the wrong hands, and the remaining provisions of the statute provide little solace.

The Fair Credit Reporting Act of 1970, the Privacy Act of 1974, the Family Educational Rights and Privacy Act of 1974, the Tax Reform Act of 1976, and the Right of Financial Privacy Act of 1978 give a fair indication how far Congress is prepared to go—or not to go—in protecting privacy. (State legislatures, when they have acted at all, have tended to follow the federal model in enacting privacy legislation.) These Acts, together with the Carter Administration's proposed Privacy of Medical Information Act, contain enough similar elements for a pattern of strengths and weaknesses to be seen.

One of the strengths of federal privacy legislation has been to allow an individual to inspect his or her own records. This does not strictly keep information private; it simply allows a person to find out what everyone else already knows. Nevertheless, it is an important right, and it meshes nicely with efforts that individuals might take on their own to protect their privacy. The Fair Credit Reporting Act (FCRA) gives consumers access to files about them that are maintained by credit or investigative bureaus, while the Family Educational Rights and Privacy Act (FERPA) gives students the same right with respect to school records. The 1974 Privacy Act allows individuals to review certain federal files that contain "personally identified" information about them but draws the line at large categories of "exempt" files. The Administration's proposed Medical Information Act would have given patients a right to see their medical files.

Equally important, each of these statutes allows the individual to challenge the accuracy of anything in such records. If the recordholder refuses to change the record, the individual is allowed to submit his or her own version of the facts and the recordholder must include that statement in the record. Once again, this is not strictly a privacy measure, but it does give the individual some control over the accuracy of what is disclosed.

Federal statutes have been less successful in giving individuals notice about the fate of their records. Both the Financial Privacy Act and the 1976 Tax Reform Act require government agents to give notice to individuals before seizing their bank records or tax records. But this notice requirement breaks down at certain key points, thus allowing, for example, the IRS to issue a "John Doe" summons to make a spot check of all the depositor records at a bank without notice to anyone. The FERPA and the Privacy Act require schools and federal agencies, respectively, to keep a list of disclosures of personal information to others and to provide that list to the affected individual on demand, but the Privacy Act requirement is subject to enough exceptions as to make its value somewhat questionable.

The weaknesses of these federal statutes extend to almost everything else. None of them does anything at all to control either the quantity, quality, or source of personal information that these various recordkeepers can amass about private individuals. The Privacy Act, for example, says that personal information in government files should be "timely" and "accurate," but virtually nothing is done to enforce that requirement. Nor do these statutes effectively control the disclosure or redisclosure of personal information in such files to others. The FCRA allows disclosure of credit and investigative-bureau files to persons having "a legitimate business need," which in practice means almost anyone. The Privacy Act allows disclosures for "routine uses"—which, in effect, has meant "business as usual." The only exemption seems to be the FERPA, which has had a significant effect on the disclosure of educational records.

Federal privacy statutes provide minor relief for a major problem. In situations in which these statutes apply, the individual is generally given some access to his files, occasional notices of disclosure of information, and some chance to correct the record. This is useful for everyday mistakes that might find their way into the records but is practically useless against serious investigations or surveillance. The federal statutory scheme is not strong enough to give anyone the assurance that private information will be protected when that protection is needed the most. The really sensitive and important information can be extracted from these files without leaving a trace and without any interference from federal privacy laws. Nor do any of these statutes come to grips with the problems posed by computers and other elements of modern technology. Rather than design legislation that copes with twentieth-century realities, Congress has reinvented Newtonian physics—something useful for dealing with ordinary-sized objects moving at slow speeds.

In reacting to society's threats, a person's first instinct may be to stand up, fight back, and demand respect for his or her personal privacy. But second thought might suggest that this is self-defeating. Privacy—like virginity—cannot be recovered once it is lost. A public struggle over a question of privacy may ultimately bring vindication, but the price is usually the privacy of the very matter being fought over. There are few things more destructive of personal privacy than a lawsuit or a press conference, and if a person decides to "go public" with a privacy problem, he or she had better be prepared to disclose just what it was in the medical record, credit report, FBI file, bank statement, or employer's files that was so upsetting.

A public struggle makes sense if personal privacy has been compromised to the extent that further disclosures make no difference. But that's not a way to handle everyday privacy problems. What is needed in most cases is a strategy of prevention—a way to seal off private information and stay out of the way of snoopers. It helps to be aware of the many ways that personal, sensitive information can be gotten at by others and the methods available for protecting it. But any strategy must take account of the fact that everyone is vulnerable to a snooper who looks hard enough. Thus, the bottom line of any defense must be to maintain such a low profile that a privacy invader won't think to look in the first place.

The greatest degree of privacy in our society is achieved by the very rich, the very poor, and the very crooked. The very rich who live off of accumulated wealth can avoid many of the intrusions on privacy that others routinely face. If you never have to apply for a job, you won't have to answer questions for a personnel file. If you don't need a professional license, you don't have to provide any data to a regulatory agency. If your credit is good enough and your bank balance high enough, you will never have to tell Mastercard, VISA, or Prudential

Life Insurance anything about your personal finances or your medical history. If you can keep your money in a Swiss bank, you might avoid many of the federal reporting requirements. If you are comfortable enough never to have had a radical idea, the FBI might not even have a file on you.

This happy state of affairs does *not* apply to those who are trying to become rich. Persons in the highest points of business or government are frequently the most exposed and the most vulnerable to society's scrutiny. It is those who have the money already who have the advantage. The efforts of Howard Hughes were perhaps an extreme example, but they point out the power of money to buy privacy. With sufficient wealth a person can employ enough intermediaries to keep the world out.

The very poor achieve a version of privacy in exactly the opposite manner. But only the *very* poor, those who are so low in the economic ladder as to fall off of it completely. These are the rural poor, the illegal aliens, and the drop-outs who are so poor, so frightened, or so strung-out that the system has missed them completely. Persons in these substrata fill out no forms, pay no income tax, acquire no credit, buy no insurance, and—in some cases—leave no trace at all within the system. Into this category one might put the "paranoid-poor"—persons who would rather give birth to a child in a rural, communal kitchen than in a maternity ward in order to avoid birth certificates and all of the records that would presumably follow the child for the rest of his or her life. Persons in these categories achieve privacy, but at the price of anonymity and sometimes grinding poverty.

This is *not* the case for those near the bottom who receive some form of welfare or public assistance. Like those near the top, they suffer frequent invasions of privacy, and these intrusions are usually both thorough and demeaning. The federal government, for example, provides extra funding under the Medicaid Management Information System to states that agree to collect additional information from Medicaid recipients. A welfare recipient must ordinarily submit to a "home visit" as a condition of receiving public aid, which becomes the source of information for everything from the person's homemaking habits to sexual activity.

What the very rich achieve through money and the very poor through anonymity, the very crooked get by the use of caution and terror. Professional criminals avoid any written documents, always call from pay phones, and pay for everything in cash. They build up no dossiers of credit reports, personnel disclosures, or insurance applications that can be used against them. Without documents they can't prove that they own anything, but that doesn't make any difference in the underworld. Professional criminals hold others in line by threats of violence, not threats of lawsuits. The result is a paperless, computerless world that lives by its own rules. FBI agents may compile a fat file from other sources, but the sophisticated criminal doesn't make their job any easier.

Most people in the United States are not rich, poor, or crooked, but the point about such groups is nevertheless significant: invasions of privacy in our society do not hit all groups evenly. Even within the same social class the impact may be different. The employee of a small company probably has a smaller personnel file than his counterpart in a large company, because the large company must rely more on written, standardized information in making employment decisions. The self-employed individual builds up no personnel file at all. Similarly, a person who pays cash or practices faith healing will build up virtually no credit file or medical record. The unlicensed "financial consultant" needn't disclose any of the information that a broker or accountant has to disclose to obtain a license. A politician may have to meet financial disclosure requirements that don't apply to a politician's-best-friend.

Personal privacy is strongly influenced by personal lifestyle, but most people aren't going to change their lifestyles drastically just to achieve privacy. The strategy of "keeping a low profile" simply means reducing the level of exposure or personal information to the lowest degree that one's lifestyle will permit. It is not a matter of total withdrawal or looking out for you-know-who. It is a philosophy of prudence—not selfishness.

Within different lifestyles, there are choices. As an individual moves closer toward the center of prominence at any level of society, the chances of restricting the flow of personal information become less and the options for maintaining personal privacy are fewer. This is an important danger signal for society, because we could be doomed to continual mediocrity in public affairs as potential leaders stay in the background to protect their private lives. Nevertheless, it is a fact of life, and the costs of fame or prominence have to be calculated in terms of loss of privacy.

A low-profile approach to privacy doesn't necessarily involve taking any drastic action. In fact, some seemingly helpful steps may be self-defeating. If, for example, a person pays cash for everything, he or she will leave no trail of checks, credit-card slips, or credit reports. But does that mean that he or she is better protected against privacy invaders? Arguably, not. Most people *do* use checks, credit cards, and charge accounts, and the person who doesn't use them may stand out as different and thus draw the attention of some investigator or snooper. The person with the low profile is probably the person with a modest credit report or bank account that tells nothing of significance.

Personal privacy is, in the final analysis, a personal matter. Individuals can make some use of privacy statutes and other legal developments on their own behalf.* But if past experience is any guide, legislators are not likely to enact the type of laws that will make the critical difference between disclosure and protection of sensitive information. The principal resource will have to be informed individuals making the decisions necessary to protect themselves.

The Harris Poll offered people six choices as to who should have "major responsibility for protecting the privacy of individuals"; the largest group (49 percent) rejected answers such as "the courts" or "the President" or "the Congress." The answer they chose was "the people themselves." It may be, therefore, that we are really getting the kind of protection of personal privacy that we want.

---

* One of the best sources of new developments is the *Privacy Journal,* edited by Robert Ellis Smith (P.O. Box 8844, Washington, D.C. 20003), a monthly publication that covers all aspects of the problem.

CHAPTER 2

"Pick Someone You Dislike and Start Investigating"

BANKS AND CREDIT CARDS

In a sense a person is defined by the checks he writes. By examining them the agents get to know his doctors, lawyers, creditors, political allies, social connections, religious affiliation, educational interests, the papers and magazines he reads and so on ad infinitum.

Justice William O. Douglas

114 PM URGENT 5-11-72
TO ACTING DIRECTOR
ATT DOMESTIC INTELLIGENCE DIVISION

THESE ACCOUNTS ARE MONITORED BY NYO FBI THROUGH MR [name deleted], ASSISTANT VICE PRESIDENT, MORGAN GUARANTEE TRUST COMPANY, MAIN OFFICE FIFTEEN BROAD STREET, NYC. FONDA'S ACCOUNTS ARE MADE AVAILABLE MONTHLY ON CONFIDENTIAL BASIS WITHOUT SUBPOENA TO AGENT OF NYO WHO REVIEWS ACCOUNTS AND SENDS PERTINENT DATA TO LOS ANGELES FOR INCLUSION IN SUBSEQUENT REPORTS.

CHECK #	DATE	PAYEE	AMOUNT
2039	11/27/70	BREMER PHOTO	$837.32
2044	12/9/70	CHELSEA HOTEL	241.57
2048	12/14/70	CAPEZIO	32.71
2047	12/12/70	MAYFAIR MARKET	15.83
2074	12/22/70	CREATIVE PLAYTHINGS	61.19

Excerpts from FBI memos re the monitoring of Jane Fonda's bank account

The FBI probably hoped to find a personal check from Jane Fonda to Ho Chi Minh; what it got was checks for groceries, clothes, and toys. The FBI was, however, successful in learning the names of groups to which she had contributed, and that information opened up opportunities for investigations and harassment of those other groups and individuals. The Fonda case illustrates as well as any the critical importance of bank records in maintaining personal privacy and the tactics investigators have used to get them. The Fonda case was hardly an isolated instance, since many other government agencies have regularly monitored bank accounts as part of their investigative process. According to James Merritt, attorney for Crocker National Bank, his client has averaged more than 2000 such investigations of customer accounts per year. He estimated that larger banks, such as the Bank of America, have had as many as 5000 or 6000 investigations per year of customer accounts from the IRS alone.

In many cases—like that of Jane Fonda—the reason for such investigation may be hard to pin down. In an FBI memo of February 6, 1972, a woman official (whose name was subsequently deleted) stated her conclusion about the reasons for the Fonda investigation: "The basis for investigation appears to be pick someone you dislike and start investigating."

If you want to investigate someone you dislike, banks are probably a good place to start. Banks have become a major storehouse of information about individuals. Bankers have become lenders, creditors, retailers, check guarantors, credit investigators, trust administrators, record-keepers, bill collectors, tax collectors, and personal advisors. Bank-affiliated credit-card companies have gone heavily into consumer credit. By the end of 1976, VISA and Mastercard had 74.6 million cardholders.

As banking has become more complicated and diverse, record-keeping has become more extensive. Before a bank will issue a loan it will usually require a complete financial statement, including the customer's income, assets, debts, and financial prospects. Additionally, however, most banks will obtain a report on the customer from a credit bureau—often through a direct computer link between the bank and the bureau. But with the addition of check guarantees, overdraft protection, and similar features to checking accounts, some banks are treating checking accounts as if they were loan applications and ordering credit-bureau reports in order to protect themselves against high overdrafts. The checking accounts themselves are a prime source of information to investigators since banks are required by law to maintain copies of all checks drawn or deposited in the account. Thus, a simple checking account may generate both a credit-bureau report on the customer and an ongoing record of all transactions run through the account.

Bank-affiliated credit cards such as VISA or Mastercard are normally issued after a loan application and financial statement are submitted by the customer and after the bank receives a favorable report from a credit bureau. The credit-card records may be maintained in the same files or computers as the customer's checking-account records. The two records together—bank cards and checking accounts—are likely to tell an investigator everything he wants to know.

Other bank functions inevitably involve information-gathering. Banks administer estates and trusts and are expected to gather complete information about the financial needs of the beneficiaries. In the case of a deceased customer, a bank representative is often present at the initial opening of the decedent's safe-deposit box. Banks and other financial institutions act as the collecting agent or paying agent for trust deeds, promissory notes, and the like for their customers. They will arrange for automatic forwarding and deposit of checks, such as Social Security checks, in the customer's account. Likewise, a bank may arrange for automatic withdrawals from a customer's account to pay certain designated creditors. Banks sell cashier's checks, certified checks, and money orders and they convert checks and drafts into cash. Each of these transactions is likely to be cross-indexed with the customer's account so that a record of each transaction is kept. If the customer has employees for any purpose, the bank will serve as tax collector for deposits to cover withholding taxes and Social Security payments. There is no question about the large accumulation of personal information by banks and other financial institutions. The important question is: What do they do with it?

Most bankers insist that they do not give out information about their customers unless they are forced to divulge it. But this doesn't square with practices in the financial business. According to a study conducted by University of Illinois Professor David Linowes, former chairman of the Privacy Commission, almost all banks give out information to other credit grantors and about three-fourths of them do it without informing the customer.

There is a disparity in attitude within banks and other financial institutions toward disclosure of information based on the function the institution is performing. Most banks will not voluntarily disclose the balance in a customer's savings or checking account, but they will report information about a customer's loan account to credit bureaus and others. When the bank is functioning as issuer of a bank card, such as Mastercard or VISA, the information in the account will normally flow even more freely—often with regularly monthly reports to credit bureaus.

Banks and finance companies are generally much freer with information about their customers in situations in which they consider themselves a creditor rather than a depository of their customer's funds. But with overdraft accounts, check-guarantee accounts, and the like there has been a blurring of the depository and credit functions. The decision of which information to disclose and which to withhold is now more difficult—and perhaps more meaningless. Disclosure of check overdrafts charged to a VISA account, for example, not only reveals information about the use of the VISA card, it also discloses a good deal about the bank balance the customer maintains (or doesn't maintain) in his checking account.

The decision whether to release personal information about a customer is largely discretionary with the bank and its employees. Despite recent federal and state legislation regulating such disclosures, there are still many situations in which the customer's only protection is the custom in the banking industry or the bank employee's sense of discretion. Disclosures by a customer to his banker are not normally privileged communications: a customer cannot prevent a banker from repeating confidential information or testifying against him in court as he might with his lawyer or doctor. This is in spite of the fact that many people turn to their banker first with their financial problems before consulting a lawyer or anyone else. The privacy of financial documents given to a banker is no better protected than information in the banker's memory; they are normally considered the property of the bank and can be copied or disclosed by the bank or grabbed by an investigator with a subpoena.

Can a bank—even with the best of intentions—maintain the confidentiality of a customer's records in the face of a government demand for disclosure? The pressures can be subtle and persistent. The Privacy Commission states that increased computerization of bank records may increase the pressures for disclosure. In the past, the Commission suggests, a banker's reluctance to cooperate with a government demand for information was based partly on an unwillingness to offend a customer and partly on the cost and time involved in assembling the information. In the Commission's words, "There was a satisfying coincidence of high-minded principle and economic interest." But the instant-retrieval capabilities of the computer removes one of the props behind this policy. According to the Privacy Commission, "When it costs the banker little or nothing to disclose detailed record information, when there are no legal barriers to such disclosure, and when the goodwill of those on whom the banker must rely for cooperation or services, such as law enforcement officers, can be increased, the pressures to disclose become enormous and often insurmountable."

How strong can these pressures be? A May 16, 1972, FBI memo that followed the adverse publicity received by Morgan Guaranty Trust over the monitoring of Jane Fonda's bank account shows that a bank representative contacted the FBI and said he thought they should stop furnishing information "for the time being." The FBI operative was sympathetic about the bank's problem and appreciative of the bank's assistance. The bank, for its part, indicated that it had "the highest regard for the FBI or it would not have made the information available in the first place." The FBI memo noted that "possibly in the future we would again be able to resume this relationship relating to the account." To be sure he didn't forget, the FBI agent put it on an "administrative tickler" for ninety days "to ascertain if we can again obtain information relating to the FONDA account."

Government Access to Bank Records

For example, let us say you were interested in the NRA [National Rifle Association] or the ADA [Americans for Democratic Action] membership list. All you would have to do as Secretary of the Treasury is find a member, trace his check for a membership to the organization, follow that to the bank that was depositing the membership checks, and in short order, literally produce with the recall of computers a photostat of every cancelled check of everybody who was sending in the $25 membership subscription. You could build on the possibilities of this sort of thing, and they boggle the mind.

Congressman Fortney H. Stark
(D-Calif.), a former banker

The possibilities do "boggle the mind." But despite the warnings of Congressman Stark and others, Congress has not done much to protect the privacy of checks or other bank records. In fact, Congress became the major source of the problem with its enactment in 1970 of the so-called Bank Secrecy Act. That statute, together with the Supreme Court's decision in *United States v. Miller,* constituted an all-out assault on the confidentiality of bank records. In the *Miller* case the Supreme Court ruled that Mitchell Miller, a suspected bootlegger, had no right of privacy in his bank records and couldn't stop government agents from seizing them. However, the fact that the bank even *had* the harmful records was due to the requirements of the Bank Secrecy Act. Since then, Congress has enacted two statutes (the Tax Reform Act of 1976 and the Right to Financial Privacy Act of 1978) with an eye toward restoring confidentiality in bank records. These two statutes have done some good, but not enough. The shattered pieces of financial privacy have still not been put back together.

The Bank Secrecy Act of 1970 created the potential for abuse by directing the Secretary of the Treasury to issue regulations requiring banks to keep photocopies of checks processed through customer accounts. A House of Representatives report found to its horror that some banks had "abolished or limited the practice of photocopying checks" and had returned to the practice of simply listing the amount of the check on the customer's bank statement without keeping a copy. It concluded that this failure by banks to keep tabs on their customers "has frustrated law enforcement personnel in securing evidence necessary to criminal, tax and regulatory investigation and proceedings." Sensing a failure by private industry, Congress jumped into the breach and made such photocopying mandatory.

Congress did not specify what use could be made of the records that banks were now required to keep. Without waiting for this other shoe to drop, the ACLU and the California Bankers Association—a somewhat unlikely pair—filed suit in 1972 to challenge the statute and the Treasury Department's regulations. They argued that the only purpose of the Bank Secrecy Act was to allow the government to snoop on its citizens and that it was therefore unconstitutional. The Supreme Court rejected their challenge in *California Bankers Association v. Schultz* for, among other things, the lack of a "concrete controversy."

But the matter was concrete enough when it reached the Supreme Court again in 1976 in *U.S. v. Miller*. Two Georgia banks had been served with secret subpoenas, directing them to provide government agents with copies of Mitchell Miller's checks, deposit slips, financial statements, and monthly account statements—all without his knowledge. When Miller tried to prevent the government from using these records against him, the Supreme Court rejected his plea and ruled that bank customers lack a "reasonable expectation of privacy" in their bank records. In the jargon of constitutional law, this meant that a bank customer lacks any protection under the Fourth Amendment to stop the government from seizing the records. The Supreme Court considered—and then ignored—the most significant fact in this whole unpleasant case: that the government had forced the bank and the depositor to create the same records it later set about seizing.

The most important thing about the Bank Secrecy Act is that it has nothing to do with "secrecy." The act sets up broad requirements for photocopying records of banks, credit-card companies, currency exchanges, and the like.

The Treasury Department regulations implementing the act include almost anything that would be of interest to an investigator:

- *each check, clean draft, or money order drawn on the bank*
- *each item . . . comprising a debit to a customer's deposit or share account*
- *each statement, ledger card, or other record on each depositor or share account*

These rules are primarily aimed at checks or drafts written by the customer, but they also extend to items *deposited* in the customer's account:

- *Records prepared or received . . . which would be needed to reconstruct a demand account and to trace a check deposited in such account . . . or to supply a description of a deposited check.*

For bigger transactions the requirements are broader and include bank loans and cash transactions. Financial institutions must photocopy records of each "extension of credit" in excess of $5000 and any "transfer of funds or currency" in excess of $10,000 either from or to a place outside the U.S.

In addition to the photocopying requirements, Treasury Department regulations require the financial institution to *report* certain transactions to the government. This adds a different dimension to the problem, since it removes any possibility that once the records are copied they may somehow remain confidential. Transactions in this category include any transportation in or out of the country of a "monetary instrument" in excess of $5000. In such a case the bank must report the amount of the instrument, the date of receipt, the form of the instrument (e.g., traveler's checks), and the person from whom it was received. Transactions involving the "deposit, withdrawal, or exchange of currency" in excess of $10,000 must also be reported by the bank whether they occur inside or outside the country. In this case the financial institution must include in its report to the government the name, address, business, and Social Security number of each person involved in the transaction.

The bank is given a little leeway, however, since it doesn't have to report immediately "transactions with an established customer maintaining deposit[s] . . . commensurate with the customary conduct of the business, industry or profession of the customer concerned." In other words, it is allowed to hold on to the records of the respectable customers but it should report the scruffy-looking ones immediately.

When the other shoe dropped in *U.S. v. Miller,* it landed on a few toes in Congress. "I don't have to recount for you here," Congressman Fortney H. Stark (D-Calif.) testified to his colleagues, "what a clear and concise and detailed record . . . even the most naive financial person could build on anyone of us here if he could take our cancelled checks . . . and credit card vouchers." Across the aisle, the House Republican Task Force noted that banks have "become the compilers and custodians of financial records which, when improperly used, enable an individual's entire lifestyle to be tracked down." Dissatisfaction with what a prior Congress had wrought in the Bank Secrecy Act led a later Congress to legislate certain changes—first the Tax Reform Act of 1976 and later the Right to Financial Privacy Act of 1978. The purpose of both laws was to restore some semblance of privacy to financial records, but Congress was unable to stuff the genie of disclosure back into the bottle.

What Congress did *not* do was repeal or modify the Bank Secrecy Act. Thus it left intact the requirement that banks copy—and in some cases report—their customers' financial records. This failure lies at the heart of the reform attempts. Congress simply imposed regulations on the manner in which federal agents seize such records. While it put some limits on the secret seizure of bank records, the end result may be to allow the federal government to do openly what it used to do surreptitiously. Moreover, the reform bills passed by Congress did *nothing* to control disclosure to state or private investigators. The records are still there, and they can still be grabbed. The basic problem is with the record-keeping requirement: as long as banks are required to maintain copies of checks and other documents the temptation for misuse may be too great.

The Tax Reform Act shows all of the effects of this compromise. The IRS must now notify the taxpayer within three days after issuing a "summons" to his bank or other record-holder. The taxpayer can stop the immediate turnover of the records to the IRS by giving notice within fourteen days to the bank, but what the taxpayer gets is just temporary relief: the IRS can usually get a court order for immediate possession of the records. There is a further problem: any effort to block IRS access to the records suspends the statute of limitations, thus extending the time during which the IRS can challenge the tax return. There is, moreover, an important type of IRS procedure—a "John Doe summons"—that is not subject to the notice requirement of the Tax Reform Act. This is a device used by the IRS when it suspects a violation but is not sure who the violator is. Under a John Doe summons, for example, the IRS can demand copies of the records of *all* depositors at a particular bank to determine which one might be responsible for a large cash deposit (presumably reflecting unreported income) appearing on the bank's financial statements. While the rules on the issuance of a John Doe summons have been tightened somewhat, the process is still carried on in secret with no notice to the bank customer whose records may be examined.

In 1978 Congress extended similar rules to other federal agencies. The Financial Privacy Act follows the same regulatory path of the Tax Reform Act, and unfortunately it includes many of the same weaknesses. A federal agency seeking to obtain an individual's bank records must now send a notice to the bank customer beforehand, advising the customer that he has the right to go to court and contest the government seizure of his records.*

---

* Congress even prescribed a form for the notice, but it is to hard to tell whether it is more informative than it is intimidating:

> *Records or information concerning your transactions held by the financial institution named in the attached request are being sought by this (agency or department) in accordance with the Right to Financial Privacy Act of 1978 for the following purpose:*

> *If you desire that such records or information not be made available, you must:*

> *1. Fill out the accompanying motion paper and sworn statement or write one of your own, stating that you are the customer whose records are being requested by the Government and either giving the reasons you believe that the records are not relevant to the legitimate law enforcement inquiry stated in this notice or any other legal basis for objecting to the release of the records.*
> *2. File the motion and statement by mailing or delivering them to the clerk of any of the following United States District Courts: _____*
> *3. Serve the Government authority requesting the records by mailing or delivering a copy of your notice and statement to _____*
> *4. Be prepared to come to court and present your position in further detail.*
> *5. You do not need to have a lawyer, although you may wish to employ one to represent you and protect your rights.*

> *If you do not follow the above procedures, upon the expiration of ten days from the date of service or fourteen days from the date of mailing of this notice, the records or information requested therein may be made available. These records may be transferred to other Government authorities for legitimate law enforcement inquiries, in which event you will be notified after the transfer.*

But there are exceptions. The CIA and the Secret Service are exempt from the law, and the Securities and Exchange Commission is exempt for the first two years. Bank records relating to a "government loan, loan guaranty, or loan insurance program" (such as FHA and Veteran's Administration loans) can be obtained by government agents without notice to the customer. Any federal agency can get "emergency access" to bank records if it is to prevent physical injury, property damage, or "flight to avoid prosecution." If the government seizes bank records by use of a search warrant, it need only notify the customer ninety days *after* the seizure. Similarly, even a federal agency that is not empowered to use a search warrant can nevertheless get a court order allowing it to seize the customer's bank records first and give notice later if it can show that advance notice would "seriously jeopardize an investigation." Also, if the investigation is directed at the bank or some other "legal entity" and not the customer himself, no notice has to be given to the customer. (If, of course, something is found while looking through the customer's canceled checks that would redirect the government's interest to the customer, there is nothing to prevent the government from using that information against him or her.) Finally, no notice has to be given to the customer if the federal agency searches a bank's records—in a manner similar to the IRS use of a John Doe summons—for an "ascertainable group of customers associated with a financial transaction or class of financial transactions."

For the most part, customers now get plenty of notice from the government about what's happening to their bank records. In the normal case they will get the previously quoted notice and a copy of the subpoena or request before the government obtains the bank records. Even when the federal agency seizes the records without notice, the law requires that the customer get a later notice explaining why he or she didn't get the earlier notice. If one federal agency transfers the customer's bank records to another agency, there is another notice form that must be sent to the customer.

The problem is not notice but what a customer can do once he or she *gets* the notice. For the most part, customers only have the right to go to court and wave goodbye to their financial records. Bank customers can, for example, only prevent the IRS from seizing their records if they can show that the government is not acting in good faith to determine their civil tax liability. Likewise, the customer can only stop other government agencies by proving that there is no "reasonable belief that the records sought are relevant to [the government] inquiry." These are very difficult things to prove. According to Congressman Stewart B. McKinney (D-Conn.), a critic of some of the important compromises in the Financial Privacy Act, the bank customer is faced with the task of "taking on the whole U.S. Government and that is, quite correctly, one terrific burden."

As long as government agents can show that they are conducting a legitimate investigation of an individual's finances, the source of his income, the things he purchases, the causes to which he contributes, and so on, they will probably be able to show that the bank records are "relevant to that inquiry." The best an individual—or his or her attorney—can hope to do is to slow down the government's inquiry, find out the reasons behind it, and try to get the government to commit itself to the purpose and scope of the investigation.

The principal benefit of these reforms is to deter the type of mindless and arbitrary harassment of dissidents that characterized the last days of J. Edgar Hoover. It is more difficult now for a federal investigator to make a secret inquiry about financial records or to conduct an investigation of an individual's finances without some definite law-enforcement purpose in mind. More difficult—but hardly impossible. In most cases it would take a rather slow-witted investigator not to figure out some seemingly legitimate purpose or some exception in the law if he wanted the records badly enough.

Despite the weaknesses of the federal reforms, individual privacy may be getting a boost from the natural conservatism of bankers. Harold Mortimer of the First National State Bank Corporation in Newark, New Jersey, who has studied the situation closely, claims that many bankers are interpreting the Right to Financial Privacy Act in a way favorable to their customers' privacy. For example, the Right to Financial Privacy Act only requires the federal agency to give notice to the customer, but many banks are also giving notice. Why? Mainly, according to Mortimer, they are afraid that government bureaucrats won't do it right and somehow they—the bankers—will get sued by an irate customer.

Many federal agencies have the authority to seek financial records by a "formal written request." Not surprisingly, some agency personnel who are now making "requests" for such information never realized they had the power to do so until the Right to Financial Privacy

Act was passed. More surprisingly, perhaps, many banks are saying "no" to such requests and forcing the agency to obtain a subpoena. Citibank of New York, for example, has adopted a policy of refusing all government requests. The reason? Mainly a fear by many bankers that government officials may not be using their powers properly and that the bank will likely be sued if it gives up the customer's records before it is legally required to do so.

Perhaps the most salutary development hinted at by industry representatives is the development at many banks of "privacy officers" who are responsible for ruling on all requests for information. If true, this is highly significant because it would affect requests by state and local governments and by private agencies—matters not covered by the federal law. The survey conducted by Professor Linowes suggests that this is not the case. Sixty-one percent of the banks responding to his survey, for example, said that they give out information to nongovernment investigators without a subpoena. But that may not fully reflect a shift in attitude both by bankers and the public that has come in the wake of the Financial Privacy Act. If so, it may help fill the gap until lawmakers catch up with the problem.

Credit Cards

Glen Wood, an executive vice president of SAR Manufacturing Company, checked into the Holiday Inn facility at Phoenix City, Alabama, during the late afternoon of February 1, 1972. When Wood checked in, he tendered payment for his room by using his Gulf Oil Company credit card. An imprint was made of his card and it was returned to him as was the normal practice. . . .

Under the system established by Gulf, Holiday Inns are authorized to contact National Data, which disperses undetailed credit information concerning Gulf credit cards. . . .

Sometime during the early morning of February 2, 1972, Jesse Goynes, the "night auditor" of the Phoenix City Holiday Inn, called National Data in Atlanta on a toll-free number provided by Gulf. . . . He received a communication from National Data advising him:

"Do not honor this sale. Pick up the credit card and send it in for reward."

Wood testified that he was awakened about 5:00 A.M. by Goynes who told Wood that he, Goynes, needed the credit card for the purpose of making another imprint, since the imprint at the time of the registration was indistinct. . . .

After 30 minutes Wood became concerned because his card had not been returned and was fearful that someone had taken it under a scheme to fraudulently secure it. Wood then dressed and went to the front desk of the motel where he was told by Goynes that the card was "seized upon the authority of National Data" and that cash payment was required.... Three days later, while he was relating the incident to a friend, he had a heart attack, precipitated apparently by the stress of the incidents surrounding the revocation of credit.

Wood v. Holiday Inns,
United States Circuit Court

Credit-card records are just as vulnerable as canceled checks and other bank records to copying, disclosure, and misuse. And they have an added hazard that other financial instruments lack: they can be cut off without warning. In Glen Wood's case, even though his account was fully paid up, Gulf Oil decided without notifying him to put his name on the "derog" list because his expenditures did not match the credit profile they had put together from their files.

Credit cards can now be used to buy drugs, pay taxes, buy from street vendors, subscribe to magazines, pay for illegal sex, contribute to causes, pay psychiatrists, retain lawyers—in short, to do almost anything a person can do with cash or checks. While multipurpose bank cards, such as VISA and Mastercard, are the most widespread, other credit cards have attempted to expand their services to become multiline sources of credit. Sears will pay you interest on any credit balance in your account. Exxon and Chevron will sell you glassware, kitchenware, silverware, television sets, clock radios, binoculars, or anything else that can be described in a brochure and stuffed in an envelope with your credit-card bill. Gulf and Mobil will allow you to charge your complete trip along with the gasoline to get you from their stations.

Credit-card records are about as vulnerable as check records to scrutiny by government investigators: they are subject to the photocopying requirements of the Bank Secrecy Act and, conversely, they are protected by the prenotification requirements of the Financial Privacy Act. But the principal difference between checks and credit cards from a privacy perspective is the frequent disclosure of credit-card information to *non*-governmental agencies as credit bureaus, authorization services, other creditors, and the like. Customers may view their credit cards as an alternate to their checkbook for a source of spending money. But to the consumer-credit industry, they are borrowers, not depositors. Consequently they are considered a legitimate source of information to be shared with other creditors.

The sharing of information about credit-card holders begins with the card issuer. Most card issuers will normally share information with a credit bureau about the customer's account. Merchants also accumulate information about card customers and share it with others. Unlike the case with checks, the merchant automatically retains a copy of the credit-card slip and the information on it. The slip may contain the details of the purchase and the phone, address, or identification from the customer. Merchants can—and often do—share this information with credit bureaus, collection agents, and others. There are virtually no restrictions on the use the merchant can make of this information. If the "merchant," for example, is a cult group selling magazine subscriptions, the information it obtains from the charge slip for its mailing list may be more important than the sale itself.

A major informational linkup is provided by credit-card authorization services. National Data, the company that conveyed the pick-up message on Glen Wood's credit card, is one such company. Credit issuers instruct merchants using their system to call for an authorization code approving any sale that is over a predetermined amount. Authorization requests on VISA cards are routed through a sophisticated system known as BASE I. The bank issuing the VISA card can direct that any merchant-authorization calls coming into BASE I be switched to its phones so that its personnel can decide whether to authorize the sale, or the bank can simply provide to BASE I a "negative file" of cardholders who will show up as unauthorized whenever a merchant calls in for approval. As an alternative, according to the senior vice president of the Colorado National Bank, the member bank "can 'interface' or link its own computers with the computer of BASE I" and then "a program based on predetermined criteria, housed in the issuing bank's computer, responds to authorization requests." Mastercard accounts are similarly linked in an Interbank Network for Electronic Transfers (INET), which in turn is administered by an independent company called International Credit System (ICS). ICS administers INET in much the same way as BASE I, providing negative-file information or allowing calls to be switched to issuing banks for approval.

Within the BASE I and INET systems, there is a two-way flow of information. At the same time the merchant is receiving the authorization code to proceed with the sale, the computer is "truncating the information on the current sales draft and recording it for future use." Thus at any given time the computers in the VISA and Mastercard systems can tell the exact status of the customer's account. In order to maintain a complete picture of the cardholder's account at any moment, card issuers have now developed countertop computerized systems that enable the merchant to record all credit-card sales—not just the ones above a minimum amount—so that the centralized computer will have a more current picture of the purchases made by the cardholder.

Information in the BASE I and INET system is of two types. There is a lot of detailed information about an individual's credit-card charges, but that information is theoretically only available to a few people in the issuing bank. There is, however, one bit of information that is available to almost anybody: whether the credit-card user has exceeded his or her credit limits. There are over 16,000 participating banks in the VISA and Mastercard system and more than 2.6 million participating merchants. Virtually any employee of any one of those organizations can find out a cardholder's credit limits by dialing a phone number and asking for authorization of a real or imaginary sale.

The possibilities for disclosure and misuse of credit-card information are greatly multiplied when a credit-card issuer or merchant uses an independent authorization service, such as National Data or Validata. Such independent services are widely used by airlines, hotels, and restaurants either as a supplement to the card issuers' own system or at the card issuer's instructions. Most independent authorization services act on behalf of several credit-card issuers and may also solicit information for their files from bank-card authorization services. Thus the authorization service is likely to have in its file information on *all* of an individual's credit-card accounts, not just the one a merchant may be calling about. The authorization services' rating of the cardholder may be based on information from several sources, and thus any problems or disputes that a cardholder has with one credit-card issuer may cause an authorization service to give out a negative authorization on the use of all other cards. Information in the files of authorization services is also freely exchanged with credit bureaus, which in turn make it available to credit-bureau subscribers for a variety of purposes. The prevalence of authorization services, in fact, completes the patterns of disclosure of credit-card information. It is as easily and casually shared as any other information in the files of a credit bureau.

The use of independent authorization services also leads to instant complications if customers try to correct any inaccurate information in their credit files. Even if they are successful in correcting the information in the card issuer's files, they will normally have no way of knowing if the correction reaches each authorization service that has information about their account. Or, as the Privacy Commission put it, "It is doubtful . . . that many of the cardholders on whom an independent service reports derogatory information . . . know that it exists." But correct information in the authorization service file is crucial, since the authorizor—not the card issuer—gives the merchant the signal whether to accept or reject the card. The wrong information can leave a traveler stranded like Glen Wood in the Holiday Inn in Phoenix City, Alabama.

Electronic Funds Transfer: Instant Banking

Seven commercial banks in Kansas have teamed with the state's largest savings and loan association to share an EFT system that supports point-of-sale banking transactions through a central switching center in Topeka. More than 40,000 banking customers in four cities have access to the network.

Described as the first EFT supermarket service in the Northeast, Stop & Shop Companies, Inc. now offers shoppers at its supermarkets in Watertown and Somerville, MA, a way to transact normal bank business through terminals in those stores.

Maine Midland Bank, with more than 30 offices throughout New York State, will be installing an on-line banking system over the next two years. It includes minicomputers, CRT display terminals and customer-operated automatic teller machines (ATMS). . . .

Frederick W. Miller,
senior editor of Infosystems

Ready or not, the country is jumping quickly into the era of electronic funds transfer systems. With EFTS comes an alphabet soup of initials, such as POS, ATM, ACH, PIN, CPU, and a host of unsolved privacy problems. For bankers, merchants, and others it is the answer to many problems. It represents the "checkless" or even the "cashless" society, and it is clearly the favorite scenario of those institutions that are in a position to shape the future.

In an EFTS system the customer initiates the transaction either through an automatic teller machine (ATM) or through a point-of-sale (POS) computer terminal at a retail outlet. The system may be card-activated, but in either case the customer must supply a personal identification number (PIN) to the computer. The information is fed to a central processing unit (CPU) and from there to a central automated clearing house (ACH), which simultaneously instructs the computer at the customer's bank to deduct the amount of the purchase from his account and the computer at the merchant's bank to add it to the merchant's account. The information transfer is one continuous process, the net result of which is to transfer automatically the funds from the customer's bank account to that of the merchant at the time of the sale.

An EFTS system is considered by bankers to be the logical outgrowth of changes in the industry. Each new banking or credit-card development—such as check guarantee systems, telephone account transfers, INET and BASE I, credit-card authorizations—is merely one step along that path. The latest development, and perhaps the last before a true EFTS system is implemented, is check truncation. In this system the bank holds on to a check it receives and transfers electronically the funds represented by that check to a predetermined list of payee accounts in other banks. This enables the bank customer, for example, to instruct the bank to pay all household bills by giving the bank a prearranged list. Bankers favor this system because it reduces the handling of the more than 27 billion checks the banking system now produces annually. Each check costs about 30 cents to process, and all of these intermediate changes in the banking system are designed to cut down on that cost. A full EFTS, bankers argue, will go further and eliminate entirely the expense and delay of handling paper checks.

Bankers stress the advantages of EFTS to consumers: instant access to cash in savings accounts, no cash or checks that can be stolen, no checking-cashing problems. Bankers do not point out that the customer will lose the "float" or interest that he might presently earn on an overdraft account while waiting for the check to clear the bank. Also gone forever will be the practice of "kiting" checks—regularly engaged in by about 5 percent of the public—in which the customer writes a check before a covering deposit is made in the checking account. Since neither of these "services" is officially offered by banks in the first place, bankers have felt no need to warn the customers about their impending loss.

The banks have not warned about loss of privacy either, a much more serious matter. While canceled checks and credit cards allow an investigator to reconstruct an individual's spending habits, EFTS presents investigative possibilities of an entirely different dimension. An EFTS investigator would not have to rely on anything as clumsy as trying to reconstruct a subject's lifestyle through canceled checks and charge slips. He could (in computer terminology) get "on line" and operate in "real time," getting into the subject's life and following it as it is being lived. A person on a shopping trip will generate an immediate computerized trail of the time, place, and nature of his purchases. An investigator tuned into the EFTS network could follow the person as easily as he could a cat with a bell around its neck.

In its report to the President the National Commission on Electronic Funds Transfer (NCEFT) worried about the amount of information an EFTS system would generate. In this it echoed a worry expressed by the Privacy Commission. According to the NCEFT, an EFTS system "will generate financial records where none existed before" and "may increase the amount of information currently included in transaction records." An EFTS record will not only show the date of the purchase but the time that the computer records it. Thus, even an investigator who is not "on line" (not monitoring the card user as the purchases are being made) could later reconstruct information about the subject's whereabouts at various times during the day.

An EFTS record is also likely to have much more detail about the goods or services that were purchased. Under the present system a store clerk in a hurry is likely to write only "merchandise" or some such designation on the charge slip. But from the merchant's point of view, an EFTS system offers a system of inventory control as well as a method of payment. Information plugged into the computer can be "truncated," with purchase information going to the customer's bank account and inventory information going to the store's own computers. The merchant will want enough information to be fed through the computer to enable him to reorder the merchandise that was sold. There is no guarantee, however, that the two strands of information will not continue to be linked in the computer's memory. The privacy implications of this are sobering. Whereas a present-day investigator can determine that an individual made a $59.99 purchase at a department store on September 12, an EFTS investigator will probably be able to tell you that he purchased black lace lingerie, size 8, at 11:45 A.M.

While proponents claim that the "cashless society" will eliminate some categories of crime, such as armed robbery, critics fear that it will only breed more sophisticated criminals. An individual linked into an EFTS system will be vulnerable to the growing wave of "computer crime." A potential thief can probably penetrate the defenses of an EFTS system as easily as those of any other computer system. The customer is thus faced with the dismal prospect of being one of a growing group of victims of crimes (approximately $27 million worth in the first half of 1973 alone) committed by persons talented enough and unscrupulous enough to gain illegal access to computerized records. Such an individual can simply program the electronic computers necessary to loot the customer's account, either at once or in small nibbles over a period of time.

But the loss of privacy to a computer criminal is an even more serious prospect. Whereas an embezzlement of funds may ultimately be detected, penetration of the computer's defenses merely to gain information about an individual probably never can be. Since an EFTS system is likely to contain important information about an individual, the temptation to tap into the computer to learn that information may be too great for some to resist. Even more frightening is the prospect of a computer criminal *altering* the individual's records. According to computer experts Stephen W. Liebholz and Louis D. Wilson, in an ordinary computer system "files can be removed and changed without leaving a trace. Data can be altered and the tracks covered in milliseconds."

If information in an EFTS system is potentially so sensitive, who can be trusted with it? The Federal Reserve system seems a logical candidate to operate the automated clearing house since it already operates ACH mechanisms for certain commercial transactions. But as operator of the central computer link in the EFTS, the Federal Reserve would have access to all of the information in the system and the restrictions on the Federal Reserve's power to disclose that information are minimal. The only restraint on the ultimate disclosure of such information would appear to be the weak notification requirements of the Right to Financial Privacy Act of 1978. According to the Privacy Commission, the Justice Department has already approached the Federal Reserve and asked it to divulge information about the financial transactions of individuals in systems it is already administering. The Privacy Commission pointed out that the IRS, "with a much more limited information resource," was "abused for harassment and political advantage" and suggested that a worse fate might await information in an EFTS system administered by a government agency. For that reason, the Commission recommended that a government agency *not* be allowed to administer an EFTS system.

The prospects for private administration of an EFTS complex are not much better. It is clear that, unless restricted by effective laws, information in an EFTS will be exploited. Experience with systems presently in use suggest just that. Telecredit, Inc., an independent check guarantee service, obtains current addresses on people who cash checks in a member store and then turns around and sells that information to any other client who wishes to locate the customer. If that information has a commercial worth, it is obvious that the information in an EFTS system would be infinitely more valuable.

Existing laws do little to control the possibility of such disclosure and exploitation. In the Electronic Funds Transfer Act, enacted by Congress in 1978 to regulate EFTS systems, scant attention was paid to financial privacy. The only requirement is that the customer be told "under what circumstances the financial institution will in the ordinary course of business disclose information concerning the customer's account to third persons." The notice is not required to be given when a disclosure is about to occur, but only at the time the EFTS account is opened—when its implications are likely to be lost upon the customer. At best, an EFTS customer gets the type of protection that a checking account or credit-card customer may get—the knowledge that someone will be investigating his account without the ability to do anything to prevent it.

Low-Profile Strategies

In adopting a strategy for financial privacy you must make a basic decision on priorities: are you primarily interested in protecting the privacy of certain expenditures or in trying to block off all information about income, assets, or expenditures? If your main concern is to keep secret a contribution to an activist group, a controversial subscription, an expenditure for drugs, or some other sensitive transaction, the best strategy may be to pay that particular transaction in cash but to pay all other ordinary expenses by check or credit card. This way you appear ordinary because you are using checks and credit cards in the way everyone else does.

On the other hand, if you're trying to block any clear trail of income and expenses, you face a more difficult dilemma. You not only face serious record-keeping and practical problems, but you also run the risk of calling attention to yourself while you are at it. The problem is to find a strategy that does not create more problems than it solves.

Take, for example, the use of odd-colored checks. The firm of Liberty Graphics in North Carolina will sell you bank checks on dark red paper that do not reproduce well when xeroxed. Presumably, this will

BANKS AND CREDIT CARDS

hinder an investigator, who won't be able to read what is on the check. But the effort is counterproductive: the Treasury Department has warned the banks that such checks violate the Bank Secrecy Act, and many banks will not honor them. Worse yet, persons using such checks can easily become the subject of an IRS audit or other government investigation. Far from being part of a low profile, a dark-red check has become more like a bull's-eye at the top of the hill.*

How about using no checks or credit cards? That may work, but the inconvenience may not be worth the trouble. Moreover, it could backfire. An investigator may conclude that the person is trying to hide something and simply redouble his investigative efforts. The strategy of maintaining a low profile seemingly requires that an investigator be tossed a bone of innocuous check or credit-card records. If he is denied that nourishment the first time around, he may come back with a bigger appetite.

The elements of financial privacy are clear even if they are not always easy to apply:

- Cash is the most private form of payment. One can look down one's nose at dope dealers, White House burglars, and the like, but they know enough to use cash when they don't want their dealings to be traced. The main problem is how to raise cash without raising eyebrows. A large withdrawal from a bank account is duly noted in the photocopied records of the bank, as is a check made payable to "Cash." If a customer cashes a third-party check at his own bank, the bank will usually require that his account number be entered on the endorsement. Even if not automatically entered in the account, it still can be later crossreferenced. Moreover, any cash transaction in excess of $5000 must normally be reported to the Treasury Department. Thus, in using cash the best advice is to acquire it in small amounts over a long period of time.
- Checks are more private than credit cards. While records of both types of transactions are photocopied by banks and other card issuers, there is a difference in the distribution of those records. Bank-

---

* Liberty Graphics has countered this setback with another idea: pens with light-green and light-blue ink that won't photocopy. Use of such ink is not as blatant a challenge to the government as use of a special check, but it may not be as effective as its promoters would like. Mark Skousen points out in his *Complete Guide to Financial Privacy* that the endorsement on the reverse side of the check is likely to be written by someone using ordinary ink. Since the Bank Secrecy Act requires *both* sides of the check to be photocopied, the back side of the check will ordinarily give an investigator all the information he wants.

account information can be seized by subpoena or other governmental demand, but banks normally do not give it to private agencies. Credit-card information is treated differently, however, and is often given to credit bureaus and others. Moreover, a credit-card customer has no control over the amount of detail about the transaction entered on the charge slip, whereas a check need only contain a bare minimum of information. EFTS, when it is implemented, should be reserved for nothing more controversial than purchasing a quart of milk.

- There are advantages to multiple accounts in different banks. Interest-bearing checking accounts are reported automatically to the IRS, so a second, non-interest-paying checking account with a modest balance in another bank may be useful. The records of such an account would have to be photocopied under federal law, but the existence of the account would not have to be reported automatically to the government by the bank. An occasional check drawn on such an account can theoretically be traced but only if an investigator knows to look for the account in the first place. A third-party check cashed in the second bank on the strength of the customer's account balance would be doubly removed from anything but the most serious type of investigation because it would not be automatically recorded anywhere.
- Other bank instruments—money orders, cashier's checks, and traveler's checks—are a useful compromise when a cash payment is impractical. These three instruments, unlike certified checks, are not normally issued on your own account number and thus are not automatically a part of your records.
- Cash certain checks rather than depositing them. A check deposited in a bank account will be photocopied as well as checks drawn on the account. If a check is cashed instead of deposited, a greater degree of privacy is achieved. It will appear in the records of the maker's account and in many cases will contain your account number on the endorsement, but it will not automatically show up in a search of your own bank records.
- Avoid multiple financial statements. Financial statements ask detailed information about your assets, income, expenses, and so on and are clearly to be avoided whenever possible. If one must be filled out, it should include as little detail as practicable. Greater difficulties arise when multiple financial statements are filed, because the sum of such information in frequently greater than its parts. One problem is inconsistency: unless you keep—and refer

back to—prior financial statements, you are likely to estimate the same item differently on different statements. This could lead to legal difficulties based on "misrepresentation" of your financial condition. However, even a series of accurate financial statements presents a problem, because it highlights changes in your financial condition. Any unexplained change in your net worth or increase in expenses can lead to further questions by an investigator.

- A corollary is that a loan or line of credit that does not require a financial statement is highly desirable. A lender who does not require a financial statement is a rarity, but the next best thing is one who doesn't require a current one. A borrower may establish a line of credit based on an original financial statement and not have to file a new one for each successive borrowing. Similarly, cash can often be borrowed on a check overdraft account or on a credit card based only on the financial statement filed when the account was originally opened or the card issued. With these latter loans there is also the advantage of being able to borrow the money without telling the lender the purpose of the loan. A line of credit based on only one financial statement avoids the problem of multiple statements and allows time to take its toll in the significance of the financial statement. The older a statement gets, the less it is likely to reveal anything important about the borrower's private activities.
- Protective letters can be important. Financial records can be grabbed by subpoena or by government investigators, no matter how many promises you extract from your banker. Nevertheless, there are gray areas in which financial officers might be persuaded not to disclose information to investigators if there are clear instructions from the customer. A friendly letter, indicating your "understanding" that the information will be kept confidential, should be sent well in advance of any anticipated trouble with a request that the letter be kept in the file. An essential element of any such letter or agreement is that the bank agree to give you notice and obtain your consent before voluntarily giving up your records to anyone.
- Use the few legal rights you have. If you receive a notice of a government subpoena of your records, there is no good reason not to go to court and challenge it. Often the government will not have complied properly with the formal requirements of the subpoena, notice, or the like and will have to start over, giving you a bit of a breather. At the very least, such an effort forces the investigator to disclose why he is investigating you and what he is after.

CHAPTER 3

"Looking for Blackberries"

CREDIT AND INVESTIGATIVE BUREAUS

> ... we know that if... [an investigator] works intelligently and carefully and conscientiously... he is going to develop a rather substantial amount of information that we term as pertinent information, pertinent to the risk.... We have a rather homespun Executive Vice-President who said that if you send a man to a blackberry field every day with a bucket and every day he came back with no blackberries, then you would notice something was wrong.
>
> Chairman of Equifax, Inc.
> in testimony before the Privacy Commission

Congressman George Hansen—who by 1979 had become the gadfly of Tehran—almost never does anything the ordinary way. When he first ran for Congress in Idaho in 1974, he unseated in the primary election a Republican incumbent with the same last name—Orval Hansen. After this happened, Orval and his friends decided it was time to look for a few blackberries.

Orval's friend asked a friend who asked a friend who was a jeweler in Pocatello. The object of all these friendly requests was to get a credit report on George. The jeweler, Melvin Morgan, later said that he thought the report was needed by Orval as part of an investigation conducted by the House of Representatives into George's campaign financing. Melvin might have been a little more astute, however, since he was also State Treasurer of the Democratic Party. The Pocatello Credit Bureau said it didn't know why Melvin requested the credit report, because it never asks questions when one of its subscribers asks for a credit report on anyone. The whole effort was wasted, however, because George and his wife came up clean.

It's not surprising that Orval could get a credit report on George; almost anybody can get one on anybody else. In 1977, the Privacy Commission estimated that there were approximately 2000 credit bureaus in the United States and that the five largest among them had more than 150 million files about individual Americans. In the short time since then that figure should be revised substantially upward. One of the largest credit reporting agencies is Credit Bureau, Inc. (CBI), which is a division of Equifax, Inc. Equifax has close to 100 million files. TRW Credit Data, another of the biggies, has about 70 million files on individuals. Three other large credit bureaus—Chilton Corporation, Trans Union Systems, and Associated Credit Services, Inc.—have huge numbers of files of their own, comparable to Equifax and TRW Credit Data. Moreover, the credit bureaus are becoming increasingly linked among themselves by becoming mutual subscribers of each other's systems. It is a virtual certainty that every person in America who has ever applied for a job, rented an apartment, or bought anything on credit has a file with his name on it in one or more credit bureaus throughout the country.

But calling it a file may not be entirely accurate; more likely than not the person's name and financial information is one of the 20 billion "bytes" of information maintained on TRW's computer or in the memory banks of some other credit bureau's computer. TRW claims that there are about 26,000 companies who subscribe to its services, and the number of companies and agencies with access to the information in other credit bureaus would appear to be comparable. The exchange of information between credit bureau and subscriber is largely computerized; TRW says that about 80 percent of the credit histories it transmits are by teleprinter terminals. With the larger subscribers (called "tape subscribers") information is transmitted directly from the credit bureau into the subscriber's office by computer linkup. The computers talk by telephone, and the human beings don't even have to get involved.

The vice president of TRW's Information Services Division claims that the nationwide hookup of credit-bureau computers is a boon to consumers. You get "instant credit," he contends, because the store can check you out through its computer terminals with a credit data bank anywhere in the country. "You may see a suit in a store where you don't have an account, and take it home with you after you've arranged for credit. The computer has made that possible."

The computer has also made a few other things possible. James

Francis Lewis* applied for a loan with Decatur Federal Savings in Atlanta, Georgia, and an employee of the bank fed the information about Mr. Lewis into a computer terminal in the bank office that linked up directly with the computer in the office of the Credit Bureau of Georgia. According to a federal judge, the Credit Bureau then fed back to the bank the names of several persons who met the "programmed minimum of correspondence" between information in the loan application and information in the computer. From this list of names, the operator in the bank directed the computer to print out a full report of James *Frank* Lewis, despite the difference in the middle name and despite the difference in former residence (San Francisco, California instead of Solano Beach, California). The James Frank Lewis file showed a prior bankruptcy, and the bank turned down the loan to James Francis Lewis because of it.

This suggests that "instant credit" may sometimes produce instant problems. The computers exchanged information at the same time they were turning down the customer's credit. The bank routinely fed all of the information it had on the right James Lewis to the credit bureau computer, which was then free to disclose that information to any of its other subscribers. The credit bureau, in turn, offered to the bank full information on several people in its memory system—none of whom, presumably, had any business with Decatur Federal Savings. The one complete file the bank did receive—that of the wrong James Lewis—was for someone who was not a bank customer.

The real zinger came later: a double check of the wrong James Lewis file at the credit bureau revealed the Social Security number of the right James Lewis! This compounded the confusion and convinced the bank, at least temporarily, that it had the file for the correct person. How did this mistake come about? The judge who eventually heard the case explained how the system was designed to break down: *". . . [the] plaintiff's James Francis Lewis social security number appeared with the bankrupt James Frank [Lewis] file because the computer was programmed to add the information when Decatur Federal's operator accepted the file of James Frank [Lewis] the first time."*

In the name of efficiency, Decatur Federal and the Credit Bureau of Georgia had designed a system that gobbled up personal information

---

* The names have been changed in this instance, as has been done occasionally throughout the book. It would not make much sense to invade a person's privacy in the process of protesting invasions of privacy.

at the first opportunity despite the likelihood of inaccuracy. While the bank was offering the customer's Social Security number for identification purposes, the credit bureau's computer took that opportunity to add the number to the information in the wrong files. The results went beyond simply an invasion of privacy and added to it preprogrammed confusion.

The Privacy Commission has characterized credit bureaus as gatekeepers because they "significantly affect not only credit relationships, but also the relationships an individual has with insurers, employers, landlords, and others who make decisions about him." Credit bureaus are in fact at the center of a hub with avenues stretching in every direction. Credit-bureau clients include collection agencies, insurance companies, mail-order houses, banks, credit-card companies, investigative bureaus, check guarantee services, oil companies, automobile dealers, employers, landlords, department stores, hospitals, grocery stores, real estate agents, public utilities, government agencies, and anyone else with a seemingly legitimate interest in the information. The consumer is not even protected in his privacy by competition between credit bureaus, because they usually subscribe to each other. If a credit bureau receives an inquiry about an individual on whom it has no information, it will often switch the inquiry to another credit bureau. The linkup between bureaus and subscribers is broad and goes well beyond the confines of the consumer-credit industry.

Each of the credit bureau's clients is a potential source of information as well as a recipient. While not all subscribers report to credit bureaus on a regular basis, the ones who do often report every thirty days, giving the customer account number, name, spouse's name, street address, account type, date of last activity in the account, scheduled payment date, date account opened, highest credit accumulated, amount owing, amount past due, any outstanding billing dispute, and the creditor's rating of the account—normally using a scale of 0–9.*

---

* 0   too new to rate; approved but not used
  1   Pays (or paid) within 30 days of billing, pays accounts as agreed
  2   Pays (or paid) in more than 30 days, but not more than 60 days, or not more than one payment past due
  3   Pays (or paid) in more than 60 days, but not more than 90 days or not more than two payments past due
  4   Pays (or paid) in more than 90 days, but not more than 120 days, or not more than three or more payments past due   (*continued on page 46*)

Subscribers who do not report regularly may only report adverse information, such as an unpaid bill, when it occurs. The total of this information is immense. TRW Credit Data, for example, receives about 1.5 billion lines of information each year from its subscribers.

The credit bureaus also obtain information from public-record reporting services, who supply them with information regarding lawsuits, judgments, bankruptcies, arrests, convictions, divorces, probates, real estate sales, motor vehicle accident reports, and anything else that may show up in the public records. Newspaper clipping services will keep the credit bureau supplied with copies of articles pertaining to the individuals in their files. Independent collection agencies provide information on delinquent accounts. And the subjects themselves provide information. Although credit bureaus are required by federal law to disclose certain information in their files to consumers when requested to do so, many credit bureaus have turned the process around. When the consumer comes to their office to look at the file, the credit-bureau personnel use this as an opportunity for finding out more information about him or her.

All of this underscores the seriousness of any disclosure of private or inaccurate information about an individual within the credit-bureau network: what is known to one may instantly become known to all. A potential employer may learn of an individual's unpaid (and perhaps disputed) credit-card bill. A landlord may learn that the individual was turned down for insurance or owes money to a hospital. A bank in New York will learn how regular he was in his payments on a department store bill in Los Angeles, and an auto dealer in Miami may subsequently learn if the customer was ever late on his payments on a bank loan in New York City. The existence of the credit-bureau network makes a problem in one part of an individual's life potentially a problem in all parts. This possibility was not lost on COINTELPRO, the FBI's former counterintelligence program, which planted false information about dissidents with credit bureaus in order to cause problems with their credit and their employment. Within such a well-organized network it is difficult to keep the cancer of false or damaging information from metastasizing.

---

5 Account is at least 120 days overdue but is not yet rated 9
6
7 Making regular payments under Wage Earner Plan or similar arrangement
8 Repossession (Indicate if it is a voluntary return of merchandise by the customer)
9 Bad debt; place for collection; skip
(For some unaccountable reason, this standard system includes no rating of 6.)

There are few rules restricting access to credit reports. The federal Fair Credit Reporting Act of 1970 supposedly limits credit-bureau subscribers to those who have a "legitimate business need" for such information. But credit bureaus can set their own standards for subscribers so long as they appear to be extending credit, providing insurance, or any of a number of seemingly legitimate operations. Individual landlords, merchants, and other small operators can become subscribers to credit-bureau information without too much scrutiny as to why they want access to the personal information in the bureau's files. More importantly, the legitimate nature of any particular inquiry is hardly ever checked out so long as the subscriber appears to be generally involved in some sort of business. The larger tape subscribers are linked to the credit bureau by a computer terminal, and this means that anyone in the subscriber's office can get direct access to the information in the credit bureau's computers without going through credit-bureau personnel. If a bank employee, for example, wants to gain information about someone—whether he is a customer or not—he usually only has to punch a button to get a credit report. His purpose can be business, but it can also be personal or illegal. Little is done to check it. Any control over the dispersal of information by the credit bureaus is largely illusory. Instead of controlling the flow of information, the credit bureaus have, in effect, placed the entire business community on the honor system.

The sophistication of credit-bureau systems has advanced to the point where businesses can know the customer's credit status before they even know the customer. The process is called "prescreening" and, according to Kenneth Larkin, Senior Vice President of Bank of America, it works like this:

> The bank provides the credit-reporting agency with its credit criteria (i.e. annual income, number of open credit accounts, lack of experience with past due accounts).... By agreement, the credit-reporting agency submits to the Bank a list of those individuals who meet the Bank's criteria. The Bank, by letter, invites these persons to become BankAmericard holders by signing and returning the lower portion of the letter.

Prescreening of lists opens up a new line of business (and a new area for potential abuse) for credit bureaus. Instead of limiting inquiries to companies and agencies that have some business connections with the consumer, credit bureaus make the information available to companies with whom the consumer has had no prior dealings and with whom he may not want to do business. It enables mail-order solicitors to gear their advertising campaigns to the weakness or sensitivities of their customers without the customers knowing they are doing so.

Put in its true perspective, a credit bureau is a generalized private information service about individuals with implications far beyond simply consumer credit. It moves information horizontally, enabling companies and agencies to share what they know about an individual, and it moves it backward and forward in time, enabling the salesman of the future to exploit the weaknesses of the past. Credit-bureau files form a private data bank that is tailor-made for the inquisitive—a jumping-off point for any serious investigation of an individual.

Investigative Reports

... proceed from the impersonal to the personal. People do not readily talk to strangers about the personal reputation and morals of their friends and acquaintances. However, after first talking about impersonal areas (identity, employment, and health), they have less hesitancy to cover more personal matters ... a sense of humor [will prove to be] a powerful instrument in the development of a warm, friendly relationship with sources. In fact, some of the most pertinent personal information is sandwiched in between homey remarks and other small talk.

Field Representative Manual,
Equifax, Inc.

The file shows that you [James C. Millstone] are very much disliked by your neighbors ... and were considered to be a "hippy type." The file indicates that you participated in many demonstrations in Washington, D.C. and that you also housed out-of-town demonstrators ... that these demonstrators slept on floors, in the basement, and wherever else there was room on your property. ... You were strongly suspected of being a drug user by neighbors but they could not positively substantiate these suspicions. You are shown to have had shoulder length hair and a beard on one occasion ... there were rumors in the neighborhood that you had been evicted by neighbors from three previous residences.

From the file of James C. Millstone
prepared by O'Hanlon Reports, Inc.

The preinsurance investigation on James C. Millstone was prepared by a commissioned investigator for the handsome salary of $1.85. Investigators for O'Hanlon Reports averaged 140 to 160 reports every two weeks. They spent from ten minutes to one-half hour gathering information for auto insurance reports; real estate or insurance reports took slightly longer. The investigation on Millstone consisted of contacting four of his former neighbors, only one of whom provided any information, and the information that was received turned out to be totally inaccurate. It was only after several long-distance calls that the information in the file was admitted to Millstone himself.

Investigative bureaus, such as Equifax, O'Hanlon's, and Hooper-Holmes, are the snooper arm of the credit-reporting industry. Instead of merely processing information from other sources, they send their own operatives into the field to dig up information. And this is snooping on a grand scale. Equifax, which owns one of the largest credit bureaus, is also the largest of the investigative bureaus. It has approximately 5000 field representatives who produce over 15 million investigative reports each year. The primary work of investigative bureaus is background checks of applicants for insurance. Equifax reportedly conducts over 80 percent of the underwriting investigations for automobile, health, and life insurance companies in the country. But investigative bureaus also conduct pre-employment inquiries, insurance-claim investigations, and similar inquiries.

In addition to the large investigative bureaus, there are smaller, specialized bureaus that gather information for particular types of creditors. The February 1980 issue of the *Privacy Journal* lists a number of these agencies, which may be well known in certain business circles but are almost totally unknown to the persons about whom they are reporting. The Professional Exchange Service Ltd. in California keeps a list of patients who have supposedly not paid their medical bills, while Inn-Guard, Inc. does the same thing for supposedly nonpaying hotel guests. The Industrial Foundation of America purportedly has a million or so files on workers who have been fired or injured on the job. Various organizations in North Carolina, Rhode Island, and California provide a clearing house for landlords with all sorts of detailed information about tenants. Telident in Southern California will tell its doctor-subscribers the names of patients who have filed malpractice claims and "who among your colleagues" has testified on their behalf.

The quality of investigations among the larger investigative bureaus is generally not much better than in the case of James Millstone. The reports of such investigators often raise hearsay to an art form, with statements such as "We are advised there is some question of his drinking and his finances while here," "suspected of being a drug user," and "an odd sort of person." There are reportedly 200,000 or so complaints each year to Equifax alone about the type of reports its company agents produce.

The investigative bureaus urge their agents to go beneath the surface and get down to the hard-core dirt about the subjects being investigated. In its report the Privacy Commission cites this memorandum from Equifax to its employees:

BELIEVE ME IT MAKES THE DIFFERENCE
THIS DOESN'T TELL THE STORY

-"*Insured drinks to excess on weekends.*"
-"*Drinks to excess on special occasions.*"
-"*Drinks to feeling good and drives afterwards.*"
-"*Drinks a few beers daily.*"
-"*Is criticized for being a heavy drinker.*"
-"*Used to drink a lot but quit.*"

WE HAVEN'T DONE THE JOB UNLESS WE'VE
FOUND OUT AND REPORTED

–What he drinks
–How often he drinks—daily, weekly, monthly, 2–3 a year?
–How much he drinks—
  If daily—how many, and where, and when?
  If on weekends—every weekend, or most, or 1–2 a month?
  If to excess—feeling good or loud and boisterous or intoxicated?
  —how often—daily, weekly, monthly,
   1–2 a month, 2–3 a year?
–Where he drinks—home, tavern, lounge, club, parties, on the job?
–When he drinks—evenings, lunch, on the way home from work?
–How long—if he quit, specifically when and why?
–Does he drive afterwards?

The company may want its agents to look for blackberries, but what it often gets from its overworked employees are zingers. A former Equifax employee described this: "*A zing means you do nothing. You do not contact the investigatee. One does not go out on the street . . . he utilizes whatever information was supplied by the insurance company, and hopefully, look up the insured in the phone book to assure that he lives there; then you just fill in the form.*"

Whether an individual is harmed more by the type of intensive investigation the company wants or by the fictitious information that the company often gets is sometimes a matter of chance. There are many reported instances of damaging stories in investigative-bureau reports that were apparently total fiction, like a Boise, Idaho, woman accused of being addicted to narcotics or a mother and daughter in South Dakota accused of prostitution. However, there are frequently instances where investigators have simply made up favorable reports because they haven't had the time to dig out potentially damaging information. The report—fact or fiction—will sit in the company's file and may be used again and again when other inquiries come in about the same individual.

Whether the investigator works the streets or just sits in his office, it is clear that he must come up with his share of "pertinent information." Investigative bureaus expect negative reports in a substantial number of cases—the investigator has to get his quota of blackberries. And the berries that investigators come up with are often of the juiciest kind. Scuttlebutt about possible immorality predominates negative reports in investigative-bureau files. A study in California showed that approximately nine out of ten insurance applications that were declined were done so on "moral grounds." The moral issues cited in the investigative reports, even when true, often had nothing to do with the insurance policy being issued. A man in New Bern, North Carolina, wasn't any greater risk on his auto or home insurance because his eighteen-year-old daughter was supposedly "running around," but it must have seemed that way to the investigative-bureau agent whose report led to cancellation of his insurance.

These types of results are virtually dictated by the economics of the industry. Investigative bureaus are a high-volume business, providing "cheapie" investigations for a client, sometimes as low as $10 or $20 per inquiry. The primary users of investigative bureaus are insurance companies seeking a quick preinsurance evaluation of a customer and, to a lesser extent, employers seeking a cheap background check on a future employee. The industry is labor-intensive, and costs are kept down by keeping that labor at a low rate of pay. The investigative jobs are often filled part-time by students, housewives, off-duty policemen, or retired persons, and they receive only minimal training. Ads for such positions sometimes indicate that the only requirement is a high school diploma and a car. Inspection-bureau investigations differ markedly from the more expensive type of surveillance conducted by experienced private investigators. Unlike the latter, the inspection bureaus provide little hard information for their clients to feed on. What they are selling is the junk food of the investigative business.

Equifax, the largest of the investigative bureaus, is more than just the author of gossipy investigative reports. It is an informational conglomerate that is virtually "information-central" within the United States. The credit-bureau arm of Equifax has close to 100 million files on Americans, while the investigative-bureau branch of the company maintains approximately 39 million files. But that isn't all. Equifax also operates collection agencies to complement its credit-bureau operations. And in addition to its consumer credit bureau, it also runs a commercial credit bureau or reporting service similar to Dun & Bradstreet. Its Dataflow Systems division now contains computerized driving record information on individuals from thirty or forty states. Finally, it has added an important division for processing computerized medical records. Each of these divisions builds up files of private information about individuals on a major scale.

The potential for abuse within such an informational conglomerate is staggering. Investigators conducting pre-employment investigations have every incentive to penetrate a system containing a subject's medical records. Collection agencies can make good use of insurance investigations, medical reports, or anything else to find a subject's weakness. The "prescreening" of a potential customer list by a credit bureau would be infinitely more valuable if it could also include medical, employment, and other personal data. The possibilities of such cross-fertilization of information are limited only by an investigator's ingenuity. Whether or not there is any immediate misuse of such information, the potential danger is there when all of the various strands of personal information have been wound together on one corporate spool.

Informational conglomerates such as Equifax stand outside any legal restrictions. The prospect of centralized data banks within government raised sufficient alarm for Congress to derail most proposals, but data banks within the private sector have gone unchecked. The problem has hardly been recognized within government circles. The Federal Trade Commission has sought to divest Equifax of its credit bureaus in a few localities, but that effort has been based on the anticompetitive effect that such holdings have had on the credit-bureau business within those communities. There has been no legal effort to break up this type of informational conglomerate because of its antiprivacy effects.

Equifax claims that it is able to keep the personal data in its various divisions compartmentalized and secure, but we have to take the company's word for it. The legal restrictions on the use of crossover of such information are inordinately weak. And given the way Equifax has misused personal information within its investigative bureaus, it is hard to be optimistic about the company's long-range ability to resist the temptation of misusing the far greater amount of information now coming under its control. Whatever restraint the company might be inclined to exhibit could be offset by the seductive ease of computer access to such information.

The entry of Equifax into the medical records business is directly related to its ability to provide automatic data processing of such information. The credit-bureau files of Equifax have, of course, long since been computerized. In theory these are separate systems, but keeping these computerized records apart may be a good deal more difficult than putting them together. Unauthorized users with computer skills—both inside and outside of organizations—have shown an amazing ability to penetrate different parts of a computerized system whenever they have had access to one part of that system. This is particularly true when the intruder merely wants to obtain information rather than alter that information, as in an embezzlement of funds. Theft or misuse of information from a computer data base is extremely difficult to detect, let alone prevent.

In an informational conglomerate it is relatively easy, for example, to run a program that reports all of the information out of the different systems relating to one name. The operator could simply run a program that picks up all the insurance, credit, and other information for a given individual. Another possibility is to start with certain characteristics and work backward to come up with a list of individuals: for example, all persons earning $50,000 per year or more who have been treated for alcoholism or all women seeking business loans who have had abortions. The combinations of information are virtually unlimited and can be tailored to the needs of the investigator, huckster, blackmailer, or anyone else with access to the system.

Can this happen? The organizational and technical apparatus for such a private data bank seems to be in place. Congress and other lawmakers have virtually ignored the problem, and nothing has been done to prevent the concentration of several different strands of private information into a few hands. The informational conglomerate sitting on the largest concentration of information has a track record of insensitivity to individual privacy. In short, it can happen. Equifax represents an informational Three-Mile Island—a privacy disaster just waiting to happen.

Misuse of credit-bureau and investigative-bureau files was one of the first privacy problems to come to the attention of lawmakers. As a result, Congress enacted in 1970 the Fair Credit Reporting Act or FCRA to regulate consumer reporting agencies. But it was a modest piece of legislation, and it has had only modest results.

The FCRA contains a prohibition against reporting "obsolete information" that "antedates the report by more than seven years." This prohibition, however, doesn't apply where the consumer is applying for credit or insurance of $50,000 or more or a job with a salary of $20,000 or more. The exception is seemingly as broad as the prohibition, and it means that the consumer reporting agency can keep out-of-date information in its files and report it to certain subscribers and not to others. As a practical matter, however, some credit bureaus have expunged information more than seven years old even though not required to do so.

Congress provided no penalty for mere disclosure of incorrect or obsolete information. A consumer reporting agency need only show that it has established "reasonable procedures" to avoid disclosure of such information, and if it does it can escape liability for any mistakes.

The FCRA defines a special kind of consumer report as an "investigative consumer report." This is a report in which information on a consumer's ". . . character, general reputation, personal characteristics, or mode of living is obtained through personal interviews with neighbors, friends, or associates of the consumer." This applies directly to investigative bureaus. Despite the breadth of the definition, there are few limitations imposed by the FCRA on what investigators can do in compiling such reports. The principal restriction is on using information from an earlier report in a later report. No adverse information in a prior investigative consumer report can be included in a subsequent consumer report unless it has been "verified in the process of making such subsequent consumer report" or unless the information is not more than three months old. There is an exception, however, that allows information that is part of a "public record" to be included without subsequent verification. But there is also an exception to the exception that requires up-to-date confirmation of information in public records on reports that will be used for employment purposes. Finally, there is also an exception to the exception to the exception that allows reporting of information in public records for employment purposes without subsequent verification so long as that fact is reported to the consumer or job applicant. The net effect is to leave open the possibility that the inspection-bureau files will continue to hold and use obsolete information unless the consumer protests loudly enough.

The various provisions of the FCRA are linked together by certain disclosure requirements to the consumer. If an "investigative consumer report" is being prepared, the agency must inform the consumer in writing "not later than three days after the date on which the report was first requested." If the consumer then requests further information, the agency must make "a complete and accurate disclosure of the nature and scope of the investigation." There is, as might be expected, an exception: disclosure is not required if "the report is to be used for employment purposes for which the consumer has not specifically applied." A credit bureau, however, doesn't have to disclose to the consumer that it has a file on him unless the report fits into the "investigative" category.

If the consumer makes a proper request to the credit bureau or investigative bureau, then the bureau must disclose "the nature and substance of all information in its files at the time of the request." The "nature and substance," however, may be a summary rather than the file itself. (The ever-present exception: "medical information" needn't be disclosed.) The agency is also supposed to disclose to the consumer the "sources of the information." But this is hedged with a broad exception, since the agency does not have to disclose the source of the information for an "investigative" report (e.g., which neighbor provided the gossip). The agency is required to disclose the names of any "recipients" of any consumer reports within the last two years "for employment purposes" and within the last six months for any other purpose.

The disclosure requirements under the FCRA are rounded out by certain requirements placed on creditors themselves. Whenever personal "credit or insurance" is denied or "the charge for such credit or insurance is increased" as a result of a report from a consumer reporting agency, the creditor or insurance company must advise the consumer of that fact and supply him or her with the name and address of the consumer reporting agency. Additionally, if credit is denied or the cost increased because of information received from someone *other* than a consumer reporting agency, the creditor must disclose that fact to the consumer and inform the consumer of his or her right to further disclosure of "the nature of the information" that led to the creditor's action.

Finally, the consumer is given an opportunity under the FCRA to exert some control over the information contained in the credit-bureau report. If the consumer disputes the "completeness or accuracy" of the information in the report, the bureau must "reinvestigate" the matter unless it has reasonable grounds to believe that the customer's complaint is "frivolous or irrelevant." More importantly, if the reinvestigation does not resolve the dispute, the consumer is allowed to file a "brief statement" (not more than a hundred words) telling his or her side of the story. In any subsequent report the bureau must include the consumer's statement or a summary of it.

The FCRA was the first significant legislation by Congress dealing with invasions of privacy. Its success says a lot about government efforts to curb abuses in the use of personal information. Its weaknesses say even more. One of these weaknesses is a total exemption for "commercial" credit reports. Despite their size and influence, commercial reporting agencies like Dun & Bradstreet are not covered under the FCRA.

Dun & Bradstreet is the biggest of the commercial credit reporting agencies, but not the only one. Other big firms such as Equifax and TRW are also in this field, and their "commercial" credit reporting is likewise exempt from the FCRA. The distinction between commercial and consumer is highly artificial, however, and many of the 2.9 million firms Dun & Bradstreet reports on are small businesses for which the distinction between personal credit and business credit is practically nonexistent. What is true of credit is true also of privacy. With small businesses, the line between legitimate information about the business and intrusions on the personal privacy of the owner becomes blurred and frequently overstepped.

A Dun & Bradstreet report will often go heavily into the owner's personal background in the "history" section of the report, including "a record of any financial difficulties that may have been experienced in the past." The reputation of Dun & Bradstreet and the methods its investigators use insure that a lot of private information will find its way into D & B reports that might escape ordinary credit or investigative reports. The name Dun & Bradstreet opens up many doors among suppliers, bankers, and others and gives a ready flow of information about the individual and his business.

But the most important source of information is from the small-business owner himself. Dun & Bradstreet investigators are highly aggressive in seeking out information from business owners, and most owners cannot afford to say no. If they do not provide the information requested, that fact can be as harmful to the business as the disclosure of derogatory information. According to the Privacy Commission, ". . . if a company does not cooperate in an investigation, that fact may be reported to its prospective credit grantors. A reported failure to cooperate, or Dun & Bradstreet's inability to produce a report because of a lack of cooperation, can arouse suspicions about a company's credit worthiness, and have a chilling effect on its ability to obtain credit."

The person being investigated has no clear right under federal law to examine a Dun & Bradstreet report or any other type of commercial credit report. If, for example, the person asks a Dun & Bradstreet agent for the source of any derogatory information in the file, he or she is likely to be told that the source of the information is "confidential." The individual in such a situation cannot even fall back on the minimal protection of the Fair Credit Reporting Act.

Credit investigations in commercial cases are not the only ones that slip through the protection of the FCRA. More surprisingly, even blatantly political investigations are often exempted. One case that found its way into federal court involved a lobbyist for the Minnesota Railroads Association who procured a credit report on Betty Henry, an aide to two state legislators. The lobbyist simply wanted the financial report to check up on a legislative adversary, and he made no bones about it. But it was the openly political nature of the investigation that prevented it from falling under the strictures of the Fair Credit Reporting Act. The federal district court concluded in 1976 that the invasion of Betty Henry's privacy was so blatantly improper that it was exempted entirely from the FCRA!

The court reached this astonishing result by reasoning that the report prepared by the credit bureau could not have been a consumer report because the Minnesota Railroads Association wanted it for a political purpose. If the misuse is open enough, the court seemed to say, then the FCRA provides no restrictions. In such a situation, the court concluded: *"Any person with access to a reporting agency account may with any motive request personal and credit information about a private individual, cause an investigation to be made without the subject's knowledge, and act on the information—without giving the subject any of the protections against inaccuracy and misuse that are provided in the Act."*

The judge apologized for the "circularity of this conclusion" and conceded that it was a loophole in the Fair Credit Reporting Act. No such apology came from another federal district court judge in Pittsburgh who ruled in a similar case in 1976 that the Retailers Commercial Credit Agency did not violate the FCRA when it gave the Boron Oil Company a credit report on an attorney, Richard G. Ley, who was simply preparing a lawsuit against the oil company on behalf of a client.

The Betty Henry and Richard Ley cases illustrate a major weakness in the Fair Credit Reporting Act—it apparently regulates the minor abuses and leaves the major abuses untouched. Not every case has reached the same result. In the case of Congressman George Hansen the court concluded that there was a violation of the FCRA when his opponents obtained a credit report about him. This legal confusion corresponds with the reality of the situation. Private investigators smile knowingly if asked whether they have access to credit-bureau information. Few of them can show a "legitimate business purpose" for the information, but they all know how to get it. This is hardly surprising, since this huge data bank of personal information is easily accessible from computer terminals all over the country. An investigator would have to be highly ethical, highly unskilled, or probably both to avoid ending up with a copy of a subject's credit report.

Controlling access to credit-bureau information is a futile effort under existing laws. The same firm or agency can have both legitimate and illegitimate uses for credit information, and no one is in a position to screen out one from another. In the case of Richard G. Ley, the Boron Oil Company already had access to the reports from Retailers Commercial Credit Agency through its credit department. When it ordered a report on attorney Ley, the credit bureau had no way of knowing it was not for a "consumer" purpose. In the Betty Henry case the distribution of credit reports was even more casual and difficult to control: the lobbyist for the Minnesota Railroads Association asked an employee of Burlington Northern Railway, a member of the Railroad Association, to obtain a report for him from the Retail Credit Company. The Burlington Northern employee thought nothing was amiss, because he had routinely supplied Forbes with credit reports for the purpose of investigating claimants with damage claims against the Minnesota Transfer Railway Company and the St. Paul Union Depot Company, two other clients of Forbes. In these types of cozy relationships it is difficult to tell who has a legitimate business need for such information and who doesn't. The one thing that is clear is that most credit bureaus make little effort to find out. In most cases where someone has been caught with credit reports for an illegitimate purpose, the Fair Credit Reporting Act hasn't even supplied a slap on the wrist.

Low-Profile Strategies

Time and again plaintiff came to the defendant's office and went over the same credit information with the defendant's employees, pointing out the errors, all to no purpose....
Like a character in Kafka, he was totally powerless to move or penetrate the implacable presence brooding, like some stone Moloch, within the Castle.

Nitto v. Credit Bureau of Rochester
New York Supreme Court

The important thing is to NEVER *check the files in the presence of the consumer....*
At the time of your appointment, ANY *and* ALL *information you may have relating to the consumer, such as copies of files, copy of your statements, index cards, etc. are to be in your desk drawer,* OUT OF SIGHT, *of the consumer. You are not to show anything, or acknowledge that you have anything, other than the Statement of Disclosure.... The statement is to be read word for word, at your normal reading speed. It is not to be read slowly enough for anyone to copy down word for word, nor is it to be read so fast that the consumer will not understand what you are saying.... The consumer and/or the person with him may not have a copy of the statement, nor may they be allowed to read the statement, or touch it.*

Handbook,
O'Hanlon Reports, Inc.

Encounters with credit bureaus aren't always Kafkaesque; sometimes they are strictly routine—but it is a routine that anyone concerned about privacy needs to get used to. It is almost impossible for an individual to avoid having a credit or investigative bureau report about him filed somewhere. In fact, the person *without* a report is the oddity—someone who is simply inviting the possibility of further investigation. The best way to maintain a low profile is to have a credit- or investigative-bureau record that is innocuous in its content—one that is generally favorable but with few details.

The main defense against misuse of personal information is to find out what everyone else already knows about you. Since credit- and investigative-bureau reports are the starting points for all kinds of other investigations, it is important to monitor the flow of information in those reports and try to control it if at all possible. The Harris Poll shows, however, that only 56 percent of the public has any awareness of a right to see credit-bureau files, and a far smaller percentage ever exercises such right.

Few people are aware of the federal Fair Credit Reporting Act, and probably fewer still are aware of laws in some states that have attempted to expand upon the FCRA's protection. Maine and New York, for example, prohibit "investigative consumer reports" unless the consumer consents in writing or unless it is part of an investigation by the person's present employer. Maine prohibits in some (but not all) instances information regarding "drug or alcoholic addiction" unless provided by a licensed physician.* Arizona requires the agency to supply the consumer with the source of any information in an investigative report. Kentucky prohibits the reporting of criminal charges that have not resulted in a conviction. Oklahoma requires a credit bureau to send a copy of its report to the consumer before sending it to the person requesting the report, while New Hampshire requires that the consumer be given a copy of any investigative report and the sources of information for the report.

The principal tool, however, is the Fair Credit Reporting Act, and it provides the starting point for dealing with credit reporting agencies:

- Credit reports can be checked periodically. The FCRA allows consumers to check the files of a consumer-reporting agency whenever they choose (a small fee may be charged for a spot check, but it is free if the person has been turned down on a credit application). The credit bureaus in any community will usually be listed under Credit Reporting Agencies in the yellow pages of the telephone book. In-

---

* Maine has also attempted to go a good deal further and to make it illegal for an investigative bureau to ask questions about "political beliefs," "personal lifestyle," "philosophy," and the like. Equifax, however, has mounted a furious legal challenge to the enactment, so its effectiveness at present cannot be measured.

spection bureaus are often harder to find and must be looked for by name (Equifax, O'Hanlon's, Hooper-Holmes, American Service Bureau, and so on). Credit bureaus will usually be more responsive to consumer requests, whereas inspection bureaus—if they respond at all—will usually give out information only grudgingly.

- Don't give out more information than you get. Most credit bureaus will require the consumer to fill out a form, ostensibly to verify identity. However, the information requested often goes beyond that. TRW Credit Data, for example, asks for the name of the present employer. The Credit Bureau, Inc. asks for the consumer's driver's license number, military identification number, credit-card numbers, and so on. TRW Credit Data provides the consumer with a form to send back with a space for additional information, while the Credit Bureau, Inc. will usually provide a personal interview in which the consumer's credit status may be discussed.
- Information in a credit-bureau file should be examined carefully. The FCRA technically only requires that the agency provide a summary of the report, so you may have to push harder to see the actual report itself. Occasionally such reports will reveal a wrong birthdate, middle name, address, or Social Security number that presents a potential for confusion. The report will also reveal which creditors report regularly to the credit bureau. Any change in payment habits with these creditors is likely to show up more quickly than any problem with a nonreporting creditor and have a more immediate effect on the consumer's credit status. A credit bureau report may also contain a reference to some other investigative report, which can be followed up.
- Find out who has been given information out of the file. The FCRA requires an agency to provide the names of recipients of any report within the last six months or—if the report was for employment purposes—within the last two years. This provides some information, but probably not as much as the bureau would like you to believe. The agency may not have much control over distribution of its reports if, for example, there is computer access to its files. It is even more difficult to determine what type of secondary distribution (a bank employee passing it on to a friendly private investigator) may have occurred.
- Follow up any notice of an investigative consumer report. The FCRA requires that anyone procuring or preparing an investigative report notify the consumer in writing not later than three days after

the investigation was requested (with the exception of an investigation that is for "employment purposes for which the consumer has not specifically applied"). If the consumer then requests further information in writing, the agency is required to make a disclosure of the nature and scope of the investigation within five days. If the agency properly complies with the FCRA, the consumer can find out quickly who ordered the investigation and for what purpose. You may want to talk to people who are likely to be contacted by the investigator and urge them to be discreet in giving out information. You might consider suggesting names of people for the agency to contact who may give positive information. You should be able to find out if there is any older material in the agency's files that should be corrected before such out-of-date material is included in the new report.

- Demand a reinvestigation of any inaccurate information in the file. Such a demand should be made in certain instances but should be avoided in others. Certainly a reinvestigation should not be demanded where the agency might pick up a bit of harmful but true information in the course of correcting a mistake.
- Demand deletion of obsolete information. The FCRA sets up different restrictions on how far back an agency can go in reporting certain items (such as arrest records for the past seven years, but bankruptcies for the past fourteen), exempts reports for certain purposes (such as life insurance of more than $50,000), and requires reverification of certain public-record information for employment investigations. Push the agency to delete any information more than seven years old and information that has not been rechecked as to accuracy. A determined consumer should be able to convince the agency that this is both cheaper and safer (since you may pounce on them with a lawsuit if they disclose the wrong information to the wrong subscriber).
- File with the agency your own statement regarding any disputed item. You can place in the file a statement up to 100 words giving your own side of the story, but be careful not to give too much. Such a statement becomes part of the record. And if you are not cautious, it can create by disclosure of private information more problems than it solves.
- Insist that corrections be forwarded to subscribers. Any changes made after a reinvestigation or any written statement prepared by you must be forwarded to anyone who previously received a report

from the agency within the last six months (or within the last two years for employment purposes). But you have to demand that it be done. You should also consider sending a copy of any such information yourself to important creditors and the like to be sure they receive it.
- Demand that the credit bureau either disclose all prescreening of mail-order lists or drop your name from such lists. Credit bureaus rarely disclose the names of the many mail-order-solicitation firms to whom they disclose your credit information. But the FCRA technically requires this disclosure in response to a consumer inquiry. According to the *Wall Street Journal,* at least one disgruntled consumer has won a substantial out-of-court settlement on this point, hence credit bureaus may be more vulnerable than they would admit. A good strategy may be to demand that the credit bureau disclose all solicitation firms to which your credit information is disclosed unless it agrees—in writing—to delete your name from such prescreened lists.
- Vary your name or address slightly on each order or subscription (when junk mail arrives with that variation you will at least be able to identify the culprit). In general, the best way to avoid junk-mail solicitation is not to respond to it. Once you buy from a direct-mail solicitor your name is moved to a more active list.
- Preventive steps should be followed. Insurance applications, employment applications, and the like may trigger investigative consumer reports, and you should try to plug any leaks of personal information or to correct any inaccuracies before making the application. Prior credit reports can be corrected, prior employers can be persuaded to delete unfair items from their personnel files, a disputed bill can be paid or negotiated, any blanket authorization for release of medical information can be revoked, or an unfriendly neighbor can be won over as a friend. All of this can be done, but the time to do it is *before* an investigator starts poking around.

CHAPTER 4

"Do you generally or frequently plan a way to kill self?"

MEDICAL AND INSURANCE RECORDS

Take the answer that first occurs to you; if in doubt, answer according to what applies to you most of the time . . .

• I get even with people	yes	no
• I omit important facts when I speak	yes	no
• I am sneaky	yes	no
• I am purposely vague	yes	no
• I threaten people to keep them in line	yes	no

. . . Place your call from a location SECURED from distraction and noise . . . state your name, phone number and full mailing address. . . . The computer will disconnect the line if you get a weak connection or if you speak too softly.

From the brochure of the
Stress Reduction Center

When complete, return this answer form to DIANETICS AND SCIENTOLOGY.

• I am well all of the time	no	yes
• I do not have accidents	no	yes
• I have all the symptoms of arthritis or kidney stones or other "depository illness"	no	yes
• I have never felt pain	no	yes
• Sometimes you have to destroy things when they threaten you	no	yes
• People who over-indulge in sex should be punished	no	yes

from a Scientology brochure

Do you generally or frequently . . .

- *currently use pot, speed, downers, acid, heroin or any similar drug?*
- *feel sad, depressed?*
- *cry without apparent reason?*
- *feel more violent than your friends?*
- *have sexual problems?*
- *plan a way to kill self?*

Enclose the completed questionnaire along with your check to Medical Datamation in the postpaid envelope and mail as soon as possible.

Good luck at college!

From Database Acquisition for Student
Health (DASH) for college preadmission examinations

All kinds of people want medical and psychological information, and not very many of them are your doctor. Employers, colleges, and the military frequently want medical information for entrance physicals and for ongoing health programs. Insurance companies want medical data for health, life, and disability insurance—both for the initial applications and to verify benefit claims. Government administrators in HEW and in various Medicaid and Medicare programs want medical information to verify that doctors' services were actually performed and to prevent fraud. Other government administrators, such as officials of the Occupational Safety and Health Administration (OSHA), want medical information to monitor industrial compliance with a variety of health and safety directives. Still other government administrations want such information to prevent the spread of infectious diseases or to make information available to medical specialists for research purposes. Lawyers want medical and psychological information to prosecute or defend cases. Social workers want it to monitor family problems or child-custody disputes. Hucksters, gurus, and faith healers want it in order to shape their formulas to fit your special needs.

Medical information is not confidential simply because it is medical information. In most states the privacy of private medical data is protected far less than is generally assumed. While virtually every state has a law stating that communications between doctor and patient are "privileged," these laws are riddled with exceptions in which the doctor or therapist can be compelled to testify about a patient or compelled to turn over his or her records. Similarly, individuals are routinely expected to sign a variety of "consent" forms each time they apply for insurance, check into a hospital, or in many other circumstances. Medical information is often routinely released on the basis of such forms.

But even the weak protection accorded to the privacy of medical and psychological information in the hands of doctors and hospitals is far better than what happens to the same information in other situations. Personal information about one's health or psyche that is divulged in an insurance application, on a college questionnaire, in a pre-employment physical, to a psychological testing service, to a quasi-religious group, or in a variety of other situations has no more sanctity or restrictions against disclosure than any other kind of personal information. The organization may keep the information confidential or it may not, but there are usually no legal restrictions that require it to maintain any standards of confidentiality. It is the context in which the information is given, not the seriousness of the information itself, that determines whether the information is privileged or not. A disclosure of medical or psychological information is normally only privileged when it is made to a doctor in the context of seeking medical advice. A disclosure of that same information to almost anyone else puts the confidentiality of that information in jeopardy.

Even within the privileged zone of doctor–patient communications there is an increasing demand for personal information and a corresponding threat to the privacy of that information. The modern-day medical specialist is usually a member of a clinic or a team with staff privileges at one or more hospitals. He or she is likely to have access to a variety of assistance from other physicians, paramedical teams, medical schools, and sophisticated medical equipment. General practitioners used to keep notes only for themselves, but the demands of modern medicine make that practice obsolete. There must be complete notes—a medical record—that can be read by others. The average patient is likely to have more than one doctor, and the same records must be available to each of them. Thus a patient's medical history may be routinely read by other doctors, by nurses, by medical-support personnel in the office, and by specialists and personnel in other offices.

A typical medical record is an overlay of many documents. At the bottom is usually an information sheet about the patient. This may be a simple questionnaire about the patient, his prior illnesses, allergies to medication, and the like, or it may be a full-scale effort to find out every possible relevant fact about the patient. Some doctors obtain so much information about a patient in the initial questionnaire that they feel confident enough to make a computer projection of the patient's future health—and even his lifespan. Another layer of information may be the doctor's handwritten notes. These range from descriptive paragraphs to random drawings or jottings. Frequently these notes will contain a doctor's informal impressions or questions ("Depressed," "Possible OD?") or information that may be only tenuously related to the medical problem ("Might be having financial problems"). If the patient's condition warrants it, the doctor's notes will be organized into a more coherent form and dictated into a memo or report. This typed document is then added to the file along with the doctor's prior notes.

Reports of consulting physicians and laboratory tests will be added to the medical file. These follow no particular form, and each may contain both precise scientific measurements and random impressions of the person preparing the report or the test. The accretion of reports, tests, and so on in the file continues when the patient is referred to another doctor or is hospitalized. Frequently, the whole file will be photocopied and passed on to the next doctor or hospital. At the hospital the record-keeping process increases dramatically. In addition to the physician's and operative reports, there now appear nurses' notes and the bedside chart. These latter are a prime source of subjective impressions along with the medical data.

Team medicine has added greatly to medical record-keeping as contrasted with the methods of sole practitioners, but the advent of the computer to medical diagnosis heralds an even greater quantum leap. Computers are rapidly being deployed by health practitioners to gather up an individual's medical history, to aid in diagnosis, and to link up different case histories for medical research purposes. A computer is frequently used as part of a "multiphasic health testing" program, designed to obtain a complete medical profile on a patient. The overall test generally consists of a blood chemistry and cell-count profile, thyroid function test, urinanalysis, serology test, chest X-ray, electrocardiogram, blood pressure and pulse, spirometry, sensory perception test, glaucoma test, and other standard measurements. The whole package of information is computerized and added to the "basic medical history" that the computer gleans directly from a one-on-one encounter with a patient.

Medical computers often have a bedside manner superior to that of many doctors. The question-and-answer sessions by which the computer digs out the basic medical history is made as painless as possible for the patient. The computer flashes a multiple-choice question on the screen and the patient responds by pushing the appropriate button. Different answers lead to different lines of questioning, as the computer is programmed to follow the patient down all the byways each answer suggests.

In a typical examination the computer may ask questions that are on the periphery of medical necessity but that lie close to the heart of personal privacy. "Have you ever been arrested?" "Have you ever smoked pot?" "What percentage of the time do you use a seat belt when riding in a car?" "How often do you date?" "Do you feel your parents are ruining your life?" "Do you have problems with an erection during sexual relations?" "Have you ever thought about ending your life?"

Doctors and psychiatrists more than anyone else can make a strong case for the necessity of compiling complete information in order to treat their patients. But a dossier is still a dossier. Computerization carries the trend one step further and greatly simplifies the methods by which that information is collected and potentially disclosed.

Good medicine accounts for only some of the growth in medical records. Good business accounts for the rest. Anyone who has been to a doctor's office since the crisis in malpractice insurance has probably seen forms and records that weren't there previously. Doctors are increasingly engaged in what is nicely called "defensive medicine." One weapon in this expensive tug-of-war between doctor and patient is the patient's medical record. It is in the doctor's interest to make that record as complete as possible so that it can later be used as evidence in the doctor's defense. Patients are routinely asked to sign "informed consent" forms for a variety of medical procedures. The principal purpose of such forms is to protect the doctor against later claims that the treatment was unauthorized, but a side effect is to create a record of a medical procedure that might otherwise have gone unnoted. Similarly, many physicians will now routinely order—and record in the medical records—tests and procedures that they might otherwise have skipped so that they will not be laid bare to a charge of malpractice in the failure to diagnose an ailment. The medical malpractice struggle has developed into a paper war, and the patient's medical record is a prime source of ammunition.

If their patients don't come back later to haunt physicians, the government might. In most states there are a variety of circumstances under which a doctor is legally required to record and report certain types of medical condition. The information required for birth and death certificates is an obvious example. Other situations involve gunshot wounds, suspected child abuse, and similar situations in which there may have been a crime. Some courts have created an affirmative duty on the part of a doctor or psychiatrist to warn a potential victim of a patient's violent tendencies. In most states there are a great many categories of infectious diseases in which the doctor is required to make a report to a public agency. In California, for example, a physician must report cases of: *"cholera, plague, yellow fever, malaria, leprosy, diphtheria, scarlet fever, smallpox, typhus, typhoid, paratyphoid, anthrax, glanders menningitis, tuberculosis, pneumonia, dysentery, hookworm, trachoma, dengue, tetanus, measles, German measles, chicken pox, whooping cough, mumps, pellagra, beriberi, Rocky Mountain spotted fever, syphilis, gonococcus, rabies, and poliomyelitis."* California doctors must as well report any disease that might cause a "lapse of consciousness."

The New York State Controlled Substances Act, which was modeled on statutes in California and Illinois, requires a physician to send a copy of the prescription form for certain categories of drug to the state department of public health. The name, address, and age of the patient is maintained in a central computer by the state. This type of program is not done for the patient's benefit but to give the state a ready-made target list in any crackdown on drug abuse. Equally sensitive (but with a more doubtful public purpose behind it) are state statutes like those in Nebraska and Maryland that require doctors to report the names of women receiving abortions and details about the aborted fetus.

But the most important nonmedical reason for doctors to keep more extensive medical records is their need to get paid. Over 190 million Americans are covered by some form of public or private health insurance. In order for a doctor or hospital to be paid they must submit certain basic information to the insuring agency to verify the claim. The information supplied to the insurer usually comes from the patient's medical record and will typically include personal and employment data, financial and employment information, clinical information, description of medical procedures, and so on. Much of this information is routine, but in some cases the requirements imposed by the insurance company will force the doctor to accumulate more information on the patient than he or she might ordinarily collect. The well-documented claim for reimbursement is a claim that will probably be paid by the insurance company with a minimum of argument.

The almost-universal practice of payment of medical claims by some form of insurance has a crucial effect on the disclosure of private information. It is ordinarily the point at which the individual's medical record first leaves the hands of the medical professionals and gets into the files and computers of claims examiners. The importance of health, accident, and other forms of insurance in the erosion of medical privacy is hard to overestimate. There are few restrictions in most states as to the information that an insurance company may demand to verify a claim and few restraints of the further use they can make of that information. Private insurance companies, as a matter of fact, get two bites at the apple: once when an individual applies for insurance and another when he or she submits a claim. In both instances insurance companies can—and often do—require doctors and hospitals to turn over substantial portions of a person's medical record. Disclosure to insurance companies in these situations is not the end of the road. It is sometimes just the first step along a path that ends up with confidential medical information in the hands of employers, bureaucrats, and investigators.

Doctor's Records

Almost anyone can put on a white coat and rifle through the secrets of your illness, be it alcoholism or tuberculosis. As a result, you may—or may not—get that job. You may—or may not—be judged minimally brain damaged for life by a fourth grade teacher. Your health insurance claim may or may not be honored; you may, or may not, get the life insurance you applied for.

Natalie Davis Spingarn, Executive
Director, National Commission on
the Confidentiality of Health Records

Unless there is a feeling between patient and therapist that what he or she reveals is confidential, there is no therapy, period. You can't help an alcoholic

if you first read him [his] Miranda rights and say that "anything you tell me is going to go to your employer."

Dr. Sheila Blume, American Medical
Society on Alcoholism

There is a tension at the heart of medical-privacy questions that is lacking in almost every other aspect of the problem. The patient has a genuine need to be as open and as frank as possible in disclosing personal information to a doctor or therapist. Complete disclosure is usually essential to good medical or psychiatric care. By contrast, when dealing with a bank, an insurance company, or a credit bureau, it is usually in the individual's interest to give out as little personal information as possible. But a person can't follow that same tactic with a doctor without seriously jeopardizing the course of treatment.

This tension is even more severe with medical or psychological problems that carry some sort of social stigma. These types of problems, such as mental illness, alcoholism, and drug abuse, are often the kinds of situation that require a great deal of communication and trust between patient and doctor if the course of treatment is to be successful. But it is precisely in these situations where confidential disclosures are so important that revelations of confidential information can do the greatest harm. "[If] a troubled gall bladder is not a sensitive issue, a troubled mind is," according to Natalie Spingarn of the National Commission on the Confidentiality of Health Records. "The same society which accepts physical illness as natural, stigmatizes mental illness; even one visit to a psychiatrist may pose difficulties for a patient and provide ammunition for those who might wish to harm him."

The same information that a psychiatrist needs to help a patient is the information that an investigator would most like to get his hands on. If the mere fact that a person has sought psychiatric help can be damaging in certain situations, the details of what is revealed to the psychiatrist can be even worse. Unless the utmost confidentiality is maintained, there is the serious danger that patient and doctor may unwittingly be creating a dossier that can do far more harm than the therapy could ever hope to remedy.

In sensitive illnesses—particularly psychiatric matters—the doctor or therapist must guarantee the patient the utmost confidentiality at the outset or the therapy cannot even begin. According to Dr. Maurice Grossman of the American Psychiatric Association, "The fear of disclosure has impeded treatment by the withholding of information." He added in his testimony before Congress: "Healing can come about only by the gradual development of trust in the therapist [allowing disclosure of] the threatening secret material which they had come to believe would destroy them if known."

The doctor or therapist may have to promise confidentiality to begin the treatment, but how well can he or she deliver on that promise? In 1973 a district attorney in California obtained a search warrant that enabled his agents to go through all of the patient files in a Palo Alto psychiatric clinic in search of the postassault psychiatric records of a crime victim. In 1978, the Attorney General of Hawaii obtained an administrative inspection warrant to go through all of the "patient history forms, medical records, reports, diagnoses and orders prescribing treatment" of an Hawaiian psychiatrist on the unsubstantiated possibility of Medicaid fraud. In many cases doctors and psychiatrists have had their records subpoenaed or been forced to testify because their patients supposedly waived the privilege of confidentiality by bringing a lawsuit for mental injuries, suing for divorce on the grounds of mental cruelty, or claiming that they are a fit parent in a child-custody dispute. In other cases, a patient's condition has become worse when the insurance company that paid for the psychiatric care reported the treatment to the patient's employer. The reason? According to one insurance company, "We are obligated to tell the employer because he pays the premium." In some reported cases of insurance-company disclosure, employers have followed up with "security investigations" in which they have asked neighbors of the employee-patient about his psychiatric problems. In other cases the information has been disclosed to other employees, who have taunted the patient. The patient's responses to these and similar disclosures have ranged from cancellation of further treatment to suicide attempts.

Given the extreme need for confidentiality, some psychiatrists have resorted to extreme actions. At least two psychiatrists, George Caesar and Joseph Lifshutz, have spent time in jail rather than divulge information about their clients in response to a subpoena. The argument of the psychiatric professionals has been that they should not be compelled to disclose information given to them in therapy sessions even though the patient may have waived his or her privilege of confidentiality. In many cases, they argue, the patient is too sick to understand the consequences of such a waiver. Mental health professionals have also raised the same argument that reporters have raised in front of grand juries: the mere threat that they might have to testify—whether or not the testimony is damaging to the individual in that particular case—is enough to deter anyone from trusting them with confidential information in the future.

The idea that psychiatrists should have an "absolute" immunity from testifying has gotten nowhere with the courts. In one instance, however, the mental health profession got a sympathetic dissenting opinion from U.S. Secretary of Education, Shirley Hufstedler, who at the time was a federal appeals court judge:

> The psychiatric patient confides [in his therapist] more utterly than anyone else in the world. . . . [He] lays bare his entire self, his dreams, his fantasies, his sin, and his shame. . . . The patient's innermost thoughts may be so frightening, embarrassing, shameful, or morbid that the patient in therapy will struggle to remain sick, rather than to reveal those thoughts even to himself. The possibility that the psychotherapist could be compelled to reveal those communications to anyone . . . can deter persons from seeking needed treatment and destroy treatment in progress.

The health-care record in many ways presents more serious problems than the testimony of the doctor. A doctor's or a psychiatrist's recollections on the witness stand can sometimes be vague—conveniently or not—but his or her notes, charts, and medical records speak for themselves when introduced in evidence. Medical records pose another hazard in that they are often not under the personal control of the person who performed the therapy. The doctor's attitude towards a subpoena or other demand may not count for much if a nurse, receptionist, records clerk, computer operator, or someone else in the health-care bureaucracy makes a quick trip to the Xerox machine without checking the matter with the treating physician.

This is a continual problem for therapists who deal with sensitive problems. They need complete records for themselves and their colleagues, but they want the records to be as skimpy as possible if they get outside the health-care establishment. Medical records will often contain impressions, tentative diagnoses, and all sorts of scribblings that may ultimately have nothing to do with the patient's actual condition. A patient's bedside chart in a hospital, moreover, may contain the same jottings from a variety of doctors and nurses, and in some cases the author of a particularly damaging comment may be unknown. All of this is harmless when kept among health-care professionals who know the value—or lack of value—of such information, but when a medical chart is paraded in front of an insurance investigator, a lawyer, or an employer, a chance comment such as "Suicidal?" or "Apparent drug dependency" can have a highly distorted effect.

Moreover, a good record for psychiatric purposes may nevertheless present a distorted picture of the patient when viewed from a different vantage point. Psychiatric records tend to emphasize the deviant behavior of a patient at the expense of information that may be more typical. Sociologists Kai T. Erickson and Daniel E. Gilbertson point out that in writing a case history about a patient, a psychiatrist is "in some ways inventing a biography that will explain his present circumstance and verify that he is a proper subject for clinical attention." The records of a mental hospital will usually not reveal those occasions when "the patient showed capacity to cope honorably and effectively with difficult life situations," according to researcher Erving Goffman, but rather it will show "the ways in which the patient is 'sick' and the reasons why it was right to commit him." Privacy expert Alan F. Westin summarizes this phenomenon:

> [If] the patient tells a psychiatrist of (a) his bedwetting, (b) his fear of a teacher, (c) of enjoying family picnics, (d) of his impulse to hit his sister with a hammer, (e) of winning a spelling bee, (f) of his terrible dreams, (g) his friendship with an unremarkable boy, (h) his parents' arguments, and (i) his exploits as a young athlete—items (a), (b), (d), (f), and (h) will no doubt be noted in his record; items (c), (e), (g) and (i) will likely be omitted as irrelevant.

Thus a psychiatrist may be doing his or her patient more of a disservice than a service by keeping a thorough patient record if there is any chance that such a record may get outside the therapy framework.

Some psychiatrists have solved this dilemma in a logical if not drastic manner. They keep no records at all. There is a substantial risk in this, because the therapist may forget a valuable point or recall an important bit of information incorrectly. Moreover, if the psychiatrist dies or becomes incapacitated, a whole line of treatment may die with him. Nevertheless, in some cases it may be the only way that a therapist can convince a patient that he or she is doing everything possible to preserve confidentiality. It is a drastic solution to an equally drastic problem.

Medical Insurance Claims

The processing of insurance claims proceeds by a perverse logic that creates the greatest disclosure of the information that is likely to cause the greatest harm to the individual. Disclosure of treatment for a sprained wrist, for example, does not cause problems for the average person, but disclosure of a condition such as alcoholism or schizophrenia might. However, in the normal processing of insurance claims the sprained-wrist claim will be approved by the insurance company with little or no verification, while the treatment for alcoholism or mental problems will not be paid until the insurance company has obtained copies of all the medical records and (in some cases) verified the claim through an independent investigator. Why? The insurance company reasons that there is no generally accepted line of treatment for the latter type of problem and that it needs verification of the actual treatment to prevent overpayments. Conversely, a sprained wrist, it is assumed, is always a sprained wrist. Thus the insurer's concern with costs runs directly contrary to the patient's concern with privacy.

The practice of Blue Cross is illustrative of this point: The company will approve a great many claims at Level One. These are routine claims based on the submission of a minimum of information about the individual and the type of treatment. But certain types of cases are automatically referred to Level Two for more intensive review. These include treatment for obesity, cosmetic surgery, alcoholism, drug addiction, mental and nervous conditions, attempted suicide, psychoneurotic and personality disorders, epilepsy, migraine, and many types of chronic diseases. In these types of sensitive medical problems, the Level Two examiner will request copies of physician's orders, history of present and past illnesses, copies of test reports, and the like before the claim is approved. If the claim is still not allowed it is sent to Level Three, where the investigator will frequently request a copy of the patient's entire medical record before the claim is approved. Once the medical record reaches the files of the insurance company, it is normally under no legal protection at all. The doctor-patient privilege that may have acted as a restraint on disclosure by health professionals does not apply to insurance companies. In most cases the insurance company's use of that information is limited only by its own sense of discretion.

The medical records that eventually find their way into insurance-company files are usually heavily weighted toward those illnesses that have some social stigma attached to them. Insurance companies claim to be more concerned about mental disorders, drug problems, alcoholism, and the like for reasons of cost control, but their motivation is not really important. The end result is that insurance companies tend only to have complete medical records on those who have the most sensitive kinds of illness, and as to those individuals they only have the records that show them at their sickest. It is an aggravation of the same problem that begins with psychiatric records themselves: the records show the periods of sickness and not what may be the longer periods of health. The entire system proceeds by a form of Gresham's Law in which the odd information tends to drive out the routine. As a result, such files are tailor-made for an investigator looking for negative information.

If the medical claim is made under a group insurance plan, there may be further routine disclosures of sensitive medical information by the insurance company. Group health insurance plans (most of them employer plans) comprise the largest number of health insurance policies in the country, covering more than 83 million Americans. It is a frequent practice, however, for insurance companies to disclose to the employer certain basic information about the employee's claim when that claim is processed. There are a variety of rationales for this. Some insurers have assumed that the employer is entitled to the information because "he pays the premium." Sometimes, however, the reasons for disclosure are more subtle than such crass reasoning would suggest. It is often argued, for example, that the employer has the right to know because the group plan is "experience-rated" and the nature and the cost of the employee's claim can affect the premium rate for the whole group. Sometimes it is suggested that an employer should know about the particular medical condition because it is one that might affect the employee's performance on the job. Frequently, however, it is not an intended disclosure but one that is simply built into the way that the group insurance claims are processed. If the claim forms are handled at some point by the individual's fellow employees, it usually doesn't take long for information about a claim for treatment for psychiatric disorder or therapeutic abortion to work its way around the office.

Psychiatrists' records are full of horror stories about group insurance plans. In several documented cases patients have been promised strict confidentiality by their therapist only to find out that other persons at work are aware of the psychiatric treatment. This has not only led to setbacks in treatment, but often the patient has ended up worse than when he or she started. Occasionally the therapist has withheld the exact diagnosis from a patient out of a fear that the patient can't handle the information, but the diagnosis is then disclosed to the patient by a fellow employee who had read the claim form. When told in advance of the possibilities of disclosure on an insurance-claim form, people in need of psychiatric treatment will often decide to forego the medical-insurance benefits to which they are entitled or skip treatment altogether.

A similar process occurs in a less visible way with government-funded health insurance programs. As an incentive to combat fraud in Medicaid programs designed for the poor, the federal government offers states additional funding if they implement a Medicaid Management Information System. Under such programs the states require healthcare providers to report extensive medical information to federal and state auditors. The State of Hawaii in 1978 carried this to its logical extreme by enacting legislation that allows state Medicaid investigators to seize by an administrative inspection warrant the medical records of any doctor or psychiatrist with patients on Medicaid. In carrying out the federal mandate, the Hawaii legislation was designed for spot checks and not to investigate any particular allegations of fraud. Federal Judge Matthew Byrne, Jr., declared the statute unconstitutional on October 22, 1979, but the matter seems headed for appeal.

Both Medicare and Medicaid are saddled with complex reporting and investigative procedures that threaten to leave privacy in the lurch. Both programs are subject to routine reviews by Professional Standards Review Organizations, which are semiautonomous professional committees in various locales. Information from PSROs and from insurance companies that have contracted to provide Medicare payments is frequently reported to the federal Health Care Financing Administration. The HCFA in turn reports medical information from these reports to various law-enforcement groups, research projects, and other government agencies. Much of the medical information in the files at these various stages can either be identified by name or some easily recognizable "personal identifier," such as a Social Security number.

The number of hands through which this medical information passes illustrates better than anything else the extraordinary difficulty of maintaining the privacy of the information. Information in the hands of the federal agencies is subject to the restrictions of the Privacy Act of 1974, but the act has a number of exceptions that allow disclosure to other government agencies for "routine uses." Information in the files of a state Medicaid agency is not subject to the federal Privacy Act, and is only kept confidential, if at all, by any state law that may apply. Information in the files of a private insurance company administering the program or a PSRO reviewing that program is generally not subject to any legal restrictions at all unless the government enforces various contractual restrictions on the use of the information.

The entire procedure by which personal medical information in federally funded programs is passed back and forth from agency to agency is far too loose to instill in anyone the idea that sensitive information will be kept confidential. This has become clear in one highly volatile issue: abortion. There are numerous instances of women being called anonymously after an abortion and being accused of "murder." The leak is usually impossible to pinpoint—whether from inside the hospital, the insurance company, government funding agency, or elsewhere. In Minnesota the State Supreme Court allowed a Catholic newspaper the right to the names of all doctors who have performed government-funded abortions. A highly sensitive issue like this tests the strength of government confidentiality provisions, and those provisions seem hardly able to stand up to the test.

Personal information flows back and forth in the medical context largely with the individual's "consent." While an individual's consent for further disclosure is generally not needed when he or she voluntarily divulges medical information on an employment questionnaire, an insurance application, or similar questionnaire, any time an investigator seeks information that is covered by the doctor-patient privilege some form of consent must be theoretically obtained from the patient. Without that, the doctor or hospital is usually not supposed to divulge the information.

This sounds fine in theory, but in practice it results in hardly any restraint at all on investigators. When a person checks into a hospital, he or she routinely signs a form that contains fine print authorizing the hospital to release to the insurance company any information necessary to process the claim. A person doesn't legally have to sign it, but few people have the presence of mind at the time they are entering a hospital to scratch out such a provision or to argue about it with the admissions clerk. Similarly, if a person applies for Medicaid or Medicare benefits, the government requires the individual to consent to government inspection of his or her medical records. Private insurance companies frequently have the same type of consent provision in their claim forms. Employers sometimes require an applicant to sign a form consenting to their examination of an employee's medical record. Insurance companies issuing health, life, or disability insurance almost always require an applicant to sign a blanket consent giving them the right to inspect medical records. These consents are often unlimited in scope and duration. The individual is not required to sign the consent form, but neither is the company obligated to issue the policy.

An insurance company may investigate an application or a claim itself, or it may call in the services of an outside investigative bureau such as Equifax, Hooper-Holmes, American Service Bureau, or O'Hanlon's. Representatives of such bureaus simply present themselves to the hospital as an agent of the insurance company and ask to see the insurance applicant's complete medical file on the basis of the consent form signed by him or her. Any information such firms obtain goes into their records as well as those of the insurance company. Such information can be used by the investigative bureau in later investigations unrelated to the one for which it was originally hired.

Although this procedure is probably legal under the laws of most states, many hospitals and doctors have become increasingly reluctant to release medical information in such a situation on the basis of a blanket release. As a consequence, some investigators have had to be more resourceful to get the information they want. According to the Privacy Commission, one investigative bureau, formerly known as the Factual Service Bureau (now known as Inner-Facts), frequently resorted to pretext interviews with hospitals in which bureau representatives misrepresented who they were and why they wanted the information. Another tactic used in the industry is to bribe a hospital employee as an informant. In one case the Denver District Attorney, posing as an insurance agent, asked a bureau to get a copy of a woman's medical records without telling the bureau that the woman was his secretary. The company got the records (the originals) by stealing them. When the company found out that the medical records were those of the District Attorney's secretary, it tried to charge extra for them.

The factors considered by the insurance company in determining whether to make a full-scale investigation vary from company to company, but an important consideration is the information disclosed by the insured on the application form. Sensitive medical conditions, such as a nervous or mental disorder, are just as likely to trigger a full-scale investigation at the application stage as at the claims stage. The applicant is faced with a dilemma at the time the application is filled out: if he or she discloses a sensitive medical condition in the application, the privacy of that information is compromised even if the policy is not issued. If the applicant does not disclose it, he or she runs the risk that such nondisclosure will give the insurance company the right to withhold payment of a claim at a later date or void the entire policy.

A disclosure to one insurance company is virtually the same as a disclosure to all. Approximately 700 U.S. and Canadian insurance companies are members of the Medical Information Bureau (MIB). Each member company is obligated to provide to MIB any medical information with any underwriting significance that it develops on individuals. The MIB functions in much the same way as a credit bureau, but in this case it is mainly medical rather than financial information that it makes available to all member companies. A company receiving information from the MIB about an individual applicant is free to contact the reporting company directly to obtain the details about the medical information. The MIB maintains reports on approximately 11 million individuals and receives about 17.5 million requests annually for information from member companies. The MIB does not investigate on its own or attempt to verify information reported to it; it acts as a clearing house for its members. There are other agencies in the insurance industry performing a similar function, but the MIB is the biggest.

Being a part of Equifax's 39 million files, the MIB's 11 million files, the Health Care Financing Administration's 25 million files, and the files of innumerable other examiners, auditors, and adjusters is not exactly what the typical patient has in mind when he or she consults a doctor. But that is what is likely to happen. Confidentiality between doctor and patient has become something that both have to fight for rather than simply expect as a matter of course.

Health and Employment

A meat inspector who's employed by the federal government, but paid for by the corporation, checks meat inside a plant. The corporation can't buy the inspector and has no control over that inspector. What's good enough for a dead carcass should be good enough for a live worker.

Anthony Mazzochi, Oil, Chemical and
Atomic Workers' Union

Worker exposure to such things as methyl chlorometer ether, nitrobiphenyl, alpha-naphthylamine, bis-chloromethyl ether, 2-acetylaminofphiorene, 4-dimenthylaminoazobenzene, betapropiolaetone, N-nitrosodimethylamine, and other unpronounceable horrors that are considered cancer-suspect agents has generated some strongly worded OSHA regulations in response. But just *how* strongly worded was a surprise even to the director of the Occupational Safety and Health

Administration. Section 1910 of OSHA regulations directed companies to give workers exposed to such chemicals a complete preassignment physical examination, "including genetic and environmental factors." Why was the word *genetic* inserted in the regulation? No one is quite sure; in fact, no one even seemed to know it was in the regulation until a *New York Times* reporter pointed it out in February 1980.

OSHA's director was not alone in not knowing of the regulation's existence. Several members of the advisory committee that created the regulations were unaware that this particular language had been inserted. Everyone was seemingly at a loss to find out where the language of the regulations originated. If there was controversy over the regulation's origin, there was even more over what it portended. The DuPont Company, for example, which does "genetic screening" for such things as "sickle trait," claims that the testing is done strictly for the worker's benefit. Anthony Mazzochi of the Oil, Chemical and Atomic Workers' Union, however, fears that such screening will be used to discriminate against certain races or categories of workers and predicts an "era of genetic confrontation." Dr. Jeanne M. Stillman, who served on the advisory committee, was not aware who drafted the final regulation or for what purpose. "If industry doesn't do genetic screening of some sort, they are apparently in noncompliance with the law as it now stands," she told *The New York Times*. "But if they try to come into compliance, the law hasn't defined for them what it is they are supposed to do."

One thing they are clearly required to do is keep records. The company must keep complete medical files on the employees and monitor their medical condition at periodic intervals. The records are supposed to include a complete personal history, family and occupational background, susceptibility to certain types of disease, as well as the "genetic" information. The company maintains such records and must make them available to various federal and state agencies. What is far less clear is what the government and industry can do with this information once they have it.

The privacy problem inherent in all this goes far beyond these particular industries and affects medical questions generally in industrial settings and in other public health situations. The genetic regulations are of particular interest both because of the way they came about—no one has claimed authorship—and because they have the capacity to penetrate the private lives of workers to the possible extent of penalizing their offspring for generations to come for having the wrong "genetic factors." These regulations have simply appeared without anyone in authority having decided that they represent good public policy. Whether genetic counseling will ultimately prove good, bad, or indifferent to workers is not at all clear. What is certain, however, is that society seems to be gobbling up such information into data banks without anyone being quite sure why they are doing it.

The normal vantage point for viewing medical questions is to start with individuals who consult a doctor because they have the symptoms of some illness. The privacy problem is to seal off that relationship as much as possible—to keep the medical information from spreading outside the confines of the doctor-patient relationship. But if one begins from the perspective of industrial or environmental health hazards and works backward to the individual, a whole different set of problems arises and the privacy solutions are more difficult to pinpoint. The potential problem may originate in a government study, for example, and the information may be passed along from the government to the company, from the company to the company doctor, and only lastly from the company doctor to the patient who doesn't suspect he or she is sick. The company doctor, in turn, may gather all the pertinent medical data from his employee-patients and forward it back up the informational chain so that the government agencies can either confirm or deny the problem.

What happens to medical confidentiality in this situation? Anthony Mazzochi takes the blunt view that "confidentiality doesn't exist, and we shouldn't talk about preserving something that doesn't exist."

Against this background, it is easier to understand the mixed reviews given to the Supreme Court's decision in *Marshall v. Barlow*. In 1978 the Court ruled that section 8(a) of the Occupational Safety and Health Act of 1970 was unconstitutional because it allowed OSHA inspectors to enter a business establishment without a warrant to look for health and safety violations. From one perspective this was a step forward for privacy; it was a ruling that protected business establishments from arbitrary entry by government agents to the same extent that private homes are protected under the Fourth Amendment. But whose privacy was being protected? Not that of the workers—or if it was, they weren't buying. From their perspective, unannounced inspections by OSHA were for their benefit and transcended any "privacy" right management might lose in the process.

What the *Marshall* case illustrates is that the normal expectations of privacy are sometimes stood on their head in matters of industrial health and safety. When OSHA proposed rules that would give government inspectors broad access to employee medical records that are in the hands of company physicians, several companies objected on the grounds that this would violate the employee's privacy. But unions scoffed at this argument and stated that their members wanted the medical information forwarded to OSHA. The privacy of the information was already compromised, the union leaders argued, and a further disclosure to government officials would help their members more than it would hurt them.

Sometimes the only person who seemingly has no access to the company medical records is the employee himself. The Oil, Chemical and Atomic Workers' Union cites a 1977 case involving the Texaco refinery at Port Arthur, Texas. Following a union complaint, OSHA conducted an inspection confirming high worker exposure to benzene, a hematologic toxin. OSHA subpoenaed the corporate medical records and had them reviewed by its doctors. Later the workers themselves wanted to conduct a more thorough review of their medical condition, but, according to the union, Texaco refused to release the medical records to the doctor designated by the affected workers.

In the setting of industrial medicine, complete privacy between doctor and patient does not seem to be one of the options. Most labor leaders and others have concluded that medical information has to be disclosed, both to protect the individual worker and others in the same situation. The only argument is over who gets the information. Labor leaders appear to want the government to have it but not the employers, and their argument has merit. Reports to company physicians suffer from the same problem as medical reports in company-administered group health plans: medical information gets leaked to other company personnel.

One solution is a separate health-maintenance organization funded by the company to carry out its required medical programs but to which company personnel do not have access. Less drastic and perhaps less satisfactory are strict company rules limiting access of most company personnel to records maintained in the medical department. But businesses in general are subject to few laws regarding employee privacy on medical or other matters. So any programs that industry initiates to seal off the misuse of such information are likely to be undertaken on a voluntary basis. Without better protection of their privacy, many employees will continue to look with one eye over their shoulder as they talk to the company physician.

Medical Records and the Law

If a stranger were to notice how many of the hospital's resources were devoted to the task of recording information about patients, he might well conclude that the main objective of the institution was to generate information and keep systematic files rather than to treat illness.

Kai T. Erikson and Daniel E. Gilbertson,
On Record: Files and Dossiers in American Life

The health-care business is an enormous record-keeping apparatus. Yet there is no federal law that has any significant impact on privacy of medical information. Congress has not enacted anything equaling even the minimal protection of the Fair Credit Reporting Act, as applied to credit bureaus, or the Right to Financial Privacy Act, as applied to banks. This has not been because of a lack of concern. Among both laymen and professionals there is widespread agreement about the need for legislation on the federal level to correct abuses of medical privacy. But good intentions have not borne fruit, and Congress has still not agreed on the terms of a medical privacy bill.

There have been no lack of proposals. The Carter Administration proposed a Privacy of Medical Information Act, and Senators Javits and Ribicoff and Congressman Richardson Preyer have also proposed statutes. The American Medical Association has proposed a "model statute," as has the American Psychiatric Society. The National Center for Health Statistics, the American Medical Records Association, and the National Commission on the Confidentiality of Health Records have all been working for legislative changes.

The bill proposed by the Carter Administration represents a modest effort to control misuse of medical records, but it falls far short of curing all the problems. The bill would directly regulate federally funded health-care facilities, requiring them to allow patients access to his or her own medical records, to include patient corrections to the medical record in the file, and to give the patients notice of certain types of disclosure. But the bill allows twenty-two different categories of disclosure of doctor-patient information *without* the patient's consent, and many of these disclosure provisions would seemingly undercut the kind of confidentiality the bill is designed to achieve. Moreover, the bill makes no attempt to regulate information practices of health-care agencies that do not receive federal funding except to regulate to some extent requests made to such agencies by the federal or state government. In short, any likely congressional action will not solve the problem of medical privacy but will only smooth some of the rough edges with the same mixed effect that federal laws have had on banking or credit-bureau practices.

State laws on medical privacy are largely a jumble of piecemeal provisions that provide for confidentiality of some medical records but leave large categories untouched. But most medical records pass through a great many hands, and disclosure is likely to occur at the weakest link in the chain. Consequently, state statues that only prohibit a certain agency from disclosing certain types of records are nothing that an individual can rely on. An investigator will simply look elsewhere in the chain of disclosure for the information he wants. The laws of several states, however, are useful in giving the patient access to personal medical records. At last count, sixteen states allowed a patient some form of access to doctors' records* and twenty-one allowed some access to hospital records.†

Both Illinois and California, however, enacted statutes in 1979 that come close to getting at the heart of the problem. The Illinois Mental Health and Developmental Disabilities Confidentiality Act applies only to doctor-patient consultation on mental health and related problems, but is probably more effective within that limited sphere than the broader California Confidentiality of Medical Information Act, which applies to all medical information. Under the Illlinois law any "personal notes" of a therapist are considered the property of the therapist and are totally exempt from any form of disclosure. Likewise, Illinois provides that even if a patient has technically waived the privilege of confidentiality, a therapist can only be required to testify after a judge conducts a closed-door hearing in which all of the potential harm to the patient-therapist relationship is evaluated. Both of these provisions go a long way toward accommodating the confidentiality needs of psychiatric treatment and make Illinois virtually unique in this respect.

Both Illinois and California allow certain disclosures without the patient's consent, but the list in both cases is considerably shorter than in the proposed federal law. Under both statutes the patient's consent is required in most cases, and both statutes put strict limits on the

---

* California, Colorado, the District of Columbia, Florida, Hawaii, Illinois, Maryland, Minnesota, Nevada, New York, Oklahoma, Oregon, Rhode Island, Utah, Virginia, Wisconsin.

† California, Colorado, Connecticut, the District of Columbia, Hawaii, Illinois, Louisiana, Maine, Maryland, Massachusetts, Minnesota, Mississippi, Nevada, New Jersey, Oklahoma, Oregon, Rhode Island, Tennessee, Utah, Virginia, Wisconsin.

language contained in any consent forms signed by patients. Such consent or release forms are valid only for a limited time, if they specify who is to receive the information and for what purpose, and if they specify the type of medical information. Blanket authorizations that allow investigators to go on a fishing expedition through all medical records are outlawed in both states. Equally important, both states limit the reuse of medical information by insurance companies or other agencies. In California further disclosure is prohibited unless the type of disclosure "appear[s] on the authorization." In Illinois, reuse of the information is prohibited unless the patient "specifically consents to such redisclosure." Both such provisions, if fully implemented, would make disclosure and redisclosure by investigative bureaus and other agencies more difficult.

Low-Profile Strategies

Privacy in medical matters requires a good deal of self-help. The goal is to have your medical record available to those who want to help you and to keep it away from those who want to help themselves.

- Find out what your doctor is required to disclose. The reporting requirements vary greatly from state to state, and it may sometimes make sense to seek treatment where the doctor is not required to disclose certain types of drug treatment, abortions, and the like. If you anticipate being haled into court for any reason or suspect some government inquiry, choose the state that gives the greatest protection to the doctor-patient privilege. You can only find this out by asking your doctor (and probably your lawyer) to be candid in telling you how well he or she can protect confidential information.
- Choose a doctor or therapist who is not likely to be investigated. The IRS audits certain taxpayers because they suspect their accountant of following shoddy or illegal practices, and the same thing is true with patients of doctors suspected of Medicaid or other fraud. The government can and will single out a patient's medical file for scrutiny based on the suspected sins of his or her doctor.
- Choose a pharmacist who can be trusted. The druggist-patient relationship falls outside the protection of most medical privilege laws. Consequently you may want to establish an understanding with your pharmacist that nothing will be disclosed without your written consent unless required by law. In the latter case, your agreement with the pharmacist should include a promise to notify you if that occurs.

- Limit your disclosures when dealing with certain doctors. A failure to be candid with your doctor can usually be hazardous to your health, but be sure he's *your* doctor. A company physician, an insurance-company doctor, and a doctor evaluating your worker's compensation are all doctors, but they frequently have divided loyalties. Doctors in these and similar positions often have an obligation to report everything they find. It is not a good idea to lie to a doctor in that position, but it may not be wise to be too candid either. Save your deepest, darkest secrets for your *own* doctor.
- Disclose sensitive information directly to your doctor. Many medical-care organizations have routine forms requesting a full medical history. It may be wise to leave sensitive information off the form and disclose it directly to the doctor. The doctor may or may not make a note of it, but it gives the patient an opportunity of discussing the impact of that information with the doctor before it gets into the file. Thus the patient and doctor can, to a certain extent, control what the doctor places in the record. This type of discretion is almost never exercised with routine office forms or hospital admission forms, which are frequently handled by nonmedical personnel and copied and distributed more casually. If you get into a discussion with a computer, you might not want to tell it anything more sensitive than your blood type.
- Ask the doctor or therapist not to keep notes in certain cases. Unless you are being treated in Illinois, a therapist's notes in any mental health problem present a serious hazard. Many therapists will not take notes or make recordings even without the patient suggesting it in order to protect the confidentiality of the patient's disclosures. Others might refrain from doing so if asked. If "noteless" therapy is not feasible in your case, the therapist may agree to destroy them after the treatment is completed or work out some arrangement to be sure that they don't fall into the hands of an investigator.
- Pay for certain sensitive medical treatment yourself. Whenever an insurance claim is made, the insurance company is likely to want more information about the line of treatment than you're going to feel comfortable giving. The company's demand for further information will normally go directly to the doctor's office, so you may not have an opportunity at that point to drop the claim rather than giving the company what it wants. Information in the hands of insurance companies is often redisclosed to investigative bureaus, insurance companies, and others. If it is group insurance, sensitive information may go to your employer. If it is Medicare, Medicaid, or

some other form of government insurance, the information may be reported to countless auditors and examiners. For sensitive medical information, an insurance claim of any sort may simply be too risky.
- Think twice before you apply for medical, disability, or life insurance. An application for such insurance is bound to involve a substantial disclosure of medical information on the application form. The insurance company will also pick up a good deal more if it uses the consent form that you sign on the application to get other detailed information from your medical records. Once this happens, the disclosure of information occurs—whether or not you get the insurance. The time to weigh the risks of disclosure of prior medical problems against the need for insurance is *before* the application is signed.
- Get copies of your own medical records if possible. Several states give a patient the specific right to get a copy of his or her records. In other states a doctor can provide the patient with a copy of the record if it is mutually agreeable. The Privacy Act of 1974 allows you to get copies of your own medical records that have progressed down the chain of disclosure to the point where they are in the hands of some federal agency. Comparable statutes in some states allow access to medical records in the files of state agencies. The Fair Credit Reporting Act gives you some access to medical information in the hands of investigative bureaus.
- Don't sign any blanket consent forms. Almost any consent or release form is trouble unless there are strict limitations on it as to the type of information, the duration, restrictions on use, and the like. Hospitals cannot require you to sign such forms, but a lot of them will try to do it. The worst that can happen if you refuse is that they will have to come back to you for your consent before they can file an insurance claim. Insurance companies may or may not be willing to modify their consent form at the time you apply, but it can't hurt to ask.
- Revoke any consent forms that have already been signed. These forms are so prevalent in the health-care business that almost no one can recall every one he or she has signed. The only practical course may be to send a letter to each doctor, hospital, and insurance company you may have had dealings with stating that you "revoke any prior consent to release of medical information that may have been given."

CHAPTER 5

"Why is this necessary to make beer?"

JOBS, POLYGRAPHS, AND EMPLOYEE FILES

As Mayor of the City of Milledgeville, it had been more or less kind of directed to me, indirectly, to what we could do as a community and elected officials to try to keep the union activities out. . . . [I asked] my Police Department to monitor the meetings of the union organizers to obtain tag numbers. These tag numbers could be scrutinized and run through our computer . . . obtaining the owner's name and registration of the vehicle. . . . As the lists were compiled [they were given to] each one of the industries: Concord Fabrics, Griffin Pipe Products, Grumman Aerospace, Meadows Industries, J. P. Stevens and Walton Manufacturing Company.

Testimony of Robert Rice,
Mayor of Milledgeville, Georgia

When I reported to the Coors personnel office I was instructed to fill out a psychological questionnaire called the "runner test" consisting of over 200 questions. . . .

Then came the biggest shock. I was scheduled for a lie detector test. When I reported, the polygraph operator was a heavy set man dressed in white. He looked like a guard in a mental institution. He attached straps around my chest, stomach and arms.

When the polygraph operator began the test he dealt with questions I had answered on the employment application. However, it didn't take long before the operator began asking extremely personal questions, like "Are you having sexual relations with your girl friend?" "Have you had sex with more than one person?" "What kind of sex?" "Are you a communist?" . . . "Have you ever committed an undetected crime?" . . . "Have you ever stolen anything from anyone in your life?" "What?" "What was it worth?" "What is the total worth of what you have stolen in your life?"

I felt helpless and wondered why all this was necessary to make beer.

David Sackler, Coors worker

The union-busting of J. P. Stevens and Co. and the psychological probing of Coors Brewery are just two of the methods that have been used by some employers to intrude upon their employees' privacy. When such intrusions occur, the disparity in bargaining power that ordinarily exists between employer and employee almost guarantees that the effect will be thorough and humiliating. An employee who wants to keep his job—or get hired in the first place—must often submit to intensive background checks, psychological testing, long questionnaires about personal information, physical examinations, on-the-job surveillance, in-house telephone taps, polygraph examinations, credit checks, pretext interviews, and the whole panoply of techniques modern men and women have devised to intrude upon their fellow's privacy. The experience of David Sackler at Coors Brewery represents the norm for many employees in many firms.

The events in Milledgeville, while hardly typical, nevertheless show the extent to which invasions of privacy can go in an employer-employee context. Surveillance of the union organizers became a major community pastime. The Textile Workers Union was only interested in organizing J. P. Stevens and Co., but that didn't stop most of the town's own employers from joining in the fun. According to the Mayor, "Grumman Aerospace had graciously consented to send two of their security men" to assist in the surveillance work. These fellows, it turns out, were ex-CIA agents.

The police and the company cops needed a room next to the union organizers at the local Holiday Inn, and the manager of the hotel obliged—for free. "We offered to [pay]," testified the Mayor, "but he would not take it." From that room and from a couple of vans parked outside they observed who came and left the room and marked down all license numbers. According to the Chief of Police, they ran them through the computer and came up with "twenty to twenty-four lists" of names. These names were eventually sent to the employers to match against their list of employees. According to the chairman of the local Community Relations Council, they did something else which they were not so free in admitting: they set up electronic recording devices to listen in on conversations in the rooms of the union organizers.

It doesn't have to be that way. Many employers conduct their businesses with a minimum of intrusion on their employees' lives. Although 25 percent of employees feel that their employers ask for too much personal information, according to the Harris Poll, that figure means that 75 percent apparently have no complaints. These figures represent the vast differences in conditions in different types of jobs. In fact, nowhere is the disparity in practices and attitudes toward privacy greater than in matters of employment. Some workers are systematically abused, while their fellow workers across town hardly have a complaint.

No one factor is decisive in shaping a firm's policy on questions of privacy. Often a difference in practice between two seemingly comparable companies may rest on the personal attitude and values of the management. But despite difficulties of generalization, some factors seem significant. The nature of the business, the hazards of the work, the degree of labor unrest, the paranoia of management—all of these tend to affect a company's attitudes toward the privacy of its workers. For example, retail chain stores—particularly middle-sized companies and fast food chains—tend to be heavy users of polygraphs and other "lie-detector" tests because of an almost obsessive concern about employee theft. Firms in the chemical industry and other hazardous industries get into frequent difficulty with employee unions over the use and misuse of employee medical information. These are simply two examples of how the type of business affects not only the attitude of management but also the type of privacy intrusion that may occur.

The size of a firm is often important. Large companies tend to rely more on personnel files and investigations than on personal evaluations of an employee. Larger firms tend to administer a wider range of employee benefit programs and fall under more governmental regulations. Big companies are also more likely to use computers for processing information about employees. All of these factors tend to increase the amount of personal information that the company maintains on its employees. But even this factor is not absolute, since some very large companies have done a better job of protecting employee privacy than many middle-sized firms.

Differences within a firm may be as great as differences between them. Some companies have different policies for white-collar workers than they do for blue-collar workers. Occasionally, the most intensive background checks are reserved for potential middle-management employees. More often than not, however, the lower-echelon employees suffer the most from intrusive practices. One type of abuse—the lie-detector test—seems to be reserved for those at the bottom. As Andrew Kahn of the AFL–CIO put it: *"Bank tellers take polygraph tests; bank presidents do not. Grocery clerks take polygraph tests; most store managers do not. . . . In short, the lie detector is used to intimidate employees or applicants on the lower rungs of the career ladder.*" Those high enough in the hierarchy to make the rules may sometimes conclude, not surprisingly, that the privacy of the people on the lower echelons is more expendable than their own.

The most important single factor in the disparity in business attitudes toward privacy has been the lack of significant government regulation of business practices. Michigan has enacted a broad Employee Right to Know law, and California, Maine, and Oregon have some legislation aimed at giving employees access to their records. But with these exceptions, neither the states nor the federal government have taken an active role in protecting employee privacy. In fact, government programs have largely been counterproductive on this issue. Much of the information gathered by employers, for example, is mandatory under a variety of governmental programs and regulations.

This situation is not likely to change very quickly. There is support in Congress for legislation to correct some specific abuses—such as lie-detector tests or dissemination of employee medical information. But there has been little effort to enact comprehensive legislation to protect employee privacy. This has been largely due to the recommendations of the Privacy Commission, which in this area advocated "adoption of most of its employment-related recommendations by voluntary action." Reflecting its business orientation, the Commission decided that businesses could do a better job of implementing privacy programs than could the government.* Congress has followed the Commission's lead and staked its hopes upon industry-initiated reforms.

Some firms have responded to the prodding. IBM, Cummins Engine, Aetna Life and Casualty Company, and others have not only adopted employee-privacy programs but have been aggressively advertising and promoting them (the Aetna program was perhaps influenced by the fact that its President, William O. Bailey, was a member of the Privacy Commission). Sentry Insurance has taken a substantial step in the same direction by commissioning and publicizing the Harris survey on public attitudes toward privacy. Of the 500

---

* The answer to this question seems to depend on who is being asked. The Harris Poll reports that 70 percent of employees thought a "law should be passed" giving an employee access to personnel files and only 23 percent thought it should be "left to employers." Employers felt just the opposite, by a ratio of 33 to 64 percent. Congressmen polled came out right in the middle: 44 percent to 48 percent.

largest companies in the United States, about 50 percent now claim to have conducted a systematic re-evaluation of their personnel record-keeping practices.

Alan F. Westin suggests that some government programs not directly aimed at privacy may nevertheless have had a beneficial effect on company practices. This has been particularly true of laws aimed at discrimination in employment. According to Westin, "[there] has been a spreading of awareness that new social attitudes about equal-employment opportunity required management to cut back sharply on the range of questions it could ask job applicants." Since questions about race, religion, sex, age, handicaps, and the like will get the company into trouble, many of them have learned to live with more diversity among their workers and, as a consequence, have tolerated a bit more employee privacy.

But these attitudes are far from being unanimous. Sensitivity to employee privacy appears to be greatest among the country's largest companies. According to Alan Westin and others, it is in the middle-sized firms outside the *Fortune* 500 mold where privacy rights of employees are in the greatest jeopardy. Employees of middle-sized firms are no small group: they comprise about 50 million out of a business workforce of 70 million. Voluntary programs may be widening the gap between different types of companies, and even within seemingly comparable companies no definite pattern is emerging. Business firms seem to be moving in two directions simultaneously—many are making an effort to protect their employees' privacy while others are figuring out new ways to intrude upon it.

Labor–management relationships at some companies are built around one word: suspicion. In that kind of atmosphere, respecting an employee's privacy is like giving aid and comfort to the enemy. "Who embezzles?" says a vice president of Perry's Drug Stores. "Any employee is suspect." The executive director of the National Association of Convenience Stores suggested darkly that "the majority of the [retail] work force is under 25 years of age, single or divorced, and grew to maturity during a period . . . when traditional institutions, values, and ethics were questioned." A person like that, he implied, can't be trusted with the company's merchandise unless there is a good deal of investigation and surveillance. He is the kind of person, according to the convenience-store executive, who "opens up a Twinkie and he is proud of it."

Employee records in most companies of any substantial size fall into similar categories. Application forms virtually all ask for name, address, Social Security number, and basic identification data. Questions about sex and age are disappearing from applications, and hardly any firm now asks questions about race.* Most application forms ask for a history of the applicant's schooling and prior employment. Although probably fewer employers are asking questions about arrest record or military record, they usually end up getting the information indirectly by asking on the application for an explanation of any gaps in the chronology of schooling and employment. After the applicant is employed, he must also routinely fill out tax-withholding forms, disability-insurance documents, and a variety of other forms relating to any health, pension, or other benefits the firm provides. This collection of documents—the minimum any employer is likely to ask—contains a rather formidable amount of personal information.

Many employers stop there, but for others it is just the beginning. If the firm is involved with government contract work requiring security clearances, the employee is required to provide a great deal more personal information, and that information is immediately placed in the files of the federal agency involved. If the job requires any special qualifications such as licensing, more information is obtained from the employee and reported to the appropriate governmental agency. If an employee must be bonded, that information is obtained and reported to the bonding company. All of these factors not only result in the company having more information about the employee but also result in that information being shared with some other agency.

Many companies attempt to delve deeper into an employee's background. The file will frequently include letters or summaries of telephone calls with persons listed as references in the application form or reports prepared by persons interviewing the applicant. These documents add to the file a number of subjective opinions the employee may not be aware of. The same is true of subjective reports and evaluations prepared by supervisors during the course of his employment. Additionally, many employers delve much deeper in personnel ques-

---

* It is not technically illegal to ask such questions, but they raise an inference of unfair hiring practices. Consequently, most firms avoid them.

In one of the quirks of federal law, these forbidden questions are usually mandatory *after hiring*. Most employers have to report information about sex, age, and race under Title VII of the Civil Rights Act to show that their hiring practices have not been discriminatory.

tionnaires, seeking information about the employee's indebtedness, second jobs, proneness to litigation, medical history, and so on. Such inquiries often dig into the employee's lifestyle, with questions about his or her living arrangements. Finally, many firms have their own security departments that develop further reports the employees may not be aware of.

What kind of information should a business be able to elicit from its employees? According to the Harris Poll, very large majorities (between 76 percent and 92 percent) of American workers feel that questions about a job applicant's friends, neighborhood, spouse, arrest record, and political affiliations are improper. By a smaller majority they are opposed to questions about creditworthiness, psychiatric counseling, and whether the applicant owns his or her own home. The majority would allow, however, questions about pregnancy, drinking habits, and drug use. Oddly enough, the employers polled apparently felt even stronger about these issues. They agreed with the employees about the question that should not be asked and they did so by consistently higher margins. A majority of employers was even opposed to certain types of questions a majority of employees would allow, such as those about marital status, drinking habits, sex, and age.

These results have to be viewed with a good deal of caution, however. One question showed that only 39 percent of workers were opposed to "evaluations of mental stability" while 57 percent of the employers thought they were improper. But 50 percent of the workers also thought that psychological tests for job applicants should be "forbidden by law" while only 25 percent of the employers agreed. The difference in the two results may be due to the words *by law*.* Some employers are willing to adopt privacy programs imposing restraints upon themselves but nevertheless oppose laws that would put the same restraints on all companies. Thus, the results may reflect not so much a consensus among employers' attitudes as their wide divergence.

Just as important as the questions is the issue of who does the asking. This is particularly important when a company wants to look into an employee's psyche as well as his background. Some companies require

---

* It may also reflect who was polled. The Harris Poll surveyed 200 businessmen from the *Fortune* list of top-1000 companies. Given the wide divergence in attitudes among businesses, it is not clear how valid these results would be for smaller firms or different types of businesses.

applicants for certain positions to go through a session with a company psychiatrist or psychologist before hiring. But fortunately for the privacy of most employees, shrinks are expensive. To substitute for this, many employers bring in a testing firm to do the same thing on the cheap—substituting "personality" or "aptitude" tests that may cost as little as $5 per applicant to administer. Many of the tests commonly used are spinoffs from the Minnesota Multiphasic Personality Inventory, but none has any scientific basis for employment purposes. According to Dr. Karl Menninger, most such tests are "not worth the paper they're printed on."

That tests are lacking in accuracy doesn't prevent them from being intrusive. One commonly used test, the ES or Emotional Stability test, is little more than simple snooping into the job applicant's personal life:

> Were you a bed wetter between the ages of 8 to 14 years?
> Do you feel you are as good as most people?
> Do you frequently suffer from bowel problems?
> Do you always sweat and get tied up in knots during examinations?

There are few people who *wouldn't* get tied up in knots if they thought they had to answer those kinds of questions.

The most devious types of tests are those designed to determine the employee's attitude. One such popular examination is called the TA, or Trustworthiness Attitude, test. It has over 100 true-false questions and may be self-graded by the employer with a grading device leased from the testing company for $60 a year. The questions are politically loaded to catch a "bad attitude" among potential employees:

> Breaking the law can sometimes be justifiable.
> Society actually encourages rebelliousness by having too many rules.
> A lot of employees steal because they are not satisfied in their job.
> Employee theft is chickenfeed compared to income tax evasion by company executives.

Many people would answer "true" to some or all of such questions, but if they did so they would end up looking for another job. Even though a "true" answer might be factually accurate, such an answer indicates a potential "troublemaker" in the value system of the test promoters. But the ethical expectations of the examiners are sometimes hard to anticipate. The head of the Personnel Security Corporation, which administers similar tests, stated that if he asked the question "It's human nature to steal," he would expect a "true" answer. "Most people are cynical enough today to answer 'true,' " he explained. "It's the thief who will answer 'false.' "

Outside firms are sometimes brought in for on-the-job snooping. Merit Protection Service, a large investigative firm, offers to businesses undercover agents who are trained to work both sides of the counter. According to its brochure,

> Merit provides professional operatives to shop your stores as regular customers and to make a series of test purchases to determine the honesty, efficiency, and courtesy of your employees....
>
> Merit will install trained investigators in your establishment as employees in shipping, receiving, warehousing, manufacturing, as sales help, stockroom help, bar boy, or in administrative jobs. The purpose here is to uncover dishonesty and inefficiency....

Merit—like similar firms—rounds off its services to employers by offering background investigations, polygraph tests, and "security surveys."

The services offered by such firms highlight a significant fact: there are almost no effective restrictions on surveillance and investigations of employees by companies that choose to do so. While there are legal limitations at the outer fringes, a company can engage in a wide range of conduct that intrudes upon its employees' privacy without violating any law. The company can bring in a security firm to search its employees as they leave the building as long as they are not too heavy-handed, listen in on telephone conversations as long as they don't tap into an outside line, and monitor them on closed-circuit television as long as they don't follow them into the bathroom. Some companies wouldn't think of such tactics, but for others it is routine.

Employers frequently use outside firms to make background checks on prospective employees. Equifax—the credit and investigative bureau—also has its finger in this pie. It does enough employment investigation work to justify a separate division of the company with investigators who are better paid and trained than its other investigators. Higher pay and better training seems to be the norm in this investigative field. This is both good news and bad news to the employee, but mostly it is bad. Such investigators are not as likely to come up with the type of distortions that can result from relying on the gossip of a neighbor, but they are likely to pick up some other investigator's distorted report and give it new currency. Such reports build on each other, and a pre-employment report may include references to an older distorted report.

The employment investigator, however, will usually conduct a background check of his own, and here it is the thoroughness of the report rather than any distortions that present the principal danger. According to the Privacy Commission, one unnamed investigative agency "routinely" contacts:

> banks; collection agencies; small loan companies; savings and loan associations; land title companies; Federal narcotic agencies; postal authorities; the Internal Revenue Service; the Immigration and Naturalization Service; the Securities and Exchange Commission; the Department of Justice; the Department of Health, Education and Welfare; State Comptrollers and tax officers; local school authorities; universities and other education facilities; and probation officers.

Investigative firms doing employment investigations have two important advantages. One is the applicant's résumé or job application. This gives them extensive leads as to where to go for further information. The other advantage is more subtle: experienced investigators in such firms often have contacts in governmental agencies who provide them with information illegally. Many investigators have developed these contacts when they were government employees themselves. The Privacy Commission noted persistent allegations about extra-legal access to files of many government agencies.

An employer's use of investigative firms enormously complicates an employee's privacy. It gives added circulation to private information and misinformation that might otherwise not have gotten into the company files. Employment investigators not only contact credit bureaus and a large range of other agencies, but they often will go back into their own files and recirculate some old information. In the case of a company like Equifax, this can be a substantial amount of information. All of this is likely to add a great deal of information to the employer's files that the company would probably not think to ask for itself.

Agencies doing employment investigations are subject to the Fair Credit Reporting Act, but the exceptions built into the FCRA weaken it considerably. The company or the investigative firm is theoretically required to disclose to the employee the fact that an "investigative report" is being prepared. But this does *not* apply to employment for which the employee "has not specifically applied." If an employee is being considered for a promotion—or for firing—he needn't be informed about the pending investigation. Moreover, an investigative report based on information gleaned out of credit records or from public records need not be reported to the employee. The same thing is true about employee rights as is true about consumer rights: the Fair Credit Reporting Act provides only a thin protection against the type of intrusions that a background investigation is capable of generating.

Polygraphs and Lie Detectors

Soon after the United Electrical workers organizing drive was discovered by management in September 1977, there was an announcement that some gold was missing from the company's vault.... A week later, after top management had attended a management anti-union session, the company announced they were bringing in a firm to do lie-detector tests.... Blatant invasions of privacy were employed in the questioning; for example: Have you ever used drugs? Did you ever steal anything from your mother? Have you ever cheated on your wife? Are you a homosexual? The questioning about the alleged theft was done in a highly accusatory manner: You stole the gold, we know you stole the gold, your friends told us you were the one who stole the gold, where did you get the money for your new car, etc. One employee snapped under this pressure, ran from the building and was found lying in a fetal position between railroad tracks, adjacent to the plant. He was admitted to a nearby psychiatric hospital.... He was not implicated in the alleged theft, nor had his test results indicated any guilt.

Hugh Harley, United Electrical,
Radio and Machine Workers of America

I don't know anything about polygraphs and I don't know how accurate they are, but they'll scare the hell out of people.

Richard M. Nixon, July 24, 1971,
Watergate Tapes

Each year anywhere from 250,000 to 2 million lie-detector tests are administered to Americans. Employers are the biggest group of users, generating about 80 percent of the income for polygraph firms. "One-fourth of all major corporations now use the polygraph," boasts the American Polygraph Association, a 1500-member industry organization. Wichita State University researchers John Belt and Peter Holden estimate that among major retail companies the percentage of use may be as high as 50 percent. This percentage seems also to apply to commercial banks. Breweries—most notably Coors—are major users of polygraphs. Fast food and convenience stores, including McDonald's (4700 outlets) and Burger Chef (900 outlets), frequently use lie detectors. Southland Corporation's 7-11 stores regularly use polygraph exams for job applicants and in-house investigations. Burstein-Applebee Company, which operates twenty-six stores in Texas, Ohio, Colorado, Kansas, and Missouri, requires anyone with a key to any store department or warehouse to submit to a polygraph exam, while Carson Pirie Scott & Co. requires pre-employment lie-detector exams for broad categories of employees in its twenty-six department stores in Illinois. The National Association of Chain Drug Stores estimates that operators of at least 80 percent of its approximately 11,500 drug stores use polygraphs. Atlanta-based Muirfood, Inc., which operates more than 1000 food stores, is reputed to conduct more than 25,000 polygraph exams each year of job applicants and employees. If voice stress analyzers (a form of "psychological stress evaluator" or PSE) are included, one could add Cumberland Farms Dairy Stores, Jim Dandy Fast Foods, Lil General Stores, Shopwell Supermarkets, and Waldbaum's 125-store grocery chain, among others, to the list of firms using lie detectors.

What have these businesses gotten for their money? They have gotten a test that William H. Winn of the Retail Clerks Union calls a "gratuitous insult to human dignity"—and one that is about as reliable as a Ouija board. According to psychiatrist and polygraph expert David Lykken, the average accuracy achieved by polygraph operators is between 64 percent and 72 percent in situations "where they could have achieved 50 percent accuracy by flipping coins." Even these low figures are probably misleading, since they derive from investigations of specific crimes. In pre-employment "fishing" investigations, where polygraph operators are looking for some generalized form of suspicious behavior, polygraphs are even more unreliable.* Voice stress analyzers have fared even worse in laboratory studies—with accuracy ratings of as low as 32 percent, or less than pure chance.

This level of unreliability is hardly surprising in light of what a "lie detector" does and does not do. Neither a polygraph nor a PSE determines "truth." A polygraph simply measures breathing movements,

---

* The difference is in the use of "control questions," one of the problems that lies at the heart of polygraph unreliability. In theory, the polygraph operator determines whether the subject is telling the truth by comparing the graph produced by the "critical" questions and the "control" questions. In order to provide an adequate baseline for the comparison, a control question should be one that is as serious and stress-producing as the critical question but that the subject will answer truthfully. This is extremely difficult to achieve even in the investigation of a specific crime, because it is essential that the subject not recognize it as a control question. However, there is rarely even the semblance of this type of controlled approach in pre-employment lie-detector tests, where the operator is not investigating any particular crime but probing the applicant's background.

blood pressure, and the electrical resistance of the subject's skin. A PSE records microtremors in the human voice (and has one ominous feature that the polygraph lacks: it doesn't have to be attached to the subject's body and, therefore, can be used without his knowledge). "What is recorded is not the subject's veracity," according to former Senator Sam Ervin, "but his physiological responses to an examiner's questions." It is the examiner's interpretation of the graphs on the machine "and not some demonstrated physical fact that determines the truthfulness of the individual's response."

Who are these polygraph examiners? On the average they have no special educational skills and have received about six weeks of training. Fewer than 1 percent of them have had any training in psychology or any related disciplines. In most states anyone buying a polygraph machine can go into business immediately. The regulation of voice stress analysis and other forms of PSE is, if anything, even weaker. Even within the lie-detection fraternity there are substantial doubts about the competence of the practitioners. According to UCLA law professor Edgar A. Jones, Jr., "at least 80 percent of the polygraph operators are publicly declared by the elite among them to be incompetent or charlatans."

Incidents of polygraph error are plentiful. In one famous case, described in the book *Death in Canaan,* an eighteen-year-old Connecticut boy was given a lie-detector test following the murder of his mother. After being told he failed the test, he gave a false confession to the police and was only acquitted years later after a new trial. In Minnesota the State Crime Bureau administered polygraph tests to a deputy sheriff and to a prisoner who accused the deputy of smuggling weapons into the jail. The prisoner passed the test and the deputy flunked. It was later proved, however, that the deputy was telling the truth and the prisoner was lying. In Los Angeles a food-store employee was asked "Did you check out items to your mother on a discount?" The operator rated her response "deceptive," and she was fired. Her emotional response, it turned out, was due to the fact that her mother was dead. In Lima, Ohio, the Allied Food Market suspended an employee after the polygraph registered hesitation in his answer to "Do you know who took the money?" The test, it turned out, failed to distinguish between a subconscious theory he had about the loss and a lack of any specific knowledge. Finally, in November 1977, the Washington *Post* reported the bizarre story of lie-detector tests taken by former Chicago Mayor Michael Bilandic and present Chicago Mayor Jane Byrne regarding Byrne's charges that Bilandic had conspired to take a bribe. The tests were administered by one of the biggest polygraph firms in the country, John E. Reid and Associates. Both mayors passed the test.

These erratic results are hardly surprising in view of the human factors involved in polygraph tests. Some subjects will produce reactions that the operator takes as guilt but in fact only show the person's anxiety about the test itself. Other persons being tested are street-wise enough to produce artificially strong reactions to control questions—such as by biting their lip or some other technique—thus throwing off the comparison data for the critical questions. Equally important is the attitude and skill of the operator. The mood created by the operator can alter the subject's response, as can the tone, manner, and timing of the questions.

The lack of reliability of the polygraph test doesn't seem to make much difference to its users. J. Kirk Barefoot, spokesman for the American Polygraph Association, suggested in testimony before a U.S. Senate subcommittee that the fear of the polygraph test prompts job applicants to disclose things about themselves—sometimes before they are even strapped to the box. According to Barefoot, of the applicants rejected "90 percent would not get the job based on their own admissions." Some of the damaging admissions may come after the testing, but "most of them come before the testing even starts." This confirms the claims of critics that the polygraph, like voodoo, is effective because people *believe* it is effective. Because of this, Andrew Kahn of the AFL–CIO points out, the polygraph examiner will strive to convince the subject that the machine works "by leaving favorable literature around the testing area, wearing clinical garb, and using scientific jargon." The operator's purpose is to create a confessional atmosphere that will do the job for him: that is, get the subject to confess or contradict himself.

Indeed, the polygraph machine itself may not be necessary. In one celebrated case the police put a colander on the head of a suspect and hooked it up with battery cables to a Xerox machine. They had previously placed a card on the photo surface that read "He's lying," so whenever they got an answer they didn't like, they pushed the copy button and got "He's lying" on the paper fed out by the machine. The suspect, a Puerto Rican youth with less than three years of schooling, cracked under the pressure and "confessed" to the crime.*

---

* This story was carried in several newspapers and in *Playboy* magazine in May 1978. It was erroneously attributed to Radnor, Pennsylvania; Robert Ellis Smith, editor of the *Privacy Journal*, confirmed that the incident occurred in Doylestown, Pa. He also found out that the detective who conceived the bright idea has gone off to polygraph school.

If polygraphs and PSE devices are so inaccurate, why are they used? To some businessmen it seems like simple economics. Polygraph exams are relatively cheap. While full background examination of a prospective employee may cost as much as $100, a polygraph exam can be done for $50, and a ten-to-fifteen-minute test may only cost $15 per employee. In these quickie exams operators tend to "play it safe" and to recommend against an employee if they have any doubts about him. The rejection rate from polygraph tests, according to J. Kirk Barefoot, is approximately 30 percent of the job applicants tested. If that seems high, it is consistent with the gloomy attitude of polygraph operators and users toward the American workforce. "Three out of four employees handling the money or merchandise steal from their employers," Barefoot says. The president of the Personnel Security Corporation goes him one better and claims that 100 percent of drug employees steal, with 80 percent stealing "significantly." Working with those kind of odds, it doesn't make any difference who is rejected. They are all presumed guilty.

From a privacy perspective, it would make no difference if lie detectors *did* work. Their unreliability should not obscure their intrusiveness and basic unfairness. A polygraph operator holds an inordinate amount of power. Once the subject is hooked to the box, there is virtually no limit to what the operator can ask and how deeply he can probe. "There is a difference," according to Birch Bayh, "between someone who has nothing to hide ... and someone who may not want to disclose everything in his or her background to a public forum or to a polygraph interrogator."

Senator Bayh's bill (S.B. 1845), which would outlaw the use of polygraph tests in connection with employment, led to extensive Senate hearings in 1977 and 1978. Testimony produced at those hearings showed the type of trauma a polygraph test engenders even in people who have done nothing illegal. Trudy Hayden of the ACLU presented the testimony of one man who "went in to have his honesty tested. He came out having to explain the entire emotional and mental history of his whole family." Some lie-detector tests may be brief, but others are frequently long and thorough.

According to Harry C. Hunter of the National Association of Convenience Stores, a typical test in that industry lasts about two hours and will cover the employee's employment and medical history with an emphasis on accidents, worker's compensation claims, alcoholism, drug problems, and the like. In addition they will ask questions designed to weed out "agitators, job hoppers, and professional and amateur thieves." There is no set line of questioning, according to Hunter, so the graphs on the machine suggest the direction they should take. "If stress is indicated in any area, new questions are formulated, retesting is conducted and results evaluated. The emphasis here is on resolution or obtaining an admission of derogatory information from the employee." The interrogation can be as intrusive as the machine operator wants it to be, and there is nothing to prevent the operator from going far afield into questions that have nothing to do with job performance. "No subject is beyond the pale," said John Shattuck of the ACLU. "Once hooked to the machine, the person must answer any question; if he hedges or denies, he will be accused of deception."

In addition to being unfair to the individual involved, lie-detector tests are frequently used as a form of political or economic warfare. Testimony of the United Electrical Workers, the Retail Clerks Union, and other labor organizations is replete with examples of how polygraph exams have been used to try to hamper union organizing efforts. Unions are not the only victims of this practice, however, as evidenced by the testimony of Don M. Blews, a former department store manager, before a subcommittee of the U.S. Senate on September 19, 1978:

> From 1973 until May of 1978, I was employed as a store manager for a department store chain which has 106 stores in Virginia, North Carolina, South Carolina and Georgia ... 2 months after I started managing my third store, my district supervisor stepped in and happened to notice that there were two black women working there.... He told me to fire them because the company had a policy against hiring blacks.... I refused and he responded by saying: "OK, Mr. Blews, we'll have to show you how our polygraph test works around here!" Two days later, the polygraph company came into the store and tested every employee, including myself. As the polygraph man left the store, he told me that two employees had failed the test. They were the two blacks. He said their printouts had shown "a sign of a possibility of deceit." This is in spite of the fact that they had already passed polygraph tests administered by the same company on two earlier occasions.

Control over the results of lie detector tests is virtually nonexistent. Operators of such tests are free to disclose the information as they see fit. The operators can give all or part of such information to the company that hired them, which in turn is free to share it with other employers, credit agencies, or anyone else. According to former Senator

Sam Ervin, "There is every likelihood that a record of the employee's responses may find its way into the personnel files of the company or agency and be transmitted as 'reference material' when the worker leaves, despite assurances to the contrary." The ACLU reports: "We know that employers keep files of polygraph test reports on both accepted and rejected applicants and on current employees ... and we know that polygraph reports are widely disseminated through credit reporting agencies." Like other information that reaches the files of credit bureaus, it becomes part of the generalized information about a person that is readily available to anyone who is interested.

Some states have laws making it illegal to require an applicant or employee to take a lie-detector test as a condition of employment.* There is, however, a catch in that only five of these states prohibit an employer from *requesting* an applicant or employee to take the exam.† Without this latter restriction, the protection is almost meaningless. According to a representative from Merit Protective Service, a large California retail-security firm, "the company sends the employees down to our office, and we always talk them into it." It takes a good deal of willpower for an employee to say no if he senses a veiled threat to his job. Moreover, some companies with multistate offices have been known to conduct all their exams in states with weak laws or no restrictions. No state has any significant restriction on the use of lie-detector results or their distribution. Once the person takes the exam for any reason, the results can be used against him in many different instances.

Union contracts provide a possible source of protection. The Retail Clerks Union, for example, estimates that about 12 percent of its contracts ban some or all use of polygraph tests. Even where an outright ban is not included in the collective bargaining agreement, unions have had some success in arbitration hearings, arguing that firings based on a refusal to take the test or unfavorable test results is an unfair labor practice. But union protection doesn't come without a price in lost bargaining power on other issues.

What is lacking is any federal restriction on the use of lie detectors. Despite extensive hearings, nothing has yet been done to control their use. There is a certain irony in this: Lie-detector tests are at least as intrusive as credit reports or surveillance of bank records. Unlike these areas, however, there is no significant government regulation. The rea-

---

* Alaska, California, Connecticut, Delaware, Hawaii, Idaho, Maryland, Massachusetts, Michigan, Minnesota, Montana, New Jersey, Oregon, Pennsylvania, Rhode Island, Washington.

† Alaska, Connecticut, Delaware, Minnesota, New Jersey.

son is the all-or-nothing nature of the dispute. Opponents of polygraphs and other lie-detector devices want to abolish them completely, or at least eliminate them entirely from use by employers. This was the position of the House Committee on Government Operations in 1976 and the Privacy Protection Study Commission in 1977, and it remains the approach of Senator Bayh's bill under consideration in the Senate. The polygraph industry, sensing its possible demise, has lobbied long and hard to prevent passage of such legislation. Although polygraph and PSE spokesmen have indicated they would accept some form of regulation (the American Polygraph Association has even proposed a model licensing act), this has had little appeal. Licensing, in the eyes of the opponents, would simply legitimize something that should be abolished. But the abolition of lie-detector tests in employment is an idea whose time is not quite at hand. Until it is, the abuses will continue.

Corporate Privacy Programs

We believe that employee privacy is something we at Cummins need to understand and pursue because it is one major way to manifest to all employees the company's basic concern for human dignity. . . . Frankly, it is our hope that other companies are also seriously addressing their privacy issues so that complex Federal regulations and reporting would not be necessary.

Theodore Marston,
Vice President of Cummins Engine Co.

Although the proportions of the two ingredients remain unclear, the mixture of concern for "human dignity" and fear of "Federal regulations" has prompted several companies to design programs to protect employee privacy. Within certain major corporations employee privacy has become a hot issue, and their policies to deal with that issue have become a source of company pride. IBM, AT&T, TRW, Polaroid, American Velvet, Prudential, Aetna Life and Casualty, Bank of America, Nabisco, DuPont, Citibank, Cummins Engine, and others have all announced privacy policies for employees and have participated in a variety of public forums about the rights and privacy of workers. One of these forums—the National Seminar on Individual Rights in the Corporation—has achieved an almost permanent status. More than 250 major corporations have attended this highly promoted event, and in 1979 it had just completed its third annual conference.

Corporate concern with employee privacy often derives from mixed motivations. Alan F. Westin suggests that IBM (a strong exponent of employee privacy) may have a few public relations points to score. The granddaddy of computer companies, according to Westin, "welcomed the chance to demonstrate that the growing data banks of personal information in use throughout the corporate world could be controlled by progressive rules on privacy." This would help shift the debate from attacks on computers to revising personnel policies. Bolstering the corporate image may have something to do with AT&T—with its phone-monitoring problems—or TRW (a major operator of credit bureaus) joining the ranks of companies trying to protect their employees' privacy.

But all is not sweetness and light in the ranks of business. Grumman Aerospace and J. P. Stevens have shown themselves willing to pull out all the stops on employee surveillance. Coors Brewery, Foremost-McKesson, and others use polygraph tests on employees or applicants. Sears, Roebuck and Co., Lockheed, Motorola, Allstate Insurance, Honeywell, U.S. Steel, and General Dynamics are all reputed to be subscribers to a private "black list" of employees maintained by a right-wing organization known as the American Security Council. Just as there appears to be a wide disparity between big businesses on matters of privacy, there appear also to be gaps between large firms. Big business in many cases is taking the lead in employee privacy, but not everyone is moving in the same direction.

Some information about the attitudes of big business toward employee privacy can be gleaned from a July 1979 survey conducted by University of Illinois Professor David F. Linowes, the former chairman of the Privacy Commission. Professor Linowes confined his survey to the *Fortune* 500 list of industrial companies, so the results are probably more indicative of big-business practices than the practices of businesses in general.* Seventy-six percent of the firms responding to the survey allow an employee to have access to his personnel-office file, but this percentage drops sharply with respect to other files. Only 16 percent allow employee access to supervisor's records and only 17 per-

---

* The survey method was to take the top thirty companies and randomly to select another 115 out of the 500 for a total sample of 145. After several contacts the response level finally reached 51 percent (74). The survey required that the companies respond affirmatively to the questionnaire, hence there may be some self-selection bias in the results. Since the survey was conducted by someone closely identified with the right of privacy, the companies who chose to respond may have been those who were proudest of their privacy policies. Based on this gloomy view, it could be that the practices of big business in general are a good deal more intrusive than these results would indicate.

cent to security records. However, a larger percentage of the firms will release information about its employees to *other* persons, such as credit grantors (85 percent) and landlords (49 percent). Sixty-five percent of the firms stated that they report information about their employees to government agencies without requiring a subpoena; 48 percent of the companies reporting indicated that they use investigative bureaus to collect or verify information about employees, and 77 percent reported that they maintain employee medical information for use in decision-making. While 72 percent of the firms claim that they get an employee's permission before conducting an investigation, 62 percent acknowledge that they don't always get the employee's consent in advance, and 71 percent say that they do not inform employees about the types of files they maintain about them or how they use such files.

The results of this survey suggest that even in the segment of the economy that may be the most attuned to employee privacy there are serious problems. Extraneous private information still finds its way into employment files, and private information in such files that is developed on the job is often leaked out. The employees themselves are often left in the dark at certain critical junctures. Despite the flurry of corporate activity about privacy, the question remains how far employers can go on a voluntary basis to protect their employees' rights.

One thing a company can do is eliminate the intake of nonessential personal information about applicants and employees. Oddly enough, two of the companies with the most advanced privacy programs—IBM and Cummins Engine—have come up with the exact same list of questions that could be deleted from their company forms: employment of the applicant's spouse, relatives employed with the company, type of military discharge, previous addresses, and arrest records. The similarity of the two lists suggests that the deleted information is probably unnecessary for most companies. But their similarity also suggests that the deletion of these items of information is about as far as a modern corporation can go in cutting back on the vast amount of information that it collects from its employees. Presumably these companies and other comparable companies feel that most of the information they collect about their employees either serves a legitimate corporate need or is mandated by some government, union, or other outside requirement.

But far more important than the elimination of specific questions is the elimination of outside agencies to collect such information. Neither IBM nor Cummins Engine uses credit or investigative bureaus to do background checks. This is a fruitful area of reform, because it doesn't require the firm to deprive itself of information about its employees but only to keep that inquiry "in-house." Elimination of outside investigators provides some check on the fairness of the procedure. A company personnel office is not likely to undertake the kind of all-out inquiry that many investigative firms pursue or to have the network of contacts that many such outside firms have. Even more important, the results of an in-house inquiry are more likely to remain within the company. There is much less chance that a report containing private information will follow an employee from job to job because a copy of it remained in some outside investigator's file.

Another area of potential reform is to limit the circulation of private information within the company. The object of this is to classify information on a need-to-know basis. IBM claims, for example, that personal documents and medical records of an employee are available only to the personnel and medical departments respectively, and that neither is available to the employee's supervisor. Cummins Engine has a similar policy, dividing the employee's principal file into a development file, which is available to his supervisor, and a personnel record, which is not. Cummins has also segregated the employee's medical files one step further from his other files by placing them with an affiliated Occupational Health Association and restricting access. Similarly, the Monsanto Company and Aetna Insurance have segregated medical, benefits payments, and other personnel files and limited access to the files within their companies. These and similar corporate policies are an attempt to limit unfairness within the company—to separate as much as possible staff and line functions. This may not limit the total amount of private information the corporation collects about an employee, but is an important attempt to restrict the use of such information.

Most corporate reform programs try to articulate the employees' right to see their own files. But that right is usually limited to certain files and not to others that the company feels may be too sensitive. Aetna Insurance has a list of forty-two files "you can see" and seven files "you can't see." The can-see list includes nineteen categories of files in the department management office, ten in the home office, seven in the employee health services offices, and six under the category of "corporate social responsibility." The can't-see list includes some, however, that might be of prime interest to an employee, including "records of security investigations by corporate audit-security control" and "background investigations conducted outside Aetna."* Another kind of record that is often closed off to the employee is "informal" supervisors' notes. Monsanto claims that the problem is alleviated by destroying such notes after a year, but at least one company (Cummins Engine) has expressed the fear that employee access to all formal company records will lead to a network of semipermanent "desk files" among supervisors containing more candid information. There has also been a reluctance to let employees see their medical records. IBM, for example, says that an employee has the right to see "factual medical data" but can only see the "primary active working medical record" at the "discretion of the medical department." Corporate practice on this point seems to reflect the problems that patients have generally in trying to see their records.

One of the most important reforms that has been undertaken by corporate privacy programs has been a restriction on disclosure of information outside the company. Aetna says that the only information it will give out is the employee's dates of employment and job title. Monsanto will also give out only final wage or salary and final location of job site. IBM and Cummins Engine have similar policies. These policies pertain to voluntary disclosures, and do not limit the type of information that will be turned over in response to a subpoena. In the latter case, however, Cummins Engine will normally inform the employee about the subpoena unless "prohibited from doing so by law" or unless the subpoenaed information applies to "literally thousands of employees." Limitations on disclosure of information about an employee not only protects that employee's privacy, but it is a reform that can be easily emulated by other companies. It is the kind of reform that doesn't cost a company anything and may even save it the time and money that would otherwise be spent in compiling information to comply with some outside request.

Is there a common denominator in all of this—a minimum level of employee privacy to which all companies should adhere? Alan Westin argues for a "minimum-rights" legislative approach similar to that accepted by Michigan. The Employee Right to Know Act adopted by

---

* Oddly enough, Aetna will give its employee the name of the company that conducted the investigation and suggest that he or she try to read it at that company's office.

Michigan in 1978 is the broadest employee privacy statute in the United States but is nevertheless quite modest in its scope. The rights it protects are a minimum—and may even be below the minimum—necessary for an effective employee privacy program. An argument can readily be made that a statute at least as strong as the Michigan one could be enacted on a nationwide basis without causing any significant disruption within the business community. The Michigan act allows employees to review their personnel record at "reasonable intervals" (generally, not more than twice a year). Sensitive material of the employer is excluded from the definition of personnel records and need not be disclosed. Among the exclusions are references and similar information if the identity of the person giving the information would be disclosed. Also excluded from the definition, and therefore not open to the employee, is "staff planning" material that refers to more than one employee. The employee is entitled to a copy of his personnel file upon payment of the duplication cost.

If the employee disagrees with any information in the personnel record, Michigan law allows him to place in the record a five-page "written statement explaining the employee's position." The employee's statement must be included along with any disclosure of the personnel record to any third party. Employers are also required to delete from the file any "disciplinary reports, letters of reprimand, or other reports of disciplinary action" that are more than four years old and to notify the employee whenever any more recent reports are disclosed to a third party.

This is a minimum, but even the minimum should have more to it. Use of outside investigative reports should be limited to specialized, sensitive types of occupation (such as security guards) and should only be allowed with the employee's written consent. Polygraphs, PSE, psychological questionnaires, and the like should be prohibited with or *without* the employee's consent. Employers should be prohibited from disclosing anything other than the mere fact of employment without the employee's written consent or a valid court order. When legislators and special interests begin carving away at any proposal, these are the things that must be left at the bottom line if the legislation is to accomplish its purpose.

The ability of employees to protect their privacy may be nonexistent if they are dependent enough on one particular job. People can usually change doctors, banks, or insurance companies if they are unhappy with their information practices. Although they can't "change" credit bureaus, they can ordinarily exert some pressure and threaten legal action if not treated fairly. But a job is another matter. A job defines a person's station in life and puts bread on the table. The stark fact is that many people have no choice but to accept a job on any terms the employer wants to offer. In such cases, privacy is a luxury—far down the list of priorities that is headed by the need to earn a living wage.

If privacy is high on the employee's list of priorities, he or she should give careful thought to the choice of career. A fast food chain, for example, is no place to choose for a job if one is determined not to take a polygraph test. Some jobs by their very nature put a person in the public eye and result in a great deal of exposure in the press. Some careers have special requirements that involve a sacrifice of some privacy. Police officer, bank teller, and many other jobs involve sensitive matters that ordinarily require divulgence of personal information beyond what is normal for other jobs. The disclosure may be medical, financial, personal, or a combination of all of them, depending upon the special needs of the job. The public has a right to insist, for example, that an airline pilot be in top physical condition, and anyone unwilling to disclose his or her medical condition for that purpose should probably consider another line of work.

But even in a career with no special needs for disclosure of personal information, there are limits as to what an individual employee can do on his own to protect his privacy. It depends upon his or her position in the company, bargaining power, and willingness to ruffle a few feathers. Conversely, the possibilities of group action to protect privacy rights are virtually unlimited. Many of the abuses that continue in certain businesses have been eliminated in others by tough collective-bargaining agreements between union and management.

Sometimes the impetus will come from within the company itself. Progressive companies have adopted privacy programs, and the desire for emulation by other, smaller companies may yet be the most potent force for reform. An employee suggestion along these lines might take root. The argument is simple: If IBM can survive employee privacy, why can't everyone else?

Low-Profile Strategies

Sometimes the most important step the employee can take is to ask the right questions.

- What information does the company obtain from outside sources? If the company uses credit or investigative bureaus to do background checks, it is important for you to examine the credit-bureau files first to clear up or correct any information that the credit bureau is likely to supply to the employer. If the company uses an outside testing service, you will want to know what happens to the test results—who keeps them and in what file. If the company makes its own verifications of personal, employment, or educational references, you may want to contact those references first to clear up any problems. The goal is to control the flow of personal information into the company so that any incorrect or highly personal information is not needlessly fed into the company files. But an additional purpose is to find out which other agencies will also be holding copies of this information for possible further dissemination.
- What information does the company disclose to outside organizations? Ideally, the company should do nothing more than verify employment and job title unless you consent to it. Many companies have never articulated a policy on this and simply give out information on an ad hoc basis. It is an area in which you may be able to exert some influence, since the company usually has no economic self-interest in giving out such information. You might indicate in a letter to the personnel office that you would prefer that information not be given out without your consent and ask that a copy of that letter be retained in your file. The letter should also ask that you be notified in case the company is forced to disclose any information because of a subpoena or other legal order. There is a possible side benefit: if the company informs you of some outside inquiry, you will get warning of what might otherwise be an unannounced investigation.
- What records can you examine? Many companies have a policy on this but don't disclose it to employees unless asked. A company without a definite policy might be willing to allow you to see most of your file if the request is couched in the form of "making sure that the company's records are complete."
- Who has access to which records within the company? In particular, does the company have a policy restricting supervisors from examining payroll, medical, credit-union, or other files? You may not be able to change the company's practices in this regard, but you will at least end up with a better idea of what your supervisor knows or doesn't know.

- Who has access to information in company benefit files? If company personnel have access to information in the company credit-union files, you might either use the credit union only for innocuous transactions or stay out of it entirely. If there is a choice of health plans, some thought should be given to how they are administered. In most cases, your privacy is best protected if the plan is administered outside of the regular company personnel.
- Can a lie-detector test be avoided? A job that requires such a test may not be worth it. But if you need the job, there are some things that should be considered. Some state laws and union contracts say that an employee cannot be forced to take such a test. Also, some employers will run a background check on the employee in lieu of a polygraph exam if the employee requests it. You have to decide which is the lesser of two evils. Finally, you should *not* assume that there is no harm in taking a polygraph exam if you "have nothing to hide." At the very least you will end up exposing private information about yourself in response to "background" questions. Any evasion or anxiety about such questions will register on the graph and encourage the operator to ask for more and more private details. This information could end up in the records of the employer, the polygraph company, and others.
- Take back any personal information that you can. If you don't take a job with a company, try to get back your résumé. (The same holds for employment agencies.) There is usually no legal limitation on what they can do with an applicant's file, so it makes sense to get back what you can. If a physical examination, psychological questionnaire, or something similar is required for prospective employees, you might consider sending the company a friendly letter indicating your understanding that the results of such procedures will be given to you or thrown away in the event you are not employed by the company.

CHAPTER 6

"A Bucket of Worms"

COURTS, LAWYERS, AND PRIVATE PAPERS

Patricia Hearst's efforts to have her bank robbery conviction overturned on the ground that her lawyer, F. Lee Bailey, bungled the defense could "open a new bucket of worms," Bailey said yesterday. . . .

"Anytime you attack a lawyer for his or her handling of the case you are inviting a response that explains why every step was taken. . . . If the judge rules that her [attorney-client] privilege has been waived by the attack and we are required to divulge everything she told us, there's a whole new bucket of worms on the table."

San Francisco Chronicle, August 8, 1978

Is F. Lee Bailey right, or can people expect their lawyers or other confidential advisors to go to jail rather than divulge private information? Sometimes a lawyer, doctor, or other confidant will risk prison rather than betray a client's confidence. In California, Joseph E. Lifshutz, a psychiatrist, spent three days in jail rather than testify about matters told to him by a patient in confidence. In 1976, Dr. George Caesar, another California psychiatrist, did the same thing. In St. Paul, Minnesota, David O'Connor, an attorney, took the same stance that attorney Edward Masry did in Los Angeles—he told the police they would have to arrest him before he would let them look through files pertaining to his client. These cases are exceptional. Most of the time lawyers or other professionals will do what they are told to do in the courtroom. If that means testifying against their client or giving up confidential information, that's what they're likely to do. For every lawyer who has spent time in the slammer on behalf of his client, there are many more clients who have done so because of their lawyers.

The problem of disclosure of confidential information is part of a larger problem that cuts through the whole legal system: courts are designed to elicit facts and they give short shrift to privacy. There is considerable irony in this, since the courtroom is the first place people usually think of heading when their privacy has been invaded. Courts and lawyers are supposed to be there to vindicate privacy rights, not to intrude upon them. Maybe so. But vindication is often lost in the informational machine that makes up the modern legal process. It may be easier to single out investigators or bureaucrats as privacy-invaders, but one should not overlook lawyers. Nobody is more thorough in digging into an individual's life than two lawyers and the person sitting across from them in the black robe.

The intrusiveness of the legal system forces a person into a number of difficult choices. Is it better not to pursue a justifiable claim in court rather than face the glare of publicity in the courtroom? How much will one have to change his or her finances, habits, or lifestyle to minimize the chances that he or she will end up in court? If forced into court, what can a person do to block disclosure of personal information and how much will it hurt the case? Whom, if anyone, can a person trust with private papers or confidential information? How much can one trust his or her lawyer?

The last question is the most important, because people must usually look to their lawyers to get the information necessary to answer all the other questions. But, like everything else, the lawyer-client relationship often breaks down in the meat-grinder of the legal system. People who are cautious must assume the worst: the legal process will force out a lot more private information than they bargained for. This is true even of information that they confide to their lawyers. Any unpleasant secret—like one of the worms in F. Lee Bailey's bucket—can eventually come slithering across the table.

Lawsuits and Courtrooms

... DOROTHY and HAROLD ALLEN: *husband pays $3000 a month spousal and child support for five months; then for the next seven months to 25 November 1980, $2500 a month; then $2300 a month ... wife gets all the net proceeds from sale of 133 Santa Maria, Tiburon, California ... husband gets 4800 shares of American Express....* FAYE and GERAND BURKE: *husband pays $2000 a month spousal support until 31 October 1982 ... wife gets proceeds from sale of 121 Broad Street, San Rafael, $45,000 in cash and $10,798 income tax refund ... husband gets professional medical practice with fixed assets valued at $48,000 and good will valued at $40,000....*

A TOTAL OF *$2,286,837 was distributed from the estate of Winnifred Aiken, who died 21 November 1976. Daughter Elizabeth Strong of 45 East 75th Street, New York, N.Y., received $186,462....*

RECEIVING *$1,105,078 from the $1,377,403 estate of Phillip Wilson, who died on 1 December 1977 was his widow, Elsa, of 271 Stoneman Road, Belvedere, California. . . .*

From the County Seat Digest,
May 1979, San Rafael, California

Both Dorothy and Harold Allen would probably prefer that no one know that he pays her $3000 per month in alimony. But there are probably several real estate brokers who are glad to know that both they and the Burkes are selling their houses as part of their respective divorce settlements. Countless salesmen (not to mention burglars) would be pleased with the information that a woman living on East 75th Street in Manhattan was $186,462 richer. And what down-on-his-luck adventurer would not perk up at the news of a widow who has just inherited $1,105,078?

This type of information and millions of other bits and pieces like it are generated daily in the public records of the courts. The growth of personal information in court records has occurred gradually, almost imperceptibly. Nevertheless, every time a person walks into a courtroom either as a plaintiff or a defendant—or even as a witness—he or she is subjecting himself or herself to some of the severest form of personal scrutiny. While this may be understandable if a person is accused of a serious crime, intrusions on personal privacy occur in many routine matters where the legitimate public interest in such information would appear to be slight. The vagaries of the legal system are such, however, that the simplest divorce or accident case can quickly get out of hand and result in both parties being required to bare their souls and their pocketbooks.

The problem of privacy in the legal system is really two problems. One problem is the wide range of information that a court will find relevant to the matter at hand. The individual may feel that the details of a fifteen-year-old operation are not pertinent to his present accident case or that investments made with separate funds should have no bearing on a divorce. But a court is likely to find otherwise and force disclosure of the information. Laymen unfamiliar with legal process are often shocked at the amount of information the court demands for seemingly simple matters.

The other half of the problem is public disclosure. Virtually every line of testimony and every document produced in evidence in a legal proceeding is part of the public record. This means that anyone who wants to can read it or copy it. Publications like the *County Seat Digest* don't do any investigative reporting; they merely repeat information compiled from the public records. A disclosure of private information that finds its way into the public record is particularly serious, because it is open to anyone interested enough to walk over to the county courthouse and look at it.

The two halves of the problem have to be considered separately but with an eye toward each other. On the question of input of personal information into the legal system, the individual is largely at the mercy of judges and lawyers who determine what information is—and is not—relevant to the particular type of case. As a general rule, the increased complexity of contemporary life is reflected in the legal system, with the result that wider and wider categories of personal information have become legally "relevant" in most proceedings. As keepers of this legal expertise, lawyers and judges are usually more sympathetic to their own needs for information than a witness or party's need for privacy. The result is often forced disclosure of information at certain critical junctures in a case. There is hardly a civil or criminal case that does not involve to one degree or another a person's state of mind or questions of reasonableness or good faith. The subjectivity of the issues gives competing attorneys the opportunity to zero in on the personal history of a party or witness to the action, probing the reasonableness of his behavior in light of his background.

The output of the legal system into the public records presents another problem. Virtually all of the personal information that must be disclosed in a legal proceeding also becomes disclosed to a far wider audience through the public records. The reasons for this are partly the result of good public policy but also partly the result of inertia. There is obviously a public interest in many legal proceedings that requires access by the press and the public to the courtroom. There have been enough abuses of judicial secrecy and star-chamber proceedings to justify public suspicion of secret trials. On many occasions when courts have tried to seal the record or exclude the press, the case has involved just the kind of issues of public concern where press scrutiny is most essential.

Nevertheless, there are many matters processed through the courts such as divorces, inheritance, and similar issues where the legitimate public interest is low. Many of these are uncontested matters where the parties have settled their dispute privately but are required to get a judge's signature on the matter. Sometimes they are matters that could have been handled privately (such as probate) had the parties been properly informed about the alternatives. But frequently they are matters that both sides would rather keep out of court but are unable to handle any other way (such as divorce). Moreover, even in disputed matters, a great deal of personal information about the parties and the witnesses is churned up that neither side needs but that nevertheless ends up in the court records. The simple fact is that the legal system forces a great deal of personal information into public records when no useful public purpose is being served.

Part of the problem stems from bad or nonexistent legal advice. At several stages in any legal matter there are decisions that can be made that will reduce the chances of exposure of private information. But clients are not often informed of these options. They don't think to ask the right questions, and lawyers don't think to volunteer the information. Lawyers are usually hired for a specific purpose, such as trying a case, forming a partnership, or dissolving a marriage. If the client doesn't mention that privacy is important, the lawyer is not likely to assume it. The lawyer will usually take the most direct route to his objective, thinking that his efficiency is in his client's best interests. The client may only find out too late if at all that there may have been different ways of achieving the same result that would have resulted in less disclosure of private information. A client's privacy will not be high on a lawyer's agenda unless the client puts it there.

Divorce is so common in contemporary America that it should generate little legitimate public interest. Many divorces, moreover, are uncontested as to all or some of the issues. Nevertheless, divorces are still conducted in the open, public records of the court. In most states the parties are each required to file with the court a list of their income and expenses, a list of their property and how it was acquired, a declaration about their fitness as parents, and other personal information. The divorce hearing itself is generally open to the public, and the transcript of testimony is a public record. The court order that grants the divorce also sets forth the division of property, child-custody arrangements, payments, alimony and child support, and a series of other orders affecting the lives of the parties, and a lot of it is usually a public record. While not too many divorces are spicy enough to be covered by the newspapers, that is not the real problem. Almost all divorces leave an inordinate trail of information in the public records that can be picked up by credit investigators and others who have a more mundane interest in the matter.

Some privacy can be gained by an out-of-court settlement, but that advantage can be dissipated if the settlement agreement containing the financial details is required to be included as an exhibit to the divorce decree in the public files of the court. It is no simple matter to keep the details of a settled case out of the public records in any event. In California, for example, each party must file in the open records of the court a complete list of income, expenses, and property before the chances for settlement of the cases are explored. In many California counties, the parties cannot avoid this even if a settlement has been agreed upon in advance; each must still file a complete financial declaration in any case involving alimony or child support. The ultimate extension of this procedure comes after the divorce when one of the parties tries to get a change in child support or alimony. This will trigger a new round of financial declarations that includes not only the income and expenses of the former spouses but also the same information from any new spouses (or live-in lovers) of the original parties. The information in such financial declarations is, of course, the very same information that many people try to prevent their bankers and others from disclosing. They are nevertheless forced to place that information in the public records in order to get a divorce.*

Probate presents similar problems. Few estates are ever contested, but legal procedures are set up on the assumption that they all will be. Consequently, property that is simply passed from one family member to another will have to be listed in detail and made available to everyone who wants to poke through the court records. As in divorce cases, the legitimate public interest in such information is slight.

Public disclosure of this type of information has not come about as a result of any plot against privacy. It is more a matter of inertia. Divorces, probates, guardianships, and the like have traditionally been matters decided in open court, and no one has bothered to change it. The fact that the social reality has changed—so that divorce, for example, is much more commonplace—simply hasn't been taken into account. Old court procedures are continued no matter how much private information is needlessly exposed.

Contested legal matters present another set of problems. When there are two sides to a dispute, it is probably essential that there be public access to all of the court proceedings and records to make sure that the courts are functioning fairly. In such a situation privacy must yield to

---

* The problem is *not* avoided by avoiding marriage in the first place. This may get you out of a divorce but land you in a legal hassle that intrudes upon your privacy even more. Lee and Michele Marvin probably never thought that they would end up being stripped of every last shred of privacy and dignity when they simply took up housekeeping.

other public policy. But once again, this is an old system that has been superimposed over a new reality. The rights of injured parties have been greatly expanded in the last few decades, giving rise to a huge number of cases clogging the courts.* These rights have grown both in breadth and in depth. Whole new areas of "liability" have been carved out by the legislatures and the courts, such as liability for defective products, tenants' rights, consumer warranties, medical malpractice, and countless other areas. At the same time the type of injuries for which a plaintiff can get recovery have been broadly expanded. The injured party can now recover for mental distress, emotional suffering, loss of consortium, and other types of injuries in addition to monetary damages for physical injuries.

All of this has given people a great impetus to take their case to court—but at a price: loss of privacy. But privacy is something that is often overlooked in toting up the pros and cons of pursuing a lawsuit. If a person claims mental or emotional suffering as a result of an injury, that entire subject is opened up to inquiry when he or she takes the witness stand. Sometimes the original suffering is not as bad as reliving it under the relentless cross-examination of an opposing attorney. While the original suffering may have been in silence, the re-enactment will probably be recounted in excruciating detail in the court records for anyone who wants to read it.

This ordeal is probably worth undergoing in serious cases where the original pain and suffering was so bad as to demand recompense. But there are a great many cases where people have had to disclose all of the intimate information about their mental state on the witness stand even though the possibility of a large verdict was slight. Often a lawyer will throw in a claim for mental or emotional injuries on top of an ordinary case involving physical injuries, thinking that he is doing his client a favor. Here again, if privacy considerations haven't been raised by the client, they may not be considered by the lawyer. A serious assessment of the risks of exposure at the beginning of a case might have convinced everyone that the game wasn't worth the candle.

The most serious problem with the legal process is not what goes on in the courtroom; the real damage to privacy often occurs behind the

---

* It has also spawned a tremendous increase in the number of lawyers. The United States is far ahead of other countries in this dubious distinction. At one point, for example, there were more lawyers in Los Angeles County than in all of Great Britain.

scenes. Each lawyer has, in effect, become the arbiter of what information does and does not remain private in any dispute. Modern legal procedures allow each attorney to force the disclosure of any records, testimony, or other information from an opponent or witness even though that information may only be remotely related to the issues of a lawsuit. It makes no difference that the information is hearsay, or immaterial, or ultimately inadmissible in the trial of the case. Federal and state rules allow an attorney to go on a "fishing expedition" to find out information he wants about a witness or an opposing party in the hope that it might somehow help his case. Most of this is done outside the courtroom, with little practical restraint on how far the attorney can go in digging into personal backgrounds. It is a perverse form of alchemy that allows an attorney to convert private facts into information on the public record.

Are you suing for an injury to your leg? The opposing attorney is likely to demand a list of every doctor you've ever seen in your life, copies of all medical and hospital records since the day you were born, a list of every sport or other physical activity you've ever pursued, the names of every school you've attended, and places where you were employed. Are you claiming a loss of wages as a result of the injury? Then you can add to that list questions about the salary for every job you've ever had, the value of your home and furnishings, the amount of money you have in the bank, and so on. If you are claiming mental anguish as a result of your injuries, you should expect to give over the names of every psychiatrist, therapist, or counselor you've ever seen and the reasons for their treatment. You should also expect to see them interrogated under oath, to have their records copied, and to have all doctor-patient confidentiality cast to the winds.

The process is called "discovery," and it is a debilitating experience for anyone who goes through it. Much information, of course, is still obtained by attorneys working off the record with private investigators. Discovery does not replace such investigations but only adds a new, court-sanctioned weapon to obtain information. Discovery often consists of hundreds of interrogatories about personal matters that a person must answer under oath, or it may be in the form of a deposition in which the same questions and answers are taken down by a court reporter. It may involve the forced production of all of a person's private papers for examination by an opposing attorney, and it may, in some instances, include a compulsory medical examination by a doctor in the employ of the opposing attorney. Often this is just the jumping-off point. The opposing attorney's main objective in any such interrogation may be to gain the names of witnesses, friends, doctors, or other confidants he can also interrogate.

The discovery process is a bit like strip mining. For every useful nugget of information an attorney turns up, he also turns up tons of personal data that are cast aside. It may not be used in the ultimate trial of the case, but that does not mean it is discarded. The records of any legal action consist of more than just the transcript of the trial; they include all of the transcripts of depositions, answers to interrogatories, and all of the volumes of subpoenaed records that were not used in the actual trial. Copies of all this material is available to anyone poking through the courthouse records or in an opponent's law office. What an attorney in his single-minded pursuit of a case may finally decide is not useful for his purposes may prove to be a gold mine for an investigator interested in other aspects of a person's life.

A person's own attorney can protect him or her to some degree from overly broad discovery by an opposing attorney. But, for a variety of reasons, this is not frequently done. Part of it is a lack of sensitivity. Lawyers grill each other's clients all the time, and it is easy for them to forget what an intrusive process it really is. Part of it is also priorities. A lawyer wants to win a case and doesn't care about personal information that doesn't affect the outcome. If he is suing over a knee injury, for example, he is likely to sit back without objection while the opposing attorney grills his client about an abortion that happened ten years earlier or a drinking problem that has since been cured. Unless the client tells the lawyer in advance that protection of his or her privacy is as important as anything else in the case, the discovery process may grind up every fact it can find.

The situation may be even worse for a person who is just a witness in a case. People who are not parties to a case may nevertheless have to sit through a deposition in an attorney's office in front of a court reporter. Unlike the parties, however, the witness will usually not have an attorney present to protect his or her interests. The witness may be asked highly personal background questions and not have the slightest idea whether or not he is required to answer them. It is not likely, in any event, that he will know that he is creating a handy dossier about himself that will be included in the public records at the courthouse.

Intrusive tactics against parties and witnesses do not complete the picture. The most gratuitous invasions of privacy in any court proceeding are reserved for the only other laymen involved: the jurors. In the interests of finding an unbiased jury (or one biased in his client's favor) an attorney is given broad latitude to question jurors about their backgrounds, attitudes, employment, religious beliefs, and so on. As with parties and witnesses, however, the most significant actions go on outside the courtroom. Most communities have various "jury reporting" services that compile dossiers on prospective jurors for use by attorneys. This includes voting registration, marital status, voting records on prior juries, and anything else that can be picked up from the public records or from other attorneys. Like everyone else involved in a legal procedure, jurors are likely to find that their private lives have become public knowledge.

The tradeoff between what is to be gained and what is to be lost in a lawsuit is no more starkly put than in an action for invasion of privacy. This type of lawsuit has come into being at roughly the same time as the other expansion of the rights of injured persons. There has never been one consistent legal theory underlying such a lawsuit, but rather a collection of torts that are all roughly related to the idea of privacy.

One such theory has given rise to lawsuits for the "public disclosure of embarassing facts," while a related legal action has been allowed for publicity that places an individual in a "false light." A more general type of privacy action has been allowed for actions that intrude upon a person's "solitude." Still other legal concepts have allowed an invasion-of-privacy lawsuit for commercial exploitation of certain private information about an individual. These doctrines have evolved through the courts and have been given refinements by various state legislatures. Congress and the state legislatures have added a few privacy rights of their own by giving an aggrieved individual the right to sue for violations of the Fair Credit Reporting Act, the Privacy Act of 1974, the Right to Financial Privacy Act of 1978, and other similar statutes.

A lawsuit can be a potent weapon against egregious invasions of privacy. Such lawsuits, however, are usually only effective against extreme examples of conduct that the law otherwise tolerates. There is no general law, for instance, that prohibits a department store from monitoring the movements of its customers by peepholes or closed-circuit television. When, however, Lord & Taylor carried its observation of a customer into the ladies' dressing room, that became part of the basis for a $51,000 jury verdict against the store for invasion of the customer's privacy. It is not generally illegal for a company to observe the activities of an employee or even to make inquiries about his home life. But when the Philadelphia Police Department maintained a twenty-four-hour surveillance on an officer because he was living with a woman who was not his wife, this led to a court award of reinstatement on his job plus back pay. Similarly, it is not illegal for an attorney or an insurance company to use an investigator to try to find information about an accident victim to defeat an insurance claim. But when an investigator in California overstepped the bounds of propriety and secured certain information from the injured party by deception while she was confined to a hospital room, the investigator and his employers were exposed to a large damage claim. Likewise, federal statutes such as the Privacy Act of 1974 or the Right of Financial Privacy Act of 1978 allow lawsuits by injured parties, but relief is generally available only for "willful or intentional" violations.

Privacy lawsuits hit at the rough edges of the problem but leave the heart of the matter untouched. Occasional verdicts for successful plaintiffs have helped ease the pain for those individuals but have not had much deterrent effect on more commonplace invasions of privacy. Someone contemplating a lawsuit, therefore, needs to think carefully about how outrageous the other person's conduct was and how much legally compensable damages he or she can show. Unless those lines intersect at a point that puts the case well into the extraordinary category, a lawsuit is probably ill-advised.

A person needs also to consider what he or she is giving up. In 1975 the man who grabbed Sara Jane Moore's arm as she was about to shoot President Ford was later described by a San Francisco columnist as a homosexual. The problem was that he hadn't intended to come out of the closet—at least not quite that way. He filed suit against the newspapers that ran the story on the grounds of invasion of privacy: public disclosure of an embarrassing, private fact. The lawsuit, however, got as much if not more publicity than the original story. As the dispute escalated, the disclosure became more widespread. The California Court of Appeals finally noted with a good deal of irony that it was becoming part of the problem. The man's privacy, the court stated, "is considerably invaded by the enshrining in hard cover of this published opinion."

A lawsuit for invasion of privacy almost inevitably reopens the old wound, and a good defense attorney will continue to pick at the scab. What was the private information you claim was disclosed? Why was this embarrassing to you? What was it in your medical report (or credit report, or government file) that you didn't want disclosed? How do you claim you were injured? Exactly what kind of emotional suffering did you go through? These kinds of questions are likely to be repeated at trial, in depositions, to the party's psychiatrist, and so on until the injured person wonders whether the lawsuit might not be more painful than the original experience. A lawsuit can almost never restore privacy; instead it can only offer recompense to make up for the suffering. The question that must be pondered carefully in each case is whether the damages that may be recovered will outweigh the further intrusions and indignities that will have to be endured in the process.

Confidential Disclosures

He was the lawyer for my divorce, a couple of lawsuits—everything. I wanted to put together a business to build FHA houses, and he came in on the deal. He took shares of stock instead of a fee.

What went wrong?

The Feds claimed we tried to pay off an FHA official. They offered me a deal if I'd testify against him. I told them we didn't do anything wrong, and I said I wouldn't do it.

Then what happened?

They offered the same deal to my lawyer, and he took it. He got up on the witness stand and told everything he ever knew about me.

Interview with Joseph Zimmer, convicted in
U.S. Federal Court in Detroit, Michigan

Communications between a lawyer and client are supposed to be privileged. The law bestows its highest forms of blessing on this type of confidential disclosure and normally will neither require nor allow such information to be revealed in court. Normally. The problem is that there are just enough exceptions to the general rule as to undermine it entirely. The entire notion of confidential disclosures is fraught with misinformation and mistaken assumptions. What starts out as an expectation of secrecy often ends up as a footrace to the witness stand.

Almost everyone who solicits sensitive information promises confidentiality, but almost no one can deliver on that promise. Insurance agents ask for medical information to help them sell life or health insurance. Brokers or investment counselors want financial information to plan your portfolio. Virtually anyone and everyone in any personal-service industry encourages clients to disclose private information on the promise that it will be held in confidence.

What does this promise mean? A good deal less than it implies. The person soliciting the information probably has in mind a certain amount of "routine" disclosure that may not violate the client's notions of confidentiality. An insurance broker, for example, will ordinarily submit such information to one or more insurance companies in an application for insurance. Information in the hands of an insurance company, however, is no longer under the control of the broker. Whatever the broker's intentions, he can no longer protect the confidentiality of the information once it reaches the insurance company and goes through the process of disclosure that is normal within the insurance industry. Is this understood by the client? Maybe—maybe not. Since there is no general standard to determine confidentiality, the client may be in for some unpleasant surprises.

What if the confidant does disclose the information in open breach of his or her promise? The injured party may have a lawsuit, but it will not be an easy one. There are no general laws imposing penalties on a faithless confidant. Deliberate disclosure of such information in most cases does not subject the guilty party to any special civil or criminal penalties. Some other legal theory, such as fraud or breach of contract, will have to be stretched to fit the situation, or the injured party will be left without a remedy.

The most difficult problem with a promise of confidentiality, however, is the inability of the confidant to protect the information. No matter how solemn the promise or how good the intentions, most confidants will have to disclose any information they have whenever a legal dispute arises. The confidant may be hit with a subpoena to produce certain documents or a search warrant. Either of these legal devices can force a disclosure. The confidant must normally give up his or her information whenever called as a witness in any criminal trial, civil trial, grand jury hearing, investigation by a government agency, or at a deposition in the offices of a hostile attorney. The law follows the precept that "the public has a right to every man's evidence." Courts usually follow that rule zealously, and they are not often impressed with a confidant's statement of a promise to keep his or her mouth shut.

Most states protect certain types of privileged communications, such as those between lawyer and client, doctor and patient, priest and penitent, and husband and wife. Confidants in these categories (with certain important exceptions) can be prevented from testifying in legal proceedings. But these testimonial privileges are narrowly construed. The importance of the information itself does not give rise to the privilege. One cannot, for example, disclose information to a bookkeeper or a financial advisor and claim that it is privileged simply because the same information would be protected if disclosed to an attorney. Indeed, many courts would even rule that such a disclosure was a "waiver" that destroyed the confidentiality of the same information that is later given to the lawyer. The law is full of these unpleasant traps.

Modern society has run right past the traditional categories of privileged communications. New relationships have grown up that lawmakers have almost totally ignored. People consult lawyers, but they also get advice from tax accountants, real estate brokers, bookkeepers, stockbrokers, investment advisors, career counselors, insurance agents, union representatives, independent adjusters, bankers, and countless other professionals and paraprofessionals. Doctor-patient communications have been supplemented by disclosures of medical information to psychologists, social workers, therapists, and many others. Priests, rabbis, and ministers have lost their monopoly over the secrets of the soul to gurus, encounter groups, and all sorts of practitioners. Even the spousal relationship has been shoved somewhat aside by people living in intimate but unmarried relationships. To persons involved in such relationships, there is seemingly little difference between them and more traditional relationships. They have the same expectation of confidentiality. But to a lawyer or an investigator trying to ferret out information, there is a substantial difference. The new-style confidants may not fit into any of the traditional legal categories and can therefore be forced to disgorge any confidential information they have acquired.

Some states have added certain privileged communications to the traditional categories, but the list is uneven and unreliable. The matter is complicated further by the fact that we live under a dual court system—one state and one federal. What is privileged in one court may not be in the other. For example, fourteen states now recognize some form of privilege for information given in confidence to an accountant,* but accountants in those states may still be haled into a federal court or into a court in a neighboring state and forced to testify against their clients. Since the federal courts are where the Internal Revenue Service does most of its business, a person runs a substantial risk disclosing confidential information to his accountant, no matter what the state law may be.

---

* Arizona, Colorado, Florida, Georgia, Illinois, Iowa, Kentucky, Louisiana, Maryland, Michigan, Nevada, New Mexico, Pennsylvania, Tennessee.

Different states have attached a privilege to other kinds of communications, but they follow no regular pattern. In Oregon a stenographer cannot be forced to testify as to any "communication or dictation" heard in the course of his or her employment. Anywhere else, a secretary is fair game for an interrogator. New York and California recognize privileged communication with social workers, but other states do not. In many states a private detective can be compelled to disclose confidential information, unless he is working under the control of an attorney. Connecticut, Michigan, and Oregon protect the confidentiality of communications from students to teachers, while Idaho, Iowa, Maine, and Pennsylvania limit the protection to "school guidance personnel." Nevada only protects such communications "concerning the pupil's possession or use of drugs or alcoholic beverages made while the teacher was counseling or attempting to counsel such pupil." Other states give no protection to confidential disclosures between students and teachers.

The uncertainty of what is and what is not confidential extends into the area of medicine and psychology. Most states recognize a doctor-patient privilege and extend it to include communications with psychiatrists and psychotherapists who are also medical doctors. However, communications to psychologists are generally not protected unless there is a specific psychologist-patient privilege, as in twenty-one states.* But only one state, Colorado, specifically recognizes the confidentiality of statements made to a psychologist in group therapy. This technique (quite common in modern psychology) has generally suffered from a lack of legal protection. If disclosures are made in a marriage counseling session, for example, the psychologist may not only be required in many states to testify in a later divorce action, but he may also have to disclose related disclosures made in private sessions. Many courts would also find a waiver of confidentiality for information disclosed at larger group therapy sessions and compel the psychologist to testify.

Breaches in the confidentiality of matters disclosed to an attorney are among the most serious because they catch the client at a point

---

* Alabama, Arkansas, California, Colorado, Delaware, Florida, Georgia, Idaho, Illinois, Indiana, Kentucky, Montana, Nevada, New Hampshire, New York, North Carolina, Oregon, Tennessee, Utah, Washington, Wyoming.

where he or she is the most vulnerable. People normally only consult a lawyer on serious matters—often matters of borderline criminality or well beyond the border. When they do so, they are encouraged by their attorney to tell all of the facts—favorable and unfavorable—so that he or she can properly advise them. If this confidence is later breached, the client is left almost helpless. Ironically, the exceptions to the lawyer-client privilege all have one other thing in common: it takes a lawyer to know when they apply.

Many exceptions to the rule of attorney-client privilege are simply traps for the unwary. If a client asks a witness to meet with the client's attorney to recount certain facts, he may be surprised to find out that the information given to the attorney by the witness isn't privileged even though the client's own summary of the witness's statement would have been. He could be in for more of a surprise if he brings the witness with him to talk to the attorney: not only would the witness's statement to the attorney not be privileged but the client's *own* statement might not be privileged either. The reason? An exception grafted onto the attorney-client that excludes communications "in the presence of a third person who is not the agent of either client or attorney." Similarly, the attorney-client privilege may be lost if a court rules—after the fact—that the information given to the attorney was intended to be transmitted to someone else, or that he was not consulted in his "attorney's capacity," or that he was only an "attesting witness" to the transaction.

In addition, there are the problems that arise when an attorney represents several individuals or an organization. If two people consult an attorney and later have a falling out, the attorney can be forced to disclose anything told to him in confidence by either in any legal action between them. If a corporate attorney interviews an employee as a witness, disclosures made by the employee would probably not be privileged if the employee himself were later sued. Moreover, there are many situations in which an attorney who represents a group or an organization is required to disclose to one client information received from another client even if not compelled by a court order. Why? To avoid getting sued himself. The Securities and Exchange Commission has, for example, been leaning heavily on attorneys in various situations to disclose any violations of law they know about or face the possibility of being charged with the same violation. The legal principles in these cases—and the possibilities of disclosure—are complex, strained, and frequently unpredictable.

While most lawyers are honest enough when they think about it to tell a client when they can and cannot protect their confidential disclosures, this cooperation breaks down in a couple of critical situations. One is when the lawyer and client turn against each other. If a lawyer has to sue his client to collect what he is owed, the Canons of Ethics of the American Bar Association allow him to disclose "confidence or secrets necessary to establish or collect his fee...." The same situation applies when the client takes the initiative and sues the lawyer for malpractice. The lawyer can reveal everything told to him by the client that would have any bearing on whether he acted negligently. This is a potent weapon. It is even more potent in a related situation where the client tries to set aside a criminal conviction on the grounds that the attorney acted incompetently. This is the point, according to F. Lee Bailey, where the client is inviting the judge to rule that the attorney-client privilege "has been waived by the attack." From that point forward, "we are required to divulge everything she told us."

Even more disturbing is the possibility of disclosure of confidential information in a situation that was initiated neither by the lawyer nor the client. The Canons of Ethics allow such disclosure by an attorney "to defend himself ... against an accusation of wrongful conduct." This is *not* limited to accusations made by the client. If an attorney faces the possibility of a serious charge against himself by a governmental agency, he may take the initiative and disclose whatever confidential information he may have to try to protect himself.

Probably the most frequent cause of the breakdown of the attorney-client privilege of confidentiality is the distressing tendency of lawyers to "jump into bed" with their clients. In many law firms throughout the country it is standard practice to cut the firm in for a "piece of the action" in new business ventures by a client. In part, this is done to save the client money; the lawyer may take shares of stock instead of a legal fee for his services. But it is also partly motivated by the feeling of many attorneys that there is more money to be made in business than in practicing law.* Whatever the motivation, it raises serious problems for clients, one of which is loss of the attorney-client privilege for confidential disclosures. The transition from lawyer to business partner may be a subtle one that is not at all clear to the client. But if a court determines after the fact that the parties had a business relationship, all privilege of confidentiality is lost. When the situation gets tight, the attorney may crack first and reveal whatever confidential information he has to save himself.

---

* Which is the exact opposite of the feeling held by most clients.

What about commercial exploitation of a client's secrets? Unthinkable? Perhaps. Nevertheless, two New York lawyers agreed to represent David Berkowitz, the "Son of Sam" killer, for $3000 and a share of the proceeds of any books, movies, or television programs that would be written about him. And in Los Angeles three lawyers had contracted with the man accused of being the "Skid Row Stabber" in exchange for an assignment of the book rights, until a judge forced them to withdraw from the case. But few have gone as far as the lawyer for accused mass-murderer Juan Corona, as shown in this excerpt of a 1978 California Court of Appeals decision:

> Corona was represented at the trial by Richard E. Hawk, a privately retained sole practitioner. Since Corona was not able to pay the substantial amount of attorney's fees chargeable in a case of such magnitude, a fee agreement was entered into between the parties. Pursuant to the agreement, Hawk was granted exclusive literary and dramatic property rights to Corona's life story, including the proceedings against him, in return for legal services. Under the agreement, Corona expressly waived the attorney-client privilege, thereby removing any impediment to the publication of the most intimate and confidential details of his life and his trial. . . . In the wake of the agreement, Hawk hired Ed Cray, a professional writer who participated in the proceedings as Hawk's investigator and sat at the counsel table during the trial. Well before the commencement of the trial, Cray and Hawk entered into a contract with the Macmillan Publishing Company to publish the book to be written about Corona and his trial. The book, entitled *Burden of Proof: The Case of Juan Corona,* authored by Cray and supplemented by Hawk's afterword, was published just a few months after the completion of the trial.

Maybe we should be thankful that it hasn't become a television miniseries.

Subpoenas and Court Orders

"*United States of America,*
Plaintiff,

              SUBPOENA DUCES TECUM

v. _____

Defendant. _____

To: _____

YOU ARE HEREBY ORDERED *to appear and testify at . . .*
YOU ARE FURTHER ORDERED *to bring with you the books, docu-*

ments, records, or other things in your possession or under your control as follows....

A government subpoena

In effect, the subpoena has become a tool that government agents can use to seize the records of an individual without being required either to give him an opportunity to dispute this action before his privacy is invaded or to establish a reasonable basis for the seizure....

The Privacy Commission

A subpoena allows an investigator to dispense with subtlety and fall back on authority; subpoenas compel testimony and order the production of private records. They may be directed at the person being investigated or—more importantly—at a bank, insurance company, hospital, accountant, lawyer, or any other "third party" who has information or records about the person being scrutinized.

The traditional function of a subpoena has been that of an adjunct to a lawsuit, and it has been justified as a necessary device to gather evidence for use in a particular case. Subpoenas are still used for that purpose, but their use has spread so that they are now often part of a much broader type of inquiry. A subpoena may be issued in connection with a trial, a deposition, or a grand jury investigation, or it may simply be issued by an administrator in some government agency. Subpoenas sweep up in their wake credit reports, investigative records, medical reports, and all sorts of other documents and records that may be available. But they do something even more important: they grab records that are otherwise *not* available. An investigator armed with a subpoena can obtain from a confidant or other third party documents that such people would not normally give up. That has become more and more the prime function of a subpoena, in fact—to punch through a promise of confidentiality.

"It looks like a court order. It acts like a court order. It will cost us money to oppose it, but it won't cost us anything to comply with. Why don't we just give them what they are asking for in the subpoena?"

Virtually all subpoenas have two things in common: They all look like they have been issued by a judge, but none of them have been. Despite the naked governmental power standing behind the subpoena, they are almost always issued without the prior approval of a judge. Grand jury subpoenas, for example, are issued under the direction of the prosecuting attorney; a judge is never consulted. Administrative subpoenas (sometimes called a summons) are usually issued by middle-echelon government employees, again without court approval. Almost any attorney in any civil action can have a subpoena issued "in blank" by a court clerk. The attorney then fills in the blanks with the name of the person and the documents he wants produced. The power of a subpoena stems from the fact that it looks like a court order, but judges have virtually nothing to do with the way in which they are issued. Subpoenas have become a game that any attorney or administrator can play.

Lawmakers justify this procedure by saying that even though subpoenas are not issued by a judge, they normally can only be "enforced" by a judge. If the person doesn't want to give up the documents called for in the subpoena, so the argument goes, he or she can simply refuse to do so and force the matter to court where he or she will get a hearing. This seemingly plausible rationale overlooks one important point: the person being investigated is usually *not* the person served with the subpoena. The prime targets at which subpoenas are aimed are bookkeepers, accountants, brokers, hospitals, employers, banks, insurance agents, credit agencies—anyone who is likely to be holding sensitive records about someone else. When, for example, a broker is served with a subpoena to turn over certain client records, he or she does not normally make plans to run downtown and see the judge. It is rare indeed that someone will want to get into a court fight over the confidentiality of *someone else's* records. It is simply human nature not to get involved in another person's fight unless one has to.

And the law says you don't have to. It is perfectly legal for the third party holding the records to copy them and turn them over in compliance with the subpoena to whoever is demanding them. In some situations, moreover, that is the record-holder's *only* alternative. Several court decisions have cut back on the right of record-holders to fight a subpoena. The rationale of the courts is that the person holding the record doesn't have "standing"—he is not a party to the dispute. Hence, even if the confidant or other person holding the records feels strongly enough about the matter to go to court, chances are he or she may lose anyway. It is easy to see that a trip to the Xerox machine usually seems a lot shorter and a lot safer than a trip to the courthouse.

How about the person being investigated? Can't he go to court and fight the disclosure of his personal records under the subpoena? Sometimes, yes. But he has to find out about it first. With certain types of subpoenas neither the person being investigated nor his attorney gets any notice that the subpoena has been issued. This is normally true with administrative subpoenas (subpoenas issued by government investigators) and grand jury subpoenas. In most of these cases the person under investigation won't even know it is happening unless the third party holding the records calls him up and tells him about it. By then it is often too late.

Notice is given for subpoenas issued in the course of an ordinary lawsuit. Theoretically, at least, the attorney for the party being investigated can step in and demand a hearing on the fairness of the subpoena before any records are turned over. In practice, he or she rarely does so. The reason? Once again, it is the attorney's attitude toward the client's privacy. Unless the client stresses the need for keeping certain records confidential, the attorney may not think it important to do so.

The problem is hopelessly intertwined with the way attorneys try lawsuits. In a personal-injury case, for example, a defense attorney will routinely issue subpoenas to every hospital and doctor the plaintiff has ever contacted and demand a copy of all medical records. The plaintiff's attorney will normally not go to court to fight such a subpoena but will simply let the records be copied. Since court appearances cost time, energy, and money, the plaintiff's attorney may see no good reason to contest the subpoena because he can always exclude the irrelevant information from the courtroom at the time of trial. Information that does not affect the case may, however, compromise the client's privacy. The defense attorney, the defendant's insurance company, and anyone who takes the time to paw through the court records may find a complete medical record on the person covering many sensitive things that have nothing to do with the case being litigated. The attorney didn't know this, because the client didn't tell him there was anything important in the records. The client didn't know, because the attorney didn't tell him the entire record would be subpoenaed and copied. While everyone focuses on the lawsuit, it is easy for privacy to slip between the cracks.

Lillian Couch, the proprietor of a restaurant, always left her bank records and business records with her accountant so that he could prepare her income tax returns. There is nothing unusual about this, except that the Internal Revenue Service decided it wanted to look at these records and issued a summons to Mrs. Couch's accountant to produce them. Her accountant protested that the documents were privileged, but in 1973 the U.S. Supreme Court ruled against her in *Couch v. United States* and allowed the IRS to seize the documents.

Dr. E. J. Mason and two other taxpayers went one step further. To protect their tax documents from seizure, they turned all of their accountant's workpapers over to their respective attorneys for legal advice. Again the IRS demanded the documents, and again the matter ended up in the Supreme Court. The taxpayers not only claimed the privilege against self-incrimination but in this instance claimed the attorney-client privilege as well; the result was the same. In 1976 in *Fisher v. United States* the Supreme Court ruled that the IRS could seize the records from the taxpayers' attorneys.

The *Couch* and *Fisher* cases have knocked the props out from under the notion of confidentiality in a person's private papers. In both cases the taxpayers did everything one would normally do to keep personal papers private, but in the end they both had to give them up. The result is an important extension of the subpoena power. An administrator armed with a summons or subpoena can now—with the Supreme Court's blessing—get at the client's most sensitive papers in the hands of his or her attorney.

The logic of the Supreme Court's argument is as chilling as the result. Justice Lewis Powell agreed that Mrs. Couch's documents would have been privileged if she had kept them but concluded that she waived that privilege when she gave them to her tax accountant: "He, not the taxpayer, is the only one compelled to do anything." Since there is no accountant-client privilege under federal law, he had to relinquish the records. Justice Powell also suggested that the accountant might want to give up her records to save his own hide: "Indeed, the accountant himself risks criminal prosecution if he knowingly assists in the preparation of a false return.... His own need for self-protection would often require the right to disclose the information given him."

In *Couch* the court concluded that the taxpayer's privileged documents could be seized because her relationship with her accountant was not privileged. But in *Fisher,* the taxpayers gave the records to their attorneys, and federal law *does* recognize an attorney-client privilege. However, it makes no difference, reasoned Justice Byron White, because what the IRS wanted were the accountant's workpapers, which the accountant—not the taxpayers—had written. Even though the taxpayers turned them over to their attorneys for advice, such papers were not protected under the attorney-client privilege. "The accountant's workpapers are not the taxpayers'. They were not prepared by him, and they contain no testimonial declarations by him." Although the accountant's workpapers were based on information supplied by the taxpayer, the Supreme Court did not think that the information was entitled to protection.

According to Justice White, the taxpayers' decision to give confidential information to their accountants was "wholly voluntary." It was, however, voluntary in the sense that eating is voluntary. The Supreme Court's reasoning overlooks the dilemma in which the taxpayer has been placed. Each individual is required under the Internal Revenue Code to file a tax return and keep such records as are necessary to compute his taxes. But if he gives those records to his accountant, they can be seized by the IRS. If he keeps the records and simply tells the accountant what is in the documents, the accountant's workpapers based on that information can be seized. If he does neither one and attempts to prepare his taxes himself, he runs the risk of serious penalties for filing an inaccurate return. Justice William Douglas, who dissented from the Court's rulings, pointed out just how unfair the situation was for the taxpayer: *"Our tax laws have become so complex that very few taxpayers can afford the luxury of completing their own returns without professional assistance. If a taxpayer now wants to insure the confidentiality and privacy of his records, however, he must forego such assistance."* It is a situation reminiscent of the double squeeze performed by Congress and the Supreme Court in which Congress required bank records to be duplicated and the Supreme Court proceeded to strip them of confidentiality. In this case the records are tax records, but the result is basically the same. The Internal Revenue Code requires detailed records to be kept for tax purposes, but the Supreme Court has followed up with a series of rulings that makes it almost impossible to protect the confidentiality of those records.

The problem is not just tax records, although there the problem is the most acute. The rulings of the Supreme Court apply to any documents given to a lawyer or other confidant and simply drives one more wedge between the client and his or her attorney. Both client and lawyer must now examine every document in the client's file and try to predict what the court is likely to do with it if the attorney were served with a subpoena. The situation is just vague and unpredictable enough that many attorneys are declining to hold on to certain documents that might otherwise be useful in helping them advise their clients. It is a situation where clients have to choose between possible loss of privacy and a possible loss of good legal advice, with the likelihood that they could end up losing both.

The evolution of the subpoena has carried it out of the courtroom and into the administrative arm of the government. The most important use now of a subpoena is as a broad research tool for government agencies, and it gives bureaucrats an added punch in their fight to grab personal information. More than 160 federal statutes give various agencies within the government the power to issue subpoenas: the Securities and Exchange Commission (SEC), the Federal Communications Commission (FCC), the Small Business Administration (SBA), the Interstate Commerce Commission (ICC), the Department of Housing and Urban Development (HUD), and the National Labor Relations Board (NLRB), for example, all have the power to issue them. (Sometimes the power is limited to certain functions within the agency. At other times, as with the Securities and Exchange Commission, it is hard to determine what limitations exist on the subpoena power.) This list, as big as it is, does not begin to cover the numerous state and local agencies that have been granted subpoena powers by state legislatures.

The power to issue administrative subpoenas, further, is usually given to middle-echelon personnel within the agency. As with other types of subpoena, no judge approves them in advance. But there is a marked difference between ordinary court subpoenas and administrative subpoenas, because the subpoenas of the administrative variety are usually issued without notice to the person being investigated. There are exceptions. The Right to Financial Privacy Act of 1978, for example, requires advance notice to the person whose financial records will be grabbed by subpoena from a federal agency. The Tax Reform Act of 1976 requires a similar notice when the IRS uses its summons power to go after various records. But there are exceptions to the exceptions, and both of the federal statutes requiring notice to the individual break down in certain key situations.

The lack of notice about the issuance of a subpoena is often compounded by a lack of notice that there is even an investigation being conducted. The government agency may have a rough idea that something is wrong but not a reasonable basis to suspect any one individual of any wrongdoing. Nevertheless most agencies can use their subpoena powers to grab personal records just to make a more-or-less random check on things to see if they can spot any law violators. A government agency may, for example, subpoena the deposit records of a bank, the client list of a broker, the files of an insurance agent, or any other broad category of otherwise private documents as part of a general investigation. The Supreme Court has given its blessing to this power, characterizing it as "a power of inquisition" in which the government can use its subpoena power "merely on suspicion that the law is being violated, or even just because it wants assurance that it is not." The government agency may not have anyone in mind as a target for further investigation until it has sifted through the documents and found a few names. Rather than starting with a list of suspects, the government often uses the subpoena to create the list of suspects in the first place.

The breadth of this power is enormous. It is no exaggeration to say that for virtually every activity an American engages in there is probably at least one agency with the power to subpoena records about it. In fact, that statement may be true for just one agency alone: the Internal Revenue Service. The IRS can compel production of virtually any document it wants to see. Supreme Court Justice Potter Stewart, objecting to the Court's refusal to clamp down on the power of the IRS, pointed out that the IRS claims the power to seize practically every document in the country. "Our economy is 'tax relevant' in almost every detail," said Justice Stewart. "Accordingly, if a summons could issue for any material, conceivably relevant to 'taxation' . . . [the IRS] could use the summons power as a broad research device."

"A broad research device" seems to be exactly what the Supreme Court condoned in the case in which Justice Stewart voiced his dissent. In *United States v. Bisceglia,* the IRS sought to enforce its summons against a recalcitrant bank officer from the Commercial Bank of Middlesboro in Kentucky. The sole basis for the investigation was the bank's deposit of a large number of old hundred-dollar bills with the Federal Reserve. On these facts alone the IRS concluded that someone may not have paid taxes on some transaction involving the bills, and consequently they issued a John Doe summons to grab all of the bank records to determine which customer may have deposited the cash. No notice was given to the bank customer, and, indeed, in the Tax Reform Act enacted by Congress the next year such John Doe summonses were specifically exempted from the notice requirements.

In an important ruling, the Supreme Court concluded that this broad-sweeping use of the subpoena power was permissible. Chief

Justice Warren Burger conceded that such a John Doe summons or subpoena could be used in an "infinite variety" of situations, but that did not in his view make it illegal or unconstitutional. But critics concluded that the Court had left the door open for widespread abuse by government agencies: *"Every day the economy generates thousands of sales, loans, gifts, purchases, leases, deposits, mergers, wills, and the like which—because of their size or complexity—suggest the possibility of tax problems for somebody."* That's pretext enough, Justice Stewart concluded, for the government to "force disclosure of whole categories of transactions" on the theory that they might be able to collect "some kind of federal tax from somebody."

Administrative subpoenas can pick up a broad sweep of private information, but they are not in the same league as grand jury subpoenas. The power of the grand jury is awesome, and as a privacy invader it is almost without equal. Grand jury procedure frequently amounts to a virtual suspension of the Bill of Rights. A potential suspect subpoenaed before a grand jury does not have to be advised of his right to remain silent or his rights to an attorney. Advising him of his right to an attorney wouldn't do much good anyway, since a witness *cannot* even bring an attorney with him when he is hauled into the grand jury room. He or she must simply match wits with a trained prosecutor in front of the grand jury while a stenographer records the testimony. Illegally seized evidence? It may be inadmissible at trial, but the Supreme Court says it is all right for a prosecutor to use such evidence in front of the grand jury to try and wrangle a damaging admission out of a witness. The Fifth Amendment is theoretically available to a witness sophisticated enough to use it ("I refuse to answer on the grounds that it may tend to incriminate me"), but even that can be undercut by a prosecutor's grant of use immunity to a witness: The government cannot use the witness' own testimony against him in court but can use other evidence developed in the case. Given these powers, it is not surprising to find that a grand jury subpoena is a more potent weapon than other types of subpoena. A witness who fails to obey a grand jury subpoena can be quickly jailed without any of the procedural protections available with other types of subpoenas.

"Ordinarily, of course, a witness has no right of privacy before a grand jury." Ordinarily, of course, Supreme Court justices are not quite so cavalier in their disregard of privacy interests as Justice Lewis

Powell appeared to be in that statement. Nevertheless, that phrase from a 1976 Supreme Court decision shows the great deference the Court has accorded to the grand jury and its powers.

But it is misleading to talk about the power of the grand jury, because what is really at work is the power of the U.S. Attorney General and the FBI. It is the behind-the-scenes link between grand juries and government administrative agencies that raises the greatest danger of abuse in investigations conducted in the name of the grand jury. This link means that grand jury investigations are more than simply inquiries directed at big-name criminals. They are part of the overall, information-gathering process of the government.

"Acting in the name of grand jury authority, a prosecutor can do almost anything," according to Congressman John Burton (D-Calif.). He can "subpoena whoever he wants without giving a reason, ask prying questions, [or] withhold evidence that might show a person's innocence." The federal prosecutor's office simply issues a subpoena in the name of the grand jury at anything or anybody it wants. According to the Privacy Commission, this is done "without the knowledge, not to mention approval, of the Grand Jury." Subpoenas issued in the name of the Grand Jury are not limited by subject matter, by person, by notice to the person being investigated, or anything else. Such subpoenas are, again in the words of the Privacy Commission, "a generalized resource for Federal investigative activities."

Theoretically, information under the seal of a grand jury remains confidential and is not released to other agencies, but that too has become a fiction. Federal agents often use the grand jury subpoena to obtain information that is never even given to the grand jury. Instead, the information is collected by investigative agents in the name of the grand jury and catalogued and copied in much the same way as any other information in government files. The Treasury Department and the FBI, for example, use the information gathered under the compulsion of a grand jury subpoena to add to the other information in their investigative files. Moreover, it is doubtful that information that is ultimately turned over to the grand jury is protected against further disclosure within government, since at least a copy of that information is usually kept in the files of an investigative agency.

Proof of the deference given to grand jury subpoenas is the exemption created under the Right to Financial Privacy Act of 1978. Unlike other federal agencies, the grand jury is not required to give notice to a customer that his bank records have been subpoenaed, nor does the customer have a chance to go to court to try to stop the subpoena. The only restriction Congress imposed on the grand jury was that bank records have to be "actually presented" to the grand jury and that they shall be "destroyed or returned" if not used in the actual prosecution of a crime. This is somewhat of a back-door admission by the federal government that information normally subpoenaed under the authority of the grand jury doesn't go to the grand jury. And it further underscores the fact that—with the possible exception of bank records—the grand jury has become a handy excuse for the wholesale collection of personal information by federal agents.

The Privacy Commission concluded that the grand jury subpoena "has become little more than an administrative tool, its connection with the traditional functions of the Grand Jury attenuated at best." An individual beleaguered by forced disclosures of private information might conclude that it is simply one of the most powerful in a long list of court and governmental weapons, second only to a search warrant in its impact on personal privacy.

Search Warrants

RAIDS: ARE CLIENTS' SECRETS SAFE?

EDWARD MASRY *was settling down to work in his suburban Los Angeles law office one day this month when two armed state investigators walked in and slapped a search warrant on his desk....*

For the next seven hours, searchers thumbed through every file in the office, removing and carrying away bushels of papers. Simultaneously, in other locations around town, other teams of agents performed similar searches at the church [a client of Masry's], at four area banks that held church accounts and at Mr. Masry's other office.

National Law Journal,
April 23, 1979

Like the man with no shoes who thought he had a problem until he met a man with no feet, civil libertarians have shifted the focus of their concern from abuses of subpoenas to abuses of search warrants. On April 12, 1971, Palo Alto police chief James Zurcher and District Attorney Louis Bergne entered the offices of the *Stanford Daily,* a college newspaper, and spent several hours disrupting that office in apparent search of photos that newsmen might have taken while covering a student demonstration. There was no claim that anyone connected with the newspaper had violated any law. Bergne followed this on June 1, 1973, with a search of all the patient files of the Psychiatry Clinic at Stanford University Medical Center, looking for information about the *victim* in another pending criminal case.

The idea took hold with prosecutors in other states and counties. In October 1974 a warrant was issued for a search of the offices of the Los Angeles *Star,* a tabloid, by police looking for unpublished articles, photos, and address books pertaining to a movie star who claimed her nude photo had been used without her permission. In September 1977 a warrant was issued for a search of station WJAR-TV in Providence, R.I., looking for outtakes of a picket-line disorder in Warwick, R.I.

In 1978, the Supreme Court upheld the constitutionality of the search of the Stanford student newspaper in the highly controversial case of *Zurcher v. Stanford Daily.* After that, the virus of search-warrant abuse spread to invasions of law offices. According to John E. Ackerman of the National Association of Criminal Defense Lawyers, "Within a week of the Zurcher decision, the FBI hit about 10 lawyers' offices in Chicago and Las Vegas." On July 25, 1978, three officers of the St. Paul police department entered the law offices of David O'Connor and demanded that he either turn over all of the files pertaining to his client or face arrest himself. In San Diego, a prosecutor was turned down by a judge in his efforts to have a defense attorney produce a letter protected by the attorney-client privilege. Not to be outdone, the prosecutor obtained a search warrant from another judge and ransacked the attorney's office until he found the letter.

On April 5, 1979, armed agents of George Deukmejian, Attorney General of California, spent over seven hours digging through every file in the two Los Angeles offices maintained by attorney Edward Masry. They carried away several boxes of papers and left the rest of the offices in total disarray. The object of this unannounced search? An investigation by Deukmejian, a Republican, into an alleged bribery charge involving Masry's client, former Democratic Lieutenant Governor Mervyn Dymally.

"They walked in the door and showed me a paper that they claimed was a search warrant," said Masry. "But it wasn't signed; it had no number on it—nothing to indicate it was legitimate. I tried to call the judge that supposedly issued the warrant, but he wouldn't take my call. I told them I wasn't going to let them have my client's files."

Masry was arrested for his efforts. "I found out they were surreptitiously taping the whole conversation," so he countered with a weapon of his own. He called the local television stations, and the newsmen arrived in time to videotape the agents going about their work and putting him under arrest.

On March 20, 1979, Attorney General Deukmejian obtained an even broader warrant to search three hospitals, two CPA firms, and the prestigious law firm of Kaplan, Livingston, Goodwin, Berkowitz and Selvin in Los Angeles. This time the purpose was to obtain information about an alleged Medicaid fraud. There was no suspicion, however, that the lawyers whose offices were being searched had done anything illegal. This raid proved to be too much for Los Angeles Superior Court Judge Perry Pacht, who ordered that the surprise search of the law office—which by then had gone on for six hours—be brought to a halt. He criticized the municipal judge who had issued the search warrant and commented that the whole thing smacked of "jackboots and armbands."

These cases involved the search of property held by third parties, parties who were not themselves under investigation. Legalities aside, this use of search warrants has shaken up a good many people because it presents the ominous picture of police officers rifling through the offices of people who have no taint of criminality about any of their activities. There were few reported cases of search warrants being used against third parties until the raid on the *Stanford Daily* in 1971. Prosecutors, even the overzealous ones, either hadn't thought of it or had apparently assumed that it would be unconstitutional. The attorneys for the *Stanford Daily* thought so too. Federal Judge Robert F. Peckham ruled in favor of the newspaper and was sustained on appeal by the United States Court of Appeals in San Francisco. But this assumption did not reckon with Justice Byron White and his colleagues on the Supreme Court of the United States.

On May 31, 1978, in *Zurcher v. Stanford Daily,* the Supreme Court, speaking through Justice White, said it was "not convinced that the net gain to privacy interests ... would be worth the candle" and reversed the lower courts. The fact that the staff of the *Stanford Daily* was not accused of participating in a crime or of concealing any evidence made no difference to the Court. Their office could be torn apart by a surprise search to the same extent as if they had been harboring fugitives in the press room. In the Orwellian logic of Justice White they had even *less* protection than a suspected criminal, since "a less stringent standard of probable cause is acceptable where the entry is *not* to secure evidence of crime against the possessor" (emphasis added).*

The pernicious consequences predicted by the newspaper's attorney, Jerome Falk, were ignored. Such search warrants, he argued, drag in everything—the specific evidence sought by the police and anything else that happens to be in the office. Privileged material—such as documents subject to lawyer-client or doctor-patient privilege or a journalist's shield law—could be seized as easily as anything else. Even use of the much-abused subpoena power was preferable to the use of a search warrant against an innocent third party. "The police do not go rummaging through one's home, office, or desk if armed only with a subpoena," he argued. At least with a subpoena there is the opportunity to come into court and assert any privilege or other reason why the information should not be turned over to the police. By contrast, the search warrant is obtained by the police without prior warning and gives the police physical access to the home or office to do virtually as they please.

Search warrants issued since the *Zurcher* decision have shown just how threatening such warrants can be to everyone's privacy. In the broadly worded search warrant obtained by the California Attorney General on March 20, 1979, the police were authorized to seize, among other things, the "outpatient medical records and financial folders" from three separate hospitals, and the financial records from various CPA offices. They were also authorized to seize from a large Los Angeles law firm all "memorandums, letters, indemnification agreements, notes, or other documents indicating transactions and/or contacts" between the suspects and any of their attorneys, accountants, or anyone else. In enforcing the warrant the police were authorized to go through all "rooms ... desks, closets, filing cabinets, safes [and] vaults" in the law offices. This warrant, like several others that have been issued, was about as broad an assault on confidential papers as one could imagine.

Third-party search warrants threaten to compromise everyone's privacy. Although the police are ostensibly in search of evidence against a particular suspect when they enter an office with such a warrant, as a

---

* The authority for this dubious proposition? In a privilege allowed to few mortals other than Supreme Court justices, Justice White cited the opinion he himself had written in *Fisher v. United States*. (The Fisher case was itself a controversial extension of the right of the government to seize information from the files of a taxpayer's lawyer.) There appears to be nothing personal in all this, however, since Justice White still draws many of his law clerks from Stanford Law School.

practical matter they can look at everything. This means not only the files of the suspect but the personal files of the doctor or lawyer as well. It also means a search of the files of everyone else who had ever been in contact with the office—all patient files in a hospital, all client files in a law office, or all reporter's notes at a newspaper. It adds a wildly unpredictable element to a client or a patient's needs for confidentiality. Not only must an individual assess the threat to his personal papers arising out of an investigation of himself or his attorney, for example, but he must also calculate the possibility that his attorney may be representing another client whose activities could trigger a police search of the whole office.

The *Zurcher* case has drawn bitter criticism. Justice Potter Stewart said in a dissenting opinion that it would lead "to the needless exposure of confidential information completely unrelated to the purpose of the investigation." *The New York Times* editorialized that the *Zurcher* case struck "a double blow at individual privacy and press freedom." The Washington *Post* stated that "the decision threatens the privacy of every home and office in the country," while editor Ben Bradlee added that it was "just plain awful.... Beyond understanding." Senator Birch Bayh (D-Ind.) called it a threat to "the citizens' right of privacy in general." The Carter Administration, having first argued that such search warrants should be permitted, reversed itself a year later in a message to Congress and said that the decision "poses dangers to the functioning of a free press...." *New York Times* columnist James Reston speculated that if the decision had been in effect earlier "the cops would have been able to come into the Washington *Post* [searching for Watergate sources]." Senator Charles Mathias (R-Md.) agreed and added: "I just don't think 'Deep Throat' would have let out a gargle, if there had been a chance of them finding out who he was." The most poignant criticism came from ABC's Howard K. Smith: "When I was a new, young reporter at the United Press in Nazi Berlin ... there was a knock on the door ... and 15 Gestapo men barged past me, began opening every desk and studying every piece of paper they could find ... six hours later they left.... I remember thanking God this couldn't happen in America. Well, now it can. It is the worst, most dangerous ruling that the Court has made in memory...."

Since the *Zurcher* case was decided there has been some backing off from some of its frightening implications. The Minnesota Supreme

Court has ruled that the use of a search warrant to go through the law office of David O'Connor violated attorney-client confidentiality rules under Minnesota law. The California legislature moved quickly to curb the excesses of California prosecutors by outlawing warrants to seize a reporter's notes and requiring an outside attorney to accompany the police whenever they search the offices of a lawyer, doctor, or psychiatrist.

But the problem is national in scope, and Congress has not yet acted to correct the situation. Stuffing the genie back into the bottle has proved a good deal more difficult than the Supreme Court's decision to let it out in the first place. But the plain, unqualified fact is that no one's privacy is safe as long as the *Zurcher* case remains the law of the land.

Low-Profile Strategies

Are we now to encourage meddling by the government and ever more ingenious methods of obtaining access to sought after materials? The premium now will be on subterfuge, on bypassing the master of the domain by spiriting the materials away or compelling disclosure by a trusted employee or confidant. Inevitably this will lead those of us who cherish our privacy to refrain from recording our thoughts or trusting anyone with even temporary custody of documents we want to protect from public disclosure.

Justice William O. Douglas

Trust no one, my friend.

Herod Agrippa to the Emperor Claudius

Some trust is essential, but an individual must keep one eye on what is likely to be revealed in any kind of a legal dispute.

- Hold on to sensitive documents. No attorney or other advisor can guarantee total confidentiality. A search warrant or a grand jury subpoena, for example, can undermine the best efforts at keeping documents confidential. Give important documents to an attorney or an accountant if necessary, but get them back as soon as possible.
- When in doubt, don't put it in writing. A damaging note in your accountant's or your attorney's handwriting is bad enough, but something in your *own* handwriting is even worse. The best rule of thumb is to imagine how your file would look if read by an investigator. Someone else's notes about a telephone conversation give you de-

niability; notes you have written yourself give you nothing but trouble.
- Check the credentials of any would-be confidant. If someone solicits medical information, for example, find out if it will be protected under a doctor-patient privilege. The doctor-patient, lawyer-client, and other testimonial privileges aren't airtight, but they give you far more protection than a simple promise of confidentiality.
- Make sure that a "privileged" communication falls within the privilege. Not every conversation with a doctor, lawyer, or clergyman is considered privileged. The protection only arises when they are consulted in their professional capacities. It is particularly important with a lawyer to ask if any information that is to be disclosed will fall within the attorney-client privilege. If there is any doubt at all, write a letter to your attorney or have him or her write one to you confirming that the information was given in confidence.
- Get your own attorney, psychiatrist, or other advisor. If you and your business partners use the same attorney, he or she may be forced to reveal confidential information if any dispute arises between the partners. The same thing may be true if you share a marriage counselor, group therapist, or the like with an ex-wife or ex-husband. The psychiatrist may be forced to testify, for example, in a child-custody dispute. Whenever it is important enough to do so, get your own advisor who has no divided loyalties and no conflicting legal duties.
- Send a protective letter with any confidential disclosure. If important information is disclosed to an advisor who does not fit within one of the privileged categories, a letter from you or your attorney should accompany it outlining the conditions under which the information is disclosed. At a minimum such a letter should spell out what further disclosures are allowed or not allowed, an assurance that the information will not be voluntarily disclosed to anyone, and a promise that you will be notified immediately if the advisor is served with a subpoena or other legal order.
- Avoid legal actions that will result in the waiver of confidential information. A lawsuit for emotional distress will allow an opposing attorney to examine your psychiatrist's records. A claim for loss of income will allow him or her to poke through your bank or employment records. Make sure that what you are asking for is worth the cost to you in terms of disclosure of private information.
- Alert your attorney to sensitive information that may show up in

certain records. If a lawsuit is filed for a back injury, for example, a defense attorney will routinely subpoena all the hospital records. However, these records may include treatment for prior illnesses that have nothing to do with the injury involved in the lawsuit. If the client's own attorney is not alerted to this, the entire medical record may be copied and sent to the opposing attorney before anyone thinks to stop it. If the client's attorney knows that it is important to his client, he can try to get the court to limit the scope of the subpoena only to the most relevant matters or get a protective order limiting the opposing attorney to looking at the documents only in the presence of the judge, not to make copies, and so on. But none of these things will ordinarily happen unless you are persistent in asking that they be done.

- Stay out of court whenever possible. Sometimes there are alternatives to settling disputes, like arbitration, that involve significantly less exposure. Certain court procedures, such as probate, can be avoided by lifetime trust and other planning devices. Other types of cases, such as divorces, can be settled in ways that minimize the exposure of private information in the public records. But the most important thing is to make sure that privacy is given as much consideration as anything else. If a realistic assessment is made of the impact of a legal action on the client's privacy, a decision may be made to go all-out to settle the matter or not to bring the lawsuit in the first place.
- Put privacy on your lawyer or other advisor's agenda, and make sure it stays there. Once an advisor understands that privacy is important to you, he or she can often bring professional skills to bear in protecting your privacy in ways you may have not thought to ask.

CHAPTER 7

"One Person's Privacy, Another Person's Cover-Up"

PUBLIC RECORDS, PUBLIC FIGURES, AND THE PRESS

As a result of the Stanford Daily *decision, we should hide our notes. As a result of the* Farber *case, we should bury our notes. The AT&T case taught us that we should make telephone calls from pay phone booths and not from the office. But what now? You can't stop them from seizing your mind.*

Jack Landau, director of the Reporters'
Committee for Freedom of the Press,
commenting on the Supreme Court's
decision in Herbert v. Lando, April 19, 1979

We are opposed to the sealing of arrest records, welfare files, and similar records. Reporters should have access to this type of information. There's an old newspaper adage that says "If you're on the dole, you're on the record."

Jack Landau, interview, March 20, 1979

In any debate over the right of privacy, the press stands in the middle facing both ways. The nature of the news business is to dig out facts that other people don't want to reveal, and reporters are naturally suspicious of restrictions placed on the news-gathering process in the name of privacy. Nevertheless, reporters and their news sources have themselves been subjected to serious intrusions of privacy that have threatened their ability to cover news stories. Consequently, members of the press have apparently mixed emotions about privacy. Reporters want unfettered access to news sources but want to be able to protect the confidentiality of their informants. They want to be free to print the documents and notes of public officials and other newsmakers but want their own documents and notes to be protected. Reporters want to probe into the backgrounds and motivations of people in the news, but they want to prevent others from delving into their own backgrounds and motivations. In short, reporters feel threatened by privacy laws to about the same extent as they feel the need for protection of their own privacy.

There is a consistency in this, but it is not the consistency of someone whose main concern is with privacy. For newspeople the guiding principle is freedom of the press. They are generally supportive of privacy measures when they view them as protecting the news-gathering process, but they oppose them when they stand in their way of writing a story. Like other groups, the press attitude toward privacy shifts, depending on the particular issue. But there is a difference: for newspeople the stakes are usually higher.

The abuse of search warrants, which gained the blessing of the Supreme Court in *Zurcher v. Stanford Daily,* has resulted in surprise raids on at least fifteen newspaper and television studios in the last eight years. Prominent newsmen, such as Joseph Kraft and Hedrick Smith, have had their telephones tapped illegally. Newsman Dan Rather's house was broken into by burglars interested only in his news files. From 1973 to 1974 the federal government secretly subpoenaed the home and office telephone toll-call records of several reporters, including Jack Anderson, Richard Dudman of the St. Louis *Post-Dispatch,* David Rosenbaum of *The New York Times,* James Polk of the Washington *Star,* Knight-Ridder bureau chief Robert Boyd, and others. A dozen or so reporters have been jailed in the last decade rather than yield information they felt would violate pledges of confidentiality to informants and news sources. In almost every instance the press has fought back hard, both individually and through the Reporters' Committee for Freedom of the Press.

But the press has fought just as hard in other cases to knock down barriers erected in the name of privacy which newsmen have thought were unjustified. In 1978 a publisher, two editors, and two reporters of the Charleston *Gazette* and the Charleston *Daily Mail* were indicted for publishing the name of a juvenile charged with a crime in violation of a West Virginia statute designed to seal the criminal records of juvenile offenders. The same year a reporter for the Topeka *Daily Capital* was convicted of violating a Kansas statute prohibiting the publication of names contained in arrest warrants. In 1978, a reporter for the Detroit *Free Press* was jailed for refusing to return a confidential investigative report in a child-custody matter. In all of these cases there is an underlying conflict between the question of privacy and the right of the press to report information contained in government records. But whether fighting for privacy or against it, there has been a common thread in the actions of newsmen: in either case they have had their necks on the line.

How has the public reacted to the press? This statement represents the opinions of many:

> The press is overstepping in every direction the obvious bounds of propriety and decency. Gossip is no longer the resource of the idle and of the vicious, but has become a trade, which is pursued with industry as well as effrontery. To satisfy a prurient taste the details of sexual relations are spread broadcast in the columns of the daily papers. To occupy the indolent, column upon column is filled with idle gossip, which can only be procured by intrusion upon the domestic circle.

This diatribe wasn't written by Frank Sinatra or Spiro Agnew, but by Supreme Court Justice Louis Brandeis in the 1890 edition of the *Harvard Law Review*. Justice Brandeis, a highly respected civil libertarian, was moved in this case by a more trivial problem than those that usually concerned him: excessive publicity given to debutantes parties by the Boston newspapers. Whatever its motivation, that 1890 article by Brandeis and Samuel D. Warren is of more than passing interest. It is the first legal publication that suggested that there is a right of privacy protected under the law.

Although the right of privacy has expanded to include many other abuses, it was originally aimed at the press. To a certain extent it still is. Newsmen recoil against the charge that they are responsible for invasions of privacy. They point out—with considerable justification—that they try to protect confidential sources, that they uncover more governmental abuses of privacy than they themselves ever commit, that they don't use private information surreptitiously, and that freedom of the press is more important than the delicate sensibilities of newsmakers. While all of this may be true, a considerable segment of the public nevertheless feels that the press is too intrusive. Thirty-one percent of the American public, according to the 1979 Harris survey, believes that the press "asks for too much" personal information.*

---

* The figures are dramatically higher for "leaders" surveyed by the Harris Poll. With the exception of the computer industry, 58 percent to 78 percent of business and government officials thought the press "asks for too much."

Credit business	75%	Doctors	61%
Credit card companies	65%	State insurance commissions	68%
Banks	78%	Congress	60%
Insurance companies	72%	Law enforcement officials	78%
Computer business	42%	Regulatory officials	58%

Two observations: This low opinion of the press comes from organizations that have

The problem involves two radically different perceptions of the press. Those fearful of press intrusions can point to the concentration of economic power within the media, newspaper mergers, and special exemptions from the antitrust laws. The press is simply another monopolistic business, critics conclude, with an almost limitless capacity to intrude on the privacy of the individual. And that's just the printed press. The advent of radio and television and the domination of television networks has added a different dimension to the problem. The "idle gossip" that bothered Justice Brandeis is nothing compared to the sensationalism of the evening news programs. To many, the image of the press is no longer Peter Zenger standing at his printing press, defying the establishment; the press and broadcast media *are* the establishment.

Newsmen understandably take a different view. In their mind what has expanded are not press abuses but press responsibilities. Modern society has achieved a complexity beyond the ability of anyone to understand, let alone control. There is increasing reliance on the press to gather, sort, and interpret information the individual is incapable of finding out on his own. Sources are harder to find, facts are harder to analyze. Thus there is a need for a certain leeway or tolerance in the news-gathering process. The public doesn't need protection from the press, newsmen argue, rather it is the press that needs protection from legal restraints. Privacy is fine in its place, but one person's privacy is another person's cover-up.

Press intrusions on privacy are different from those of other institutions. On one hand, revelations of private facts in the press are likely to reach the widest audience. If invasions of privacy are measured by the number of people who suddenly become aware of what used to be a secret, then private revelations in the press would rank at the top of the list. Any major newspaper or television station, for example, is likely to have a wider audience than the largest of the credit or investigative bureaus. On the other hand, what the press does, it usually does openly. If the more important harm comes from surreptitious surveillance

---

often been criticized themselves for invasions of privacy. Moreover, the criticism that has been leveled at them has often come by way of the press. If one may be permitted a garbled metaphor, it may be a case of the pot calling the kettle black because its ox has been gored.

or from the gathering of secret dossiers about individuals, then the press is nowhere near the top in the list of privacy invaders. News articles may cause public embarrassment, but only rarely will they give rise to private vendettas or blacklisting.

The news media differ from other institutions in another fundamental sense. The press is just as likely to be exposing invasions of privacy as it is to be exposing private information. A good argument can be made that press revelations, on balance, have assisted the right of privacy more than they have harmed it. This is particularly true in relation to news stories about the actions of government and other large institutions. Beginning with the Watergate period, the news media have uncovered vast programs of government surveillance. This has enabled individuals to follow up with more specific actions to protect their rights.

But on the bottom line, as any good media person knows, the question is one of image. The press has developed a mixed image: on the one hand it is a privacy-protector and on the other it is a privacy-invader. The degree to which the press is a privacy problem is largely a function of which image will prevail at any given time. Is it Woodward and Bernstein exposing a government "enemies" list? Or is it some paparazzi hounding Jackie Onassis for a few intimate photos?

Protection of News Sources

- In 1974, reporter Jay Shelledy of the Lewiston (Maine) *Morning Tribune* was jailed for thirty days for refusing to disclose information obtained from a confidential source about the shooting of a suspect by an Idaho narcotics agent. In October 1977, the U.S. Supreme Court declined to review the case, thereby upholding his conviction.
- In 1978, reporter John Hammarley of the Sacramento *Union* was ordered jailed for refusing to turn over notes and tapes of a confidential interview with an informant in a murder case.
- In 1978, reporter Joe Pennington of KAKE-TV was ordered jailed for sixty days for refusing to disclose the confidential source of a rumor regarding a pending murder case.
- In 1976, reporter Myron Farber of *The New York Times* was jailed for refusing to turn over to defense attorneys notes and recordings from more than 100 witnesses in a murder case that Farber had obtained in confidence. He ultimately served forty days in jail and *The Times* paid fines of $285,000 after the U.S. Supreme Court declined to review the conviction.

Whatever else can be said about the ability of the press to protect confidential disclosures, one thing is clear: reporters are frequently willing to go to the mat to protect their sources. Even when a case has not involved the jailing of a reporter, it has often meant expensive and frustrating litigation. The Des Moines *Register and Tribune,* the Twin Falls *Times-News,* and Station KOB in Albuquerque, among others, have engaged in lengthy lawsuits to protect confidential sources.

Newsmen claim a right to protect confidential sources based on the First Amendment's guarantee of freedom of the press. At first glance it is a strange argument, since the First Amendment seemingly has nothing to do with the right to privacy but is aimed instead at the right of public debate through "free speech" and a "free press." Much of what a newspaper does is done at the expense of privacy—it publishes information that others want to keep quiet. Freedom of the press and the right of privacy would therefore seem natural enemies.

Nevertheless, the press argues, freedom to publish is inseparably linked to the right to protect what is *not* published. There is an interdependency between the two rights, so that the right of a free press cannot succeed unless the right of privacy is also protected.* Often, a reporter cannot obtain the lead to a story without promising an informant confidentiality. Without this promise—and the ability to back it up—there is a "chilling" effect on valuable news sources. The First Amendment therefore implies an element of privacy. Newsmen argue that a vigorous and independent press only comes about through the constant balancing between confidential sources and public disclosure. The link between the two is the newsman's promise of confidentiality. If a "deep throat" has to speak for the record, he won't speak at all.

It is an eloquent and persuasive argument, but one that has gotten virtually nowhere with the Supreme Court. In November 1970 Paul Branzburg of the Louisville *Courier Journal* was subpoenaed by the Jefferson County grand jury in Kentucky and ordered to reveal the names of the operators of a marijuana "laboratory" who had allowed him a confidential interview. In the same year, Paul Pappas, a television-news photographer, was supboenaed before the Bristol County

---

* This is, moreover, a two-way street. The right of privacy depends, to a large extent, on a free press. The massive intrusion on privacy committed during the Watergate era might never have been brought to light without the persistent efforts of the press. Jane Fonda, for example, didn't find out that the FBI was copying her address book, monitoring the bank account, and shadowing her children until she read about it in Jack Anderson's column in 1973.

grand jury in Massachusetts and ordered to disclose what he had seen and heard inside the New Bedford Black Panther headquarters despite his pledge of confidentiality to the Panthers. Also in 1970, Earl Caldwell of *The New York Times* was subpoenaed before a federal grand jury in Northern California and ordered to disclose information gathered in confidence from the Black Panthers over a period of months. All three cases reached the Supreme Court at the same time, and in August 1972 the Court gave a resounding "no" to the privacy claims of the press based on the First Amendment. Justice Byron White, speaking for the Court in *Branzburg v. Hayes,* said that the public interest in law enforcement was sufficient "to override the consequential, but uncertain, burden on news gatherers" that might result if reporters are forced to testify. The dissent called this a "crabbed view" of the First Amendment and predicted that law-enforcement agencies would try "to annex the journalistic profession as an investigative arm of government."

The failure of the Supreme Court to recognize a constitutional underpinning to the newsman's privilege has forced the press to go to the various state legislatures for the adoption of shield laws to protect confidential sources. A majority of states now have laws stating that a reporter cannot be compelled to disclose his sources of information. In other instances courts have developed a qualified privilege for confidential disclosures, allowing them to be withheld in some cases and disclosed in others. But the protection given by these laws is far from clear. One weakness is the lack of a federal shield law. While some federal courts have allowed reporters to invoke a state shield law in federal court proceedings within that state, others have not. Thus a reporter might safely decline to testify at a statehouse inquiry only to be called across the street and forced to testify about the same facts before a federal court or grand jury. Also important are the exceptions that have been read into the various shield laws by the courts. Some exceptions have come about through technicalities, as in New York, where the seemingly absolute protection given to a news source has been held to have been waived when a portion of the confidential information was previously published.

The most difficult situations, however, are those where a reporter has information that may assist the *defense* in a criminal trial. The Myron Farber case, for example, arose as the result of a series of articles in *The New York Times* by Farber suggesting that a doctor may have murdered several of his patients. When the doctor's attorney subpoenaed him, Farber invoked the protection of the New Jersey shield law. Farber and *The New York Times* asserted the familiar press argument that if he were forced to reveal his confidential sources in this case, it would dry up all confidential sources for reporters in other types of investigations. But there was an element in this case that was not present in cases like *Branzburg*. A forced disclosure in this type of case would not make the press "an investigative arm of the government": disclosure was requested by the defendant. The question, in effect, was whether the shield law would be used to help the prosecution by keeping information from the defense. The courts anguished over the dilemma and finally decided that the defendant's right of a fair trial overrode the right of a newsman to protect his sources. The issue was only resolved after the doctor was acquitted without the testimony of Farber, after which Farber was released from jail on his contempt-of-court citation.

Cases like Farber pit the privacy of a reporter and his sources against the loss of privacy to a defendant that would result from his unjustified imprisonment. That conflict became even more difficult to resolve in a 1977 case involving the *60 Minutes* investigation of teenage use of "angel dust." The Santa Clara County Narcotics Bureau allowed the *60 Minutes* news team to "wire" two of its undercover agents while they attempted to purchase the hallucinogenic drug PCP from two suspects. In order to get the Bureau's cooperation, *60 Minutes* agreed that it would use only voice recordings and camera shots that did not reveal the agents' identities. In a subsequent criminal prosecution of the alleged drug dealers, the defense attorney sought to have the television film and the outtakes produced to see if they contained any information helpful to his client's defense. CBS resisted on the grounds of newsman's privilege, arguing that the California shield law prevents a forced disclosure of confidential information given to newsmen—no matter who wants to use it. From the point of view of the network, it made no difference that the pledge of confidentiality was given to an undercover cop. As a privacy issue, it makes quite a difference: undercover agents are a frequent source of intrusion on the privacy of others. What appears to be emerging from these cases is a doctrine that allows a court to override journalist shield laws when the information is essential to the defense of a criminal case and cannot be obtained in any other way. Thus the person disclosing confidential information to a reporter cannot be sure in every instance that the reporter will be able to protect that confidentiality.

But even in cases where a reporter can protect the confidentiality of information, he or she may decide not to. The journalist shield laws protect the reporter, not the informant. A reporter is basically free to pick and choose which information to print and which to keep confidential. In this respect a journalist privilege is quite different from an attorney-client, doctor-patient, or other privilege. A person supplying information to a reporter on the assumption that it will remain confidential must either get a legally enforcible agreement with the reporter or make sure that he or she is confiding in someone with a great deal of integrity.

Public Records

Large majorities of both the public and leadership groups feel that publication of the following items would be an invasion of privacy:
- *the details of an extramarital affair that a public official is having with another person*
- *the names of people on welfare*
- *a photograph of a well-known politician entering a pornographic bookstore. . . .*

The publication of the following items would not be an invasion of privacy:
- *the names of doctors who have received large sums of money under Medicare and Medicaid*
- *the names of persons arrested for possessing illegal drugs*
- *the contents of confidential government papers that reveal incompetence or dishonesty by public officials. . . .*

While strongly supportive of the freedom of the press on several key issues, most people believe there are real limits beyond which the press should not go.

The Harris Poll

How far can the press go? Most people in the press argue that they should be able to go as far as their instincts tell them—that the only limit is what is newsworthy. Others (particularly those in a position to be embarrassed by press revelations) feel that there must be a line somewhere that can't be crossed.

There apparently is a line, but no one is quite sure where it is. There is a rule of law that holds the press liable for "public disclosure of embarrassing facts." This rule, of course, it not as broad as it seems. If it were, Richard Nixon would probably still be in the White House and the press would be printing only wedding announcements. Instead, the courts have limited it to situations that are somehow different from ordinary news coverage. It has been a difficult concept to define, but several courts have taken a crack at it. "The line is to be drawn when the publicity ceases to be the giving of information to which the public is entitled," says the Ninth Circuit Court of Appeals, "and becomes a morbid and sensational prying into private lives for its own sake." According to the Supreme Court of Missouri, the press becomes liable for invasion of privacy when "the intrusion has gone beyond the limits of decency." Several courts agree that the test is whether the disclosure is offensive to persons of "ordinary" or "reasonable" sensibilities.

But these are all generalities. Without an authoritative Supreme Court decision, no one knows exactly what they mean and how much the press is limited. Are there any limits as to what the press can reveal in following a legitimate news story? What is a legitimate news story? How current does a news story have to be to be legitimate; do the same rules apply, for example, to a story about a man arrested ten years ago and a man arrested last week? How much does the person's prominence affect what can be revealed? Does the source of the story—a private investigator's file, a police blotter, an interview with a neighbor—make a difference as to what can be said? None of these questions has been resolved, and they all involve issues the press will probably be battling for years to come.

One area in which the press has great latitude is with information in the public records. Generally speaking, newspapers can publish any government record that they can get hold of. Thus the principal question is what information in government records is open to the press and the public?

Access to government files has become largely institutionalized under the federal Freedom of Information Act and similar laws in each of the states. The press has been a frequent user of the FOIA and has financed much of the litigation pushing for a broad interpretation of that act. Many disclosures under the FOIA have revealed government programs that have invaded individual privacy on a massive scale. FOIA disclosures have included the CIA's twenty-five year program to experiment on human beings with mind-control drugs, the "pumpkin papers" from the Alger Hiss case, documents from the Rosenberg spy case, the CIA training of local policemen as burglars, the Nixon tapes, the FBI surveillance of Jane Fonda, the FBI harassment of the Socialist Workers' Party, and many other similar documents. The FOIA in these and other instances has been mainly used to flush out government documents in privacy-related cases.

The problem is that government files also contain a great deal of personal information. The FOIA tries to solve this problem by exempting "personnel and medical files and similar files, the disclosure of which would constitute a clearly unwarranted invasion of personal privacy." The legal language was left deliberately ambiguous because Congress was unable to decide exactly what it wanted to do. The question of what types of files are "similar" to a personnel or medical file can be argued indefinitely. What the congressional draftsmen appeared to have in mind was to try to protect both privacy and public access to records, but to let the federal courts decide each request on a case-by-case basis.

The most significant danger in press access to government files, however, comes with the addition of a factor that has changed so much else: the computer. In one sense the computer doesn't change anything, because all it does is process information that is already in the files in a different form. But in another sense it changes everything. The computer can pick up isolated bits of information and reprocess it into new patterns. When this technique is applied to personal information in government files, the computer can easily come up with lists of all persons who fit into various controversial categories.

The informational battles of the future may come to resemble a dispute recently decided by the Minnesota Supreme Court. *The Bulletin,* a Catholic newspaper, demanded under Minnesota's Freedom of Information Act the names of all doctors who had received Medicaid money for abortions, how much they received, and how many abortions they performed. The Minnesota Department of Public Welfare agreed, but only if the newspaper paid the $2500-to-$4000 cost of duplicating the computer data. The state relented on the fee demand when the newspaper agreed to provide its own computer programmer. When the Minnesota State Medical Association got wind of the plan, it filed suit on behalf of its members to stop the disclosure. Organizations that would otherwise be allies chose opposite sides on this one: The Minnesota Civil Liberties Union filed a brief in support of the medical association, while the Minnesota Newspaper Association lined up behind the *Bulletin.*

The newspaper argued that this was a simple case of finding out who received certain government payments, i.e., payments through Medicaid. That, argued the newspaper, should be a matter of public record. The doctors argued for the privacy of their patients as well as their own. They pointed out that disclosure of such information would be extremely harmful to their own privacy because it could spark boycotts and protests by anti-abortion groups. Although the names of the patients would supposedly not be revealed, the doctors claimed that the privacy of their patients could also be compromised by an inadvertent disclosure of personal information and by the publicity surrounding the doctors' offices. The computerized records that were being demanded also contained patient names, descriptions, and other data. With a slight reprogramming the computer could spew forth all of that confidential data. In the highly charged atmosphere of this type of dispute, medical privacy could depend on which button is pushed. Despite these dangers, the Minnesota Supreme Court decided the matter in favor of the newspaper and ordered the information released.

The dispute was made both possible and more complicated by computer technology. The computerized data base made it a relatively simple and inexpensive task to sort out the doctors who received Medicaid payments for abortions from the total number of Medicaid payments. The newspaper could gain access to these records by simply asking one computer one question. Information that might have taken a reporter weeks to dig out while pounding the pavement could be obtained in a matter of minutes. The newspaper, in fact, doesn't even need a reporter—only its own computer programmer. It is all very efficient, but efficiency and privacy have never been close friends.

There is a strong argument to be made for a right of privacy in arrest records. An arrest by itself proves nothing. It simply means that the person has been detained by the police. But disclosure of an arrest can have serious consequences for the person involved. It is a badge of infamy that may affect his or her personal and professional life. On the other hand, an arrest is an action by a government official and the public has a right to know how government officials are going about their business.

The solution? In most states arrest records are available when indexed one way but not when they are indexed another way. Reporters generally have access to chronologically arranged arrest records—police blotters showing who was arrested on any given day. While this is useful for keeping up with current crimes, it is an extremely cumbersome way of checking on the arrest record of a specific individual. It is just this type of background check, however, that raises the privacy problems. As a consequence, almost all states have restrictions on disclosure of name-indexed arrest records or "rap sheets." The federal Law Enforcement Assistance Administration has entered the picture by issuing regulations prohibiting states from disclosing arrest information unless done within LEAA guidelines.

With the question of criminal convictions the issue becomes stickier, because a conviction *does* signify something. Nevertheless, a persuasive argument can be made for sealing or expunging criminal records where the crime is only a minor one or a significant amount of time has elapsed. California allows for expunging marijuana-related offenses. Illinois allows records to be sealed following parole. Maryland permits an expungement of a conviction that was followed by probation. In Massachusetts, Nevada, New Jersey, and Rhode Island misdemeanors and felonies can be sealed after five, ten, or fifteen years, provided there are no other convictions. Ohio, with certain exceptions, allows first offenders to have their convictions sealed, while West Virginia allows the same thing for first offenders on marijuana charges. Many states that do not allow records of convictions to be sealed or expunged allow arrest and related information to be sealed so that anyone making inquiries will get only the bare fact of an arrest, if that. All in all, thirty-nine states at last count allowed for sealing or expungement of some or all of various criminal records.*

The problem is that no one knows for sure whether any of these laws are constitutional. In the two cases involving similar laws that have come before the Supreme Court the press has won and the laws have been struck down. WSB-TV convinced the Supreme Court to overturn a Georgia law that made it a crime to publish the name of a crime victim following the 1971 murder of a young girl. A few years later the Charleston *Daily Mail* and the Charleston *Daily Gazette* got the same

---

* Alabama, Alaska, Arkansas, California, Colorado, Connecticut, Delaware, the District of Columbia, Florida, Georgia, Hawaii, Idaho, Illinois, Indiana, Iowa, Kansas, Louisiana, Maine, Maryland, Massachusetts, Michigan, Minnesota, Missouri, Montana, Nevada, New Hampshire, New Jersey, New York, North Carolina, Ohio, Oklahoma, Oregon, Puerto Rico, Rhode Island, South Carolina, Tennessee, Vermont, Virginia, and Washington.

result with respect to a West Virginia law that made it a crime to publish the name of a juvenile offender. What does this do to the elaborate procedures that many states have evolved for sealing or expunging criminal records? No one can say with any authority. It may be that if any of these laws are challenged by the press, the whole system of sealing and expunging records could become unraveled.

Public Figures

Some men are born great, some achieve greatness, and some have greatness thrust upon them.

Shakespeare, Twelfth Night

Since 1964 the courts have attempted to define and redefine just who is a public figure, but they would probably have done just as well to fall back on Shakespeare and leave it at that. Prior to 1964 the notion of a "public figure" did not even appear in our jurisprudence, but in that year the Supreme Court decided the first of a series of cases in which it attempted to differentiate public figures from everyone else. The difference has become an important one, because with public figures the press has been given a much greater latitude of what it can say and how it can say it than with anyone else.

Differentiating public figures from others has, however, proved anything but easy. The best way to determine who fits into the category of public figure is to look at the cast of characters the Supreme Court has considered. The first case in 1964 was New York Times *v.* Sullivan, involving an Alabama police commissioner who claimed he had been libeled by *The New York Times.* The Court reasoned that since he was a "public official" the newspaper had a wide latitude in what it could say about him. Two years later the Court expanded the doctrine to two public figures who weren't officials. General Edwin Walker, a radical-right figure of the period, and Georgia football coach Wally Butts, who faced the somewhat bizarre accusation that he had sold his team's plays to Alabama's Bear Bryant, were both found to be prominent enough to be considered public figures. In 1971, the Court went one step further and held that a man arrested for selling allegedly obscene material was a public figure.

Since then the Supreme Court has marched in the opposite direction. *Gertz v. Welch* in 1974 involved a Chicago lawyer who had sued Robert Welch, the publisher of the John Birch Society's *American*

Opinion magazine, for labeling him a "Leninist" and "Communist-fronter" and as the architect of a frame-up against a Chicago policeman convicted of murder. Welch, discovering somewhat belatedly the virtues of the First Amendment, argued that Gertz was a public figure by virtue of the fact that he was the attorney for the family of the murder victim.* The Supreme Court rejected that argument and adopted a more limited definition of public figures as applying only to those who have "thrust themselves to the forefront of particular public controversies in order to influence the resolution of the issues involved." The Court conceded that hypothetically there may be cases where individuals become public figures involuntarily by the rush of events but added the instances of truly involuntary public figures "must be exceedingly rare."

Since *Gertz* the Supreme Court has found one reason or another to conclude that the individuals who have come before it were not public figures. In 1976 it held that Mary Firestone, who was married to "the scion of one of America's wealthier industrial families," was not a public figure "other than perhaps [in] Palm Beach society." In 1979 the Court concluded that Ilya Wolston was not a public figure even though he had been convicted of contempt of court for his refusal to testify before a grand jury. The same day the Court ruled that Ronald Hutchinson, who had received a federal grant to study aggression in animals (and—much to his dismay—Senator William Proxmire's "Golden Fleece" award), was not a public figure.

The lower courts, at the same time, have seemingly been moving in the other direction. Various lower courts have imposed the dubious honor of being a public figure on a contractor who did business with a local government, a state social worker, a chemistry teacher, an alleged mobster, the operator of a "close-out" sale business, and a disbarred attorney seeking reinstatement. Somewhat oddly, one U.S. district

---

* I must confess a certain bias against that type of assertion. In 1969, the Oakland *Tribune* was engaged in a vendetta against welfare recipients and attorneys who represented them, and one Saturday morning the front-page headline read:
JUDGE ACCUSES LAWYER OF WELFARE CASE LIE
Since I was the lawyer mentioned in the news story and no one had accused me of a lie, I sent a demand for retraction to the newspaper (a preliminary step that is required in California and many other states before a libel suit can be filed against a newspaper). The *Tribune*'s attorney called me and hinted darkly that I might be a public figure. I responded that I was a humble neighborhood poverty lawyer and that the case described in the article was only a routine guardianship. He must have decided I was right, because on the last day allowed for a retraction the newspaper headline read:
JUDGE DIDN'T ACCUSE LAWYER OF WELFARE CASE LIE
I've often wondered what a casual reader that morning thought about that as a news story.

court has held that an undercover narcotics agent is a public figure, while another U.S. district court has refused to impose that same status on a narcotics informant. From a reading of the cases, it is doubtful whether the press can tell what it can or cannot do to avoid getting sued. An individual would not have much better luck finding out what he or she should or should not do to stay out of the limelight.

Public-figure status—however it comes about—has a great importance in actions for invasion of privacy and for defamation of character. These are closely related torts, but the significant difference is that a defamatory statement—whether in writing (libel) or oral (slander)—must be shown to be false. An action for invasion of privacy, on the other hand, may involve a true statement that is nevertheless a "public disclosure of an embarrassing fact." There is, however, a hybrid form of tort that arises from statements that place an individual in a "false light." This suggests that the distinction between defamation and invasion of privacy may not be as great as it seems, particularly in the heat of gathering the news. In the haste of covering a story a reporter can easily misstate a few facts as he or she pokes into a sensitive area.

Despite an uncertainty as to who is a public figure, the Supreme Court has been reasonably precise in defamation cases in specifying the legal consequences of misstatements about public figures and others. If the newspaper uses reasonable care to prevent mistakes, then it will not be liable to anyone for defamation even if the story is inaccurate. If the press is negligent in its gathering of the facts, then it may be liable to a private individual for that person's "actual injuries" as a result of the story. But the press will only be liable to a public figure if the person can show that the news media acted with actual malice—a "subjective awareness of probable falsity." For the press, this means that they do not have to hold up fast-breaking stories about important people until they have verified every fact. For someone prominent enough to be a public figure, however, there is probably no recourse against the press unless he can show that the news medium was out to get him.

While not as clearly articulated, the rules regarding public figures seem to apply in invasion-of-privacy cases as well. Six members of the University of Maryland basketball team, for example, sued the Washington *Star* for revealing that they were getting failing grades. The Maryland Court of Appeals threw out the case, concluding that while a newspaper's revelation of a student's grades might ordinarily be an invasion of privacy it wasn't so in this case. The players, by participating in a nationally publicized sport, had become public figures.

The public figure–private person distinction seems to be an underlying rationale in an otherwise unintelligible array of decisions. If a person is drawn into an otherwise legitimate news story, the courts have generally been quite lenient in how far the press can go in revealing otherwise private facts. A Florida court upheld the St. Petersburg *Times'* right to publish the name of a patient in a drug treatment program, despite a law making such information confidential, because there had been allegations that the drug program had been holding patients against their will and that particular patient had tried to run away. Similarly, an Iowa court allowed the Des Moines *Register and Tribune* to publish the name of a woman who had been sterilized in a county health home because the revelation was part of an investigation of abuses at that county facility. On the other hand, if the press singles out someone for coverage without any particular reason for doing so, the individual probably has a recourse in a privacy action. The Alabama Supreme Court, for example, let stand a judgment against a newspaper for publishing a photo of an otherwise unknown woman whose dress was blown over her head while leaving a fun house. A Kentucky court allowed a private individual's claim against a newspaper for publishing a notice from a store implying that he was a deadbeat.

But the line between legitimate news stories and invasions of privacy is incredibly difficult to draw. Sometimes it appears to depend on the timing of the story. California courts have allowed privacy lawsuits to stand against the press when the stories have involved the revelation of old crimes by persons who have since been rehabilitated, but the issue is far from resolved nationally. Does the mere passage of time create a right of privacy in matters that would otherwise be on the public record? A New York court upheld a judgment against CBS because its news team entered a restaurant that had been cited for health code violations and filmed its patrons (many of whom crawled under the table to avoid being filmed) having dinner. In its ruling the court emphasized the manner in which the press acted—entering the restaurant without notice. Far from resolving the matter, however, the case raises more unanswered questions. How much does the right of privacy depend upon the manner in which the press goes about its business?

Privacy and defamation lawsuits sometimes come full circle to a familiar question: Whose privacy is being protected? There is a real danger in many cases that when one person seeks redress for loss of privacy he or she may force the revelation of private information about others. This problem lies beneath the surface of a 1979 Supreme Court decision that ostensibly favored protection of privacy at the expense of the press.

The decision in the 1979 *Herbert v. Lando* hit the news media like a bucket of ice water. Lt. Col. Anthony Herbert had presumably become a public figure when he accused his superior officers of covering up atrocities in Vietnam and when his story was presented by Barry Lando and Mike Wallace on *60 Minutes.* What shocked newsmen was the Supreme Court's conclusion that reporters could be subjected to the entire meatgrinder of discovery and disclosure in libel suits initiated by public figures. Prior to the case reaching the high court, CBS had yielded to the discovery demands of plaintiff's attorney and had produced the transcripts and films of interviews, Lando's notes, and pretelecast conversations between Lando and Wallace. Lando was deposed for twenty-six sessions over the course of more than a year, and the transcript ran about two thousand pages. Lando finally refused to answer a relatively small number of questions about his beliefs and opinions on the story on the ground that such questions interfered with the editorial process in violation of the First Amendment. But the Supreme Court stated that he had to answer the questions and that the First Amendment offered no special protection.

Justice White, speaking for the Court, recognized that the Supreme Court may have taken back with the left hand what it had given with the right. By requiring a public figure to prove "actual malice" on the part of the reporter, the Court had opened the reporter's state of mind to judicial inquiry. White conceded that "the costs and other burdens of this kind of litigation have escalated and become much more troublesome for both plaintiffs and defendants." He might have added that others could be dragged in as well when the reporters are grilled by attorneys in an effort to find the source of a story.

Following *Herbert v. Lando* the Supreme Court let stand a New Mexico decision that ordered reporters to disclose all notes, documents, and confidential sources in a libel suit initiated by a political figure against the Albuquerque *Journal* and *Tribune.* The information that was ordered to be revealed hit not only at the reporter's privacy but at the privacy of those who supplied confidential information to the reporter. As this case indicates, the courts seem to be increasingly faced with the problem of weighing the privacy of the person mentioned in a news article against the privacy of persons who were not. Does one always prevail over the other; and, if not, how are they to be balanced? It is a delicate calculation, but one that the Supreme Court seems unwilling to make.

But looking at public-figure status and its implications from the point of view of court cases probably provides too narrow a focus. The fact is that there are gradations of public exposure in almost every walk of life. In many cases there is an almost invisible threshold that, once crossed, will mean disclosure of more and more personal information in the public records and a greater likelihood of publication of information by the press.

Sometimes the line is crossed deliberately—much the same thing that happens when a small corporation decides to go public with its stock. Hiring a press agent, calling a news conference, slipping items to the press (all the tactics that one does to improve one's "image") brings an individual closer to public-figure status. Indeed, if privacy is a major concern among many Americans, anonymity seems to be just as big a problem to many others. And it is not unusual to see one person exploiting in the media the same bizarre sexual, religious, or other beliefs that someone else is trying to keep private.

But most people don't set out deliberately to expose themselves. Instead, they sometimes wake up to find themselves getting more public attention than they wanted. They crossed the threshold, but they weren't aware that they had done so.

Sometimes the nature of the occupation makes the difference. A policeman will normally be subject to more legitimate public scrutiny than a plumber whether he or she likes it or not. The public, sensitive nature of the work means that there are fewer private facts that can be shielded from the press. But sometimes the degree of exposure seems purely arbitrary. This is true with respect to the bewildering array of occupational licenses found at all levels of state and local government. A beer salesman in New Jersey is required to have an occupational license, as does a dry cleaner in California. In order for persons in these and other regulated occupations to obtain licenses they must file certain personal information with the licensing agency, and this information to one degree or another is open to the public. Because these occupations are regulated by law, the press has a more legitimate reason to scrutinize the licensing process and the individuals who are licensed.

The same gradations often exist within the same business or occupation. The owner of a small store may simply have to record his or her name with some local government agency. A director of a middle-size corporation in the same line of business, however, may have to file certain financial documentation with the securities regulatory agency in the particular state. But if the company is a large department store with stock that is publicly held, the director may have to report his or her salary and extensive other information in a public statement.

These same gradations of exposure exist in unions, government, and similar areas. The more important the activity—and the more important the individual's role in it—the more potential there exists for exposure of private information.

Many of these disclosure laws are based on sound public-policy considerations in which individual privacy is only one factor. The question of what are excessive or not excessive disclosure requirements cannot be determined without a careful look at each occupation or profession and a weighing of the public's right to certain information in each instance.

What *can* be decided without challenging the whole regulatory system is whether the individual wants to play the game. A person who wants to prevent disclosure of personal information might decide to be an unlicensed financial advisor instead of a licensed stockbroker or accountant, an unlicensed counselor rather than a licensed therapist. A person with a small business might decide to expand in a different direction or not to expand at all rather than make the public financial disclosures that are necessary to bring in outside investors.

The decision in any case is a highly individual one, and there is no right answer. The important point for anyone involved in these decisions, however, is to be aware of the privacy factors involved and to make them a conscious part of the decision-making process. The alternative is to keep making disclosures of personal information at various junctures in life in order to get ahead, when all you may really be doing is getting exposed.

Low-Profile Strategies

Anytime the press gets involved in a matter it's pretty clear that something is going to get published somewhere. The problem for the individual is to control the flow of information.

- Don't talk to the press unless it makes sense to do so. No one has to talk to a reporter, and an individual may have greater protection in a later legal action for invasion of privacy if the story was written without a personal interview. Once the individual is interviewed on any aspect of the story, a court may conclude that he or she consented to the entire story—including matters not covered in the interview.
- Any promise of confidentiality should be in writing. If the information is given for background purposes only and is not to be used in the story, that should be spelled out in a written document. The same is true of a promise to withhold your identity. The object is to create a form of contract—a release of information in exchange for restricted use—that will hold up in court later. This promise should include a written commitment by the reporter to invoke any shield laws. Shield laws basically protect the reporter, not the news source. But a written commitment by the reporter to invoke the protection of that law may give both you and the reporter a better chance to use that shield in front of a sympathetic judge.
- Evaluate the reporter's ability to protect confidential information. No matter how many promises you extract from a reporter, there may be situations when he or she cannot prevent disclosure. Who is likely to want the information? A state grand jury? A federal grand jury? The parties to a civil action? A defendant in a criminal action? The results may vary in each case. In this complicated world, it may sometimes be best to take your chances on a confidential disclosure to your attorney for advice before making a confidential disclosure to the press.
- Get any promises as to review of the story in writing. If the reporter is willing to give you review or editorial rights to a story, the details of the agreement should be spelled out in writing before the interview. It doesn't make much sense to wait to work out the details after the reporter has everything written down in his or her notebook.
- A demand for a retraction should be made in most defamation cases. In many states such a written demand is a legal prerequisite to a successful lawsuit, since the newspaper is given the right to correct its mistake in a later edition. Even when not required, it is probably advisable. A refusal to print a retraction after the correct facts are pointed out to the editor may be evidence of "actual malice" and a basis for punitive damages. Weighed against this is the practical

problem that the retraction is often phrased in such a way that it may give further circulation to an unpleasant story (such as JUDGE DIDN'T ACCUSE LAWYER OF WELFARE CASE LIE).
- Get an admission of your non-public-figure status. Along with the other things that you ask to be put in writing, you should consider having the reporter admit in the written release that you are not a public figure. In a close case that might convince a judge. If nothing else, it will probably ensure that the reporter will be careful in what he or she reports about you.

CHAPTER 8

"The Counterspy Shop"

BUGS, TAPS, AND SURVEILLANCE

Bugged?

Are your conversations "bugged"? Protect yourself with pocket-size "Bug" Detector, light signals presence of transmitter worn by visitor in your presence.

Also inquire about our revolutionary electronic lie detection systems, kidnap recovery system, anti-wiretapping, bomb detection, bulletproof apparel, and night vision viewing equipment. Call Mr. ——— in Los Angeles.

San Francisco Examiner, *November 11, 1979*

The quiet contest between eavesdropping and countermeasures is a technological tug of war. Like living insects, electronic bugs develop a resistance to whatever is used against them. No sooner is one generation of eavesdropping device wiped out by a new countermeasure technique than a hardier strain appears, immune to that particular insecticide.

George O'Toole, The Private Sector

Its offices stretch from Wilshire Boulevard in Beverly Hills to South Audley Street in London. The people who run it claim that it is the biggest and best in the field of countersurveillance equipment, and they have adopted for CCS Communication Control the motto "There's more than one way to beat a bug." They should know. Like a reformed whore who can finger all the other hookers, the folks at CCS are former CIA agents who have come in from the cold to show their clientele how to beat the bugs, taps, and surveillance equipment they spent so many years implanting.

There is nothing cold about the way CCS operates. Its storefront shop in London's fashionable Mayfair district is a model of good taste and discretion. At first glance it looks like a hi-fi store, and only the most sophisticated windowshopper would notice that the Security Recording System STR 440 or the Voice Stress Analyzer Mark IX-P are not items you would plug into your ordinary components system. Their product line doesn't seem too unusual given the surroundings: a collection of foreign embassies, high-priced hotels, and headquarters of multinational businesses where concern about personal security and privacy has reached crisis proportions. Toys for the paranoid? Perhaps. But CCS must have an unshakable faith in the strength of its product market to choose such a semiserious name for its store as The Counterspy Shop.

Bugs and Counterbugs

One of the favorite CCS products is the Bionic Briefcase. This ordinary-looking attaché case emits a discreet red light seen only by its owner when a hidden transmitter is in the area. The same briefcase gives off a *loud* noise if anyone other than its owner tries to pick it up, and it gives off a *silent* radio transmission to a home-based receiver if its owner is kidnapped. The price? A mere $6000, which includes a bomb blanket.

CCS employees are not without a certain whimsey in their work. Their cable address in New York is ANTIBUGSYS, but they freely admit that until the Watergate crisis they sold many more bugs than antibugs. Their brochure notes without apology that "The officers of our firm are the inventors of much of today's eavesdropping equipment." It goes on to boast, however, that the company is now working the other side of the street: "Now we hold the patents on the anti-bugging equipment being introduced to the public." The Counterspy Shop also wears the Olympic logo. It achieved that distinction by becoming the "exclusive security supplier" to the 1980 Winter Olympics at Lake Placid.

CCS claims that it has gotten out of the surveillance business entirely and that it is now marketing only defensive equipment. But that is a matter of definition. It still sells infrared cameras, recording systems, wireless TV monitor systems, and the like. In one sense these are defensive devices, since they are mainly designed to protect the CCS clientele from unwanted callers. But the client's privacy is often protected at the expense of someone else's. The caller, for example, may find *his* privacy being invaded by a hidden recording device or voice stress analyzer, which tries to determine his veracity by measuring "microtremors" in his voice. But that is a philosophical distinction that doesn't count for much in this business. The point is to give the client all the hardware he needs to protect his privacy and security. If the other person needs protection, let him get his own supplier. Better yet, let him come by the shop the next day and CCS will sell him what he needs.

A transmitter no larger than George Washington's nose on a quarter, a microphone in a pack of cigarettes that can pick up a normal conversation at thirty feet and transmit it two miles, a "shotgun" microphone that can record a normal conversation from the vibrations in a wall—at first glance the instruments of surveillance seem so fearsome as to instill paralysis. It is easy to assume that anything can be bugged at any time and nothing can be done about it.

In part, this is true. If someone is willing to pay the price and run the risks, it is technically feasible to monitor almost any conversation. But all bugs are not the same. Each technique has certain technical and legal limitations, and each is vulnerable to certain countermeasures. From a private perspective it is useful to know these differences and to try to devise a counterstrategy.

Probably the most common form of bugging device is the "infinity transmitter" or "harmonica bug." This device uses the telephone as a transmitter for conversations carried on near the phone. The range is theoretically infinite, since the conversation can be monitored from another telephone anywhere in the world. A switching device is implanted in the subject's telephone receiver and is activated by a preset tone or series of tones sounded by a harmonica or other musical-toning device. The eavesdropper simply dials the number of the subject telephone and sounds the toning device before the telephone rings. This opens up the telephone line without anyone in the room being aware of it. The eavesdropper can then listen to a conversation in the room as if he were listening to a phone call. Despite the capacity for mischief in such devices, they are often sold openly and legally on the pretext that the user may want to monitor his own home or office for burglars when he is away from the premises.

A cheaper device that accomplishes the same thing is a "listenback" or "keep-alive." Like the harmonica bug, it is installed in the telephone, but it is a less complicated mechanism because it is not tone-activated. The eavesdropper dials the subject telephone and waits for it to be answered. When the telephone is hung up, the device keeps the line alive so that the person on the other telephone can hear conversations carried on nearby.

Harmonica bugs and keep-alives are not without their limitations. When either device is activated, the telephone is unusable. Anyone calling in will get a busy signal, while anyone picking up the telephone will not get a dial tone until the eavesdropper hangs up. The keep-alive must be activated by a pretext call that might arouse the subject's suspicions. If the user of a harmonica bug doesn't activate the tone-controlled device quickly enough before the telephone rings, he may also have to come up with a phony story for the person answering the phone.

A keep-alive can be detected by simply dialing the subject telephone from another telephone and listening to see whether it continues to transmit sounds after it is hung up. A harmonica bug is more difficult to detect. If it has not been activated, it can usually only be detected by a professional "sweep" of the instrument either to locate the device itself or run through all the possible tonal signals to activate it. However, an active harmonica bug can be detected more easily. A relatively inexpensive device attached to the telephone will emit a light signal whenever the voltage drop indicates that the line is open, and persons near the subject telephone will know they are being bugged.

There are other practical problems with such devices. Harmonica bugs and keep-alives, like many other bugging devices, require that the eavesdropper have prior access to the subject's telephone. This means that they are most useful when the eavesdropper has the cooperation of the building or telephone owner.

There are similar practical limitations on other types of bugging devices. A "mike and wire" system installed in a wall gives the greatest range, but the eavesdropper needs a substantial amount of time and freedom of movement within the premises to install the device and conceal the connecting wires. A "drop" transmitter may be easier to install (it is quickly attached to a picture frame or a table) but its range is more limited. Since a drop transmitter operates by radio rather than wires, it usually requires a receiving set within a hundred yards or so. Normally, the radio link is with a van or panel truck near the building. This is a workable arrangement, but it is not exactly inconspicuous to someone who has seen more than a few spy movies.

But this is big-league bugging. Most of these devices require either a warrant or a surveillance team that is willing to run certain legal risks. There are cost factors as well, both in the hardware itself and the personnel needed to install and monitor it. As a practical matter, an individual is not likely to encounter electronic surveillance of his private conversations by a third party unless he is under serious scrutiny by some law-enforcement agency or is involved in a financial deal for very high stakes. Bugging of a conversation by an outsider is, fortunately enough, reserved for the relatively few.

Minor-league bugging is another matter. The most common form of electronic surveillance the average individual is likely to face is a secret recording by the *other* party to the conversation. The other person may be a paid informer, a faithless confidant, or someone who simply wants to make a secret record of the conversation. But the result is the same—a record of the conversation without the individual's knowledge or consent.

A secret recording by a participant to a conversation is much more common than third-party surveillance. In most states this type of bugging of a conversation is legal—the person is considered a participant rather than an eavesdropper. It is also technically simpler, since the hardware is cheaper and easier to install. The person who places a recording system in his own home or office only has to conceal it well enough to hide it from the occasional visitor he wants to record. This is a good deal easier than trying to hide a bug in another's home. The person who wants to record a conversation in which he is involved can also carry a recording unit on his body. He thus avoids many of the technical problems associated with bugging, since he can maneuver his subject close to the microphone, operate without a receiving unit nearby, and record a conversation in the other person's home or office.

Fortunately for the person whose conversation would be taped, there are reasonably effective countermeasures. Suppliers such as The Counterspy Shop allow the buggee to match the bugger tit for tat. If the bugger, for example, enters a room carrying a hidden taping device in a cigarette case, the person being recorded can match that with the Bug Alert EJ8, a desktop pen set that emits a small red light, seen only by the person behind the desk. Conversely, if the bugger has a hidden recorder in *his* desktop pen set to record office visitors, the visitor can defend himself with an antibugging device in *his* cigarette case that vibrates whenever he enters a room with a hidden recorder. The balance between the bugger and his victim can be maintained—for a price. In fact, The Counterspy Shop will let you play the game both ways at the same time for a mere $675:

EXECUTIVE SURVEILLANCE SYSTEM B405
A desktop system that records your conversation by voice activated control, monitors your telephone and detects concealed body transmitters. Attractive and discreet, this system poses as an innocent cigar humidor with all components concealed beneath a removable tray.

The cigars, presumably, are not included.

"If a person voluntarily talks to someone else, why should he be able to deny what he said?" argues Hal Lipset, a noted San Francisco detective. There is nothing wrong with one party making a secret tape recording of a conversation, Lipset contends, because all the tape recorder does is preserve an accurate record of what was said. Otherwise, he argues, you give a person a "license to lie." Lipset, who looks more like someone's favorite uncle than a sleuth, gets indignant about laws that might restrict his right to make a secret recording during an investigation. Almost as if to prove his point, Lipset openly turns on his tape recorder during an interview so there will be no mistaking what he has to say.

The object of Lipset's wrath is a California law that makes it a criminal offense to use any electronic device to "eavesdrop upon or record" any "confidential communication" without the "consent of all the parties." This law has been blamed by some for making it impossible for an investigator to do his job—allowing, for example, a key witness to change his testimony with no backup tape to refute him. On the other hand, it has been credited—rightly or wrongly—with deterring former President Richard Nixon from installing a secret taping system in his office in San Clemente. California, along with Alaska and Pennsylvania, are almost unique in trying to regulate this widespread practice.

The controversy over this law ultimately resolves itself into a philosophical question: Does tape-recording of a conversation by one party involve any real invasion of privacy? Opponents of the law say no. The information being recorded is not truly private, they would argue, since the person making the statement intended that the other person hear it. The recording only verifies what was said and deters either party from lying about it later. They point to the practical benefits of secret tape recordings, such as recording secret threats made against an individual. In a seeming concession to this point of view, California law exempts secret tape recordings involving extortion, bribery, and other serious crimes. Opponents of the law contend that all secret tape recordings should be legal where one party to a conversation is merely trying to preserve an accurate record of what was said. What's wrong, they argue, with honesty and accuracy?

The answer to this ultimately involves a fundamental concession: privacy presupposes some room for lying. Sometimes honesty and accuracy come at too high a price, and the harm done by secret tape recordings usually exceeds their value. The issue provides a good litmus test for a person's attitude toward privacy. Proponents of stricter privacy laws instinctively rebel against secret tape recordings of conversations despite the seemingly plausible arguments in favor of allowing people to do so. They take a broader view of privacy—one that looks to the proper balance between the individual and society, between man and machine. In this view of things a world in which all statements are "on the record" is frightening to contemplate. Widespread recording of every utterance leaves no room to backtrack, recant, or deny an indiscreet remark. It allows no room to be blunt or uncivil—no chance to be intimate or foolish—without the nagging fear that the words will be played back later. The threat of a secret tape recording violates the speaker's normal view of reality: that is, that the person within earshot is the only person listening. It substitutes for it a paranoid view of the world that assumes there are unseen ears everywhere. Such a view may sound reactionary to persons weaned on the benefits of technology, but a concern for privacy is often a mixture of radical and reactionary ideas.

Telephones

There is a crime so heinous that merely to be suspected of it is legal grounds for the wiretapping of your telephone without a warrant. Your every telephone conversation will be tape-recorded for as long as it takes to establish your guilt or innocence. If no evidence against you is overheard, you will never know that your privacy was violated. If your telephone conversations indicate you are guilty of this crime, there will be a knock on your door. It won't be the police, the FBI, the CIA, or any official law enforcement agency, for the law does not grant them this kind of power over a person suspected of this crime. The men on the other side of the door will be from one of the most powerful private police forces in the country —the telephone company cops. And the crime they are empowered by law to investigate through wholesale warrantless wiretapping is not murder, kidnapping, espionage, or treason; it is telephone fraud—cheating Ma Bell out of a dime.

George O'Toole, The Private Sector

If you don't want it known, don't use the phone.

Nelson Rockefeller

Each year more than 10,000 Americans complain to the telephone company that their telephone is being tapped. There are millions more who believe they are being wiretapped but who do not report it. According to the Harris Poll, almost one out of every ten Americans believes his or her telephone has been tapped at one time or another. Yet, wiretapping is supposedly prohibited by federal law, and there are only about 600 legal taps instituted by law-enforcement officials each year. This means one of two things: either the average American is becoming paranoid or he knows something that the official figures don't reflect.

One thing the official figures don't stress is that wiretaps placed on a relatively small number of phones nevertheless result in the recording of a large number of people. In 1976, for example, 635 legal telephone taps resulted in the recording of approximately 34,290 people and 431,370 conversations. Nor do the official figures include a good many "unofficial" taps. Some of them are arguably legal: a company monitoring the calls by its employees on its in-house phones or a husband recording the amatory adventures of his wife on their home phone. Some of them are accidental or incidental, such as a telephone repairman tapping into the wrong line or a service representative listening in on a call to see if the line is functioning properly. Some of them are blatantly illegal: a telephone security cop recording a conversation for a buddy down at the police station or an eavesdropper splicing into the line. But—most of all—the official figures do not reflect AT&T's own monitoring of phone lines to see if anyone is trying to cheat the company. More than 1.8 million calls were monitored and recorded for this purpose by the phone company over a five-year period.

A telephone tap by the phone company is as simple as picking up a receiver. In many cases phone company personnel do just that: they pick up a phone and listen to the conversation. But AT&T also uses more sophisticated methods. In an effort to catch Phone Phreaks—home-grown electronic wizards who get a thrill out of things like calling Australia on a dime—the phone company devised a scanning system to tap into their calls. The problem is that it tapped into a great many more innocent calls as well. The device monitors all telephone calls, searching for a tone at 2600 cycles—the frequency at which Phone Phreaks operate. When the scanning device hears that tone, it automatically taps into the line and records the conversation. This is fine for catching Phone Phreaks. But of the estimated 1.8 million telephone calls the phone company monitored and recorded in this fashion in five years, fraud was proved in less than 2 percent of the cases. The great majority of the rest were simply ordinary calls that happened to involve that same tone. If this monitoring of phone calls to catch a group of pranksters seems like a bit of overkill, it does not appear that way to Ma Bell.*

For those not employed by the phone company, telephone eavesdropping is more difficult but far from impossible. The favorite technique for illegal telephone taps is an in-line transmitter. This is a low-power FM transmitter attached to the phone line somewhere between the telephone and the telephone pole. Ordinarily, it is linked to a voice-activated tape recorder located within a few hundred feet. Installation of an in-line transmitter requires tapping into the telephone wires, and for that reason it is almost always illegal unless done with the consent of the owner. There are countermeasures, however. For $2375 the Counterspy Shop will sell you a Tap Alert B409 that will supposedly detect an in-line transmitter.

A more sophisticated eavesdropper will tap into the line between the telephone pole and the phone-company office. This type of tap is more difficult to detect, because it is farther from the telephone. The problem, however, is finding the right lines. At some point the individual lines from a home or office go through a junction box, where they merge with lines from all the other buildings. Only the employees at the telephone company have the "cable and pair" information needed to find the right lines. The solution to the eavesdropper's problem is implicit in that fact: find a friend in the phone company. Since many telephone-company security cops are former policemen or FBI agents,

---

* Some may view Phone Phreaks operating under colorful names like Captain Crunch as jolly anarchists, but the phone company takes a much more somber view. According to AT&T's general counsel in his testimony before Congress, the onslaught of the Phone Phreaks with their black boxes "was a breakthrough almost equivalent to the advent of gunpowder, where the hordes of Genghis Khan faced problems of a new sort, or the advent of the cannon."

it is not unusual to find such information passed along in a buddy network.

But this too has its countermeasures, even though they are a good deal more expensive. The Telephone Analyzer TA 2000 is the pride and joy of The Counterspy Shop. "It checks both telephone sets and lines for irregularities up to 10 miles," according to the brochure, "and then not only reveals an eavesdropping device but helps pinpoint its location." According to the salesman, "it does everything but bark and climb trees." The price? A hefty $38,750. But, according to CCS, it is "the ultimate in telephone analyzing equipment . . . [and] no other countermeasure system is necessary."

Not quite. Although a sophisticated telephone analyzer can sweep the line back to the telephone company, it will not pick up on eavesdropping conducted at the telephone company itself. The telephone-company cops—or the police when armed with a warrant—can simply listen in on a conversation at the phone company office. There is no mess and no fuss, and there is no tapping device for the telephone analyzer to detect. Thus, countermeasure devices may work against illegal taps, but they are not effective against those who can listen in with legal impunity.

The problem of privacy in telephone conversations is more complicated than simply a game of cat and mouse played on the telephone wires. Many calls don't even use wires. About 70 percent of all long-distance calls are relayed by microwave transmission between towers stationed about twenty miles apart across the country. The implications are scary even to eavesdroppers. Many government agents and telephone security teams have begun to worry about the privacy of *their* phone calls carried over microwaves. The eavesdropping technique that concerns them is called "plucking," because the receiving equipment simply plucks the conversation out of the microwaves in the air. It involves no wires, no surreptitious entries, no detectable emissions—and there is virtually no defense against it.

The Soviet Union intercepts telephone conversations carried over microwaves. The Soviets have a monitoring device on their embassy in Washington, their UN mission headquarters, and at various consulates and locations throughout the country. The U.S. National Security Agency has also perfected the technique and uses it to intercept calls. As a foremost user of this method, the U.S. government knows how vulnerable the telephone lines are to penetration by the Soviets or any one else with the proper equipment. Consequently, the U.S. government has earmarked substantial sums of money to try to rechannel its vital telephone lines through the old-fashioned cable system or something else less vulnerable.

The plucking of telephone calls would not be effective without the help of a computer. No matter how carefully an interceptor station is placed, it is still likely to pick up huge numbers of unwanted telephone calls from different phones in the area. Left to itself, the interceptor station would record everyone—indiscriminately. As bad as that sounds, it would probably be a good thing. The information would overload the circuits. The system would give the eavesdropper too much information to sort out and would therefore be impractical to use.

What actually happens is less broad-sweeping but more sinister. A sophisticated computer enables an eavesdropper to sort out the important telephone calls. The U.S. government, for example, has developed the HARVEST computer, which allows it to glean certain calls from the airwaves according to preestablished criteria. The computer can be programmed to record only the calls being made to certain telephone numbers, based on the digits picked up from transmission. It can also be programmed to pick up certain voiceprints or to tune into a call only when it hears certain buzzwords or key phrases.

The techniques for microwave interception of telephone calls were detailed in a report prepared for the White House by the Mitre Research Corporation in 1977. According to Ford Rowan, author of *Technospies*, the date is significant, because if the technique had been known five years earlier it would not have been necessary for the Watergate team to have burglarized the Democratic National Headquarters to implant a wiretapping device. They could have done it all without leaving the White House. The Howard Hunts and G. Gordon Liddys of the future will probably sit in their offices, look at their scanners, and never get caught.

Following the orgy of wiretapping in the Nixon years, Congress finally closed the "national security" exception to the wiretapping laws in 1978. But troubling exceptions remain. One of these exceptions is for a listening device installed with the user's consent. Wiretapping is permitted without a warrant when it is done by a "party to the communication" or with his "prior consent." In other words, a person can tap his own line or authorize it to be tapped. Fine for him, but how about the person on the *other* end of the line? He has not given *his* consent to being recorded, but the tap is nevertheless exempt under federal law.

Wiretapping or recording with the consent of only one party raises the same practical problems that confront the person walking into the room with the hidden tape recorder. But the problem has an added wrinkle. Unlike the person in a bugged room who can perhaps detect such a device with his own bug alert, the person on the other end of the telephone has no way to know if he is being recorded. The other party needn't actually tap into his own line but can simply attach a recording device that cannot be detected. The ubiquitous answering machines are sometimes used for this purpose: the person simply has the machine answer the telephone and then cuts in on the conversation while leaving the machine running to record what is said.

What happens when a husband plants a tapping device on the home phone to catch his wife in her infidelities? Not much, according to former Attorney General Griffin Bell, who before that was a judge on the Circuit Court of Appeals. In a 1974 decision he ruled that such a wiretap was not illegal because the couple lived in the same house and the husband alone could legally "consent" to it. Other courts have been troubled with this result and have hinted that such wiretaps might violate federal law. A similar problem arises with a company's tapping of telephone calls within its own offices. Courts have allowed such monitoring so long as it doesn't involve the external lines leading out from the switchboard. These cases illustrate that the "owner" and the "user" of the phone may be quite different individuals with conflicting interests.

The phone company's monitoring of telephone calls is exempt from the search-warrant requirement, and this presents all kinds of problems. In addition to the 1.8 million or so calls Ma Bell monitors to catch cheaters, there are countless calls that the phone-company employees listen to as part of its routine maintenance and training. Pacific Telephone, for example, now carries the following notice in its telephone books:

> For training and quality control purposes, a sampling of telephone calls ... between telephone company employees and customers are monitored, without notice to the customer or the employee, by supervisory or management personnel.

Phone-company employees also listen in while working on the equipment. Theoretically, this is done at random. In practice? One former

Pacific Telephone Company operator revealed that company technicians search the lines until they find an interesting conversation—usually one involving sex—and then put it on the loudspeaker around the shop for everyone's enjoyment.

The issue gets stickier when the telephone-company employee comes up with something more than mere titillation. In November 1976 a troubleshooter for Pacific Telephone in Escondido, California, cut in on a line while testing for a malfunction. While on the line he allegedly heard one of the callers offer the other 100,000 "bennies" for $5000. The telephone company informed the police, who subsequently arrested the callers. The California Supreme Court in a highly controversial decision threw out the evidence against the defendants, but they did so on narrow grounds. Judging by the heat the California Supreme Court took from law-enforcement agencies for its decision, it is unlikely that such a ruling will be followed by courts elsewhere. For most people the assumption must be that the contents of their private phone calls can be revealed by a telephone workman who wanders across their line and government agents can act on that information.

While the phone company's purpose in monitoring calls is usually benign, occasionally it can turn vicious. James Ashley, a former general commercial manager for Southwestern Bell in Texas, claimed in 1974 that phone-company agents listened in on phone conversations of city councilmen and other public officials with whom they had to negotiate rate increases. The information they got was (to say the least) useful in later negotiating sessions. Ashley claimed he would know "How much they owed, who they were sleeping with, or how they could be gotten to.... If we didn't have the information on the councilman, the company would just tap a few telephones." This type of monitoring by phone-company officials is by no means legal, but the blanket exemption for phone-company surveillance makes it difficult to detect when a phone-company employee might cross the line from routine monitoring to extortion.

It is difficult also to detect how much unofficial cooperation there is between telephone-company cops and law-enforcement agencies to circumvent the warrant requirement for wiretaps by the police. The police are required to show probable cause—some substantial facts to show that a law is being violated—before a judge can issue a warrant. Vague suspicions are not supposed to be enough, but they were enough in Baltimore, Maryland, in 1975. During that period Baltimore vice-squad officers would contact their friends at the security office of the Chesapeake and Potomac Telephone Company whenever they had a notion that a residence might be being used for gambling. The security cops would obligingly listen in on the telephone calls to and from the residence to confirm the vice squad's suspicions. If they struck gold, they would report back to the police, who would then go into court for a warrant to tap the telephone based on information from a "reliable informant." With the warrant they would then go through the charade of listening in on the telephone to pick up the evidence they already had in their back pockets.

Despite the exceptions, loopholes, and evasions, federal law does prevent unrestricted eavesdropping on telephone calls. But the law covers only the calls themselves. Any other information about the use of a telephone is a no-man's-land that is open to any investigator. For example, a telephone user can get an unlisted telephone number for an extra charge. But unlisted to whom? Pacific Telephone has routinely turned over unlisted phone numbers to the IRS, FBI, CIA, and many other agencies without a subpoena or court order. The California Public Utilities Commission is considering rules that would require the phone company to inform the subscriber, but only within thirty days *after* it has given out the number. Other states have simply left the matter up to Ma Bell's sense of discretion.

Telephone toll-call records present a more serious problem. These records provide a good indication of a person's friends, interests, vices, and the like. These records have at times been systematically invaded by government agents, particularly against reporters. In almost every case the government's motive was to find out the source of a leak that led to an unfavorable news story.

Since 1974 it has been AT&T's policy to turn over toll records to government agents only in response to a subpoena (although no subpoena is required from the FBI). A subpoena, however, is not much protection to the subscriber, since an administrative or grand jury subpoena can usually be obtained by the government without notice to the telephone user. The phone company could give notice to the telephone subscriber when it receives the subpoena, but it will not do so for ninety days if requested not to by the government. The Reporters' Committee for Freedom of the Press challenged in court the phone company's practice in giving out toll records to the government, but their case was unsuccessful.

The reporters' challenge probably wouldn't have made any difference anyway, since the Supreme Court opened up an even bigger can of worms less than a year later. In *Smith v. Maryland,* the Supreme Court upheld a government practice that makes the seizure of phone records almost obsolete—that is, the installation of pen registers without a search warrant. A pen register is an electronic device that automatically records each telephone number dialed from the user's phone. With such a device in place, an investigator can determine each person the phone user has called as well as the date, time, and length of the call. It is obviously a potent weapon of surveillance, but the Supreme Court gave short shrift to the privacy problems it raises. As it now stands, government agents and the telephone company can simply monitor all the numbers called from an individual's phone without any prior approval of a court or anyone else.

Mail

The New York Regional Office of the IRS had become concerned over possible losses of United States income taxes through the use of secret Swiss bank accounts. It occurred to someone that taxpayers having such accounts might be identified by their receipt of statements from the banks. However, detection was impeded by the fact that, in the interest of secrecy, the Swiss banks used envelopes not bearing the banks' names or return addresses. Some agents penetrate this shield by writing various Swiss banks about establishing accounts and observing the postal meter numbers on the answers. Armed with these numbers, IRS requested the Postal Service, in a communication not in the record, for permission to conduct a mail cover during the first four months of 1968. On the evenings of about 60 days during that period, a Postal Inspector and IRS Special Agents, working at the main New York City Post Office, photostated with high speed copiers the faces of all air mail envelopes without return addresses mailed from Switzerland to New York. Thereafter postage meter numbers on these photostats were examined to see if any matched those known to have been used by Swiss banks. This group, which amounted to thousands of envelopes, was converted into a print-out containing the recipients' names, addresses, dates of envelopes and the identities of the banks. From the several hundred names in the print-out . . . [the IRS] selected a group of 100 in the Manhattan and about 50 in the Brooklyn District.

From United States v. Leonard, *United States Circuit Court of Appeals, 1975*

In the same year (1975) the U.S. Circuit Court was giving its approval to an elaborate use of mail covers by the IRS to detect possible correspondents with Swiss banks, the Chief U.S. Postal Inspector was assuring Congress that no such thing could happen.

> CONGRESSMAN ROBERT W. KASTENMEIER (D-Wis.): Do you people in the field ever require agencies requesting mail cover to provide any sample evidence of the possible commission of a crime?
> WILLIAM J. COTTER (Chief Postal Inspector): Yes.
> MR. KASTENMEIER: And you take that at face value.
> MR. COTTER: Indeed, they do. And they go back, I'm quite sure, regularly, and turn down requests if they don't satisfy the requirements.

In a mail cover government agents record the name and address of the sender, the place and date of postmark, the class of mail, and any other information appearing on the outside cover of any item of mail. Postal Regulations supposedly limit mail covers to situations involving national security or obtaining evidence of the commission of a crime. But the Postal Service has not been too inquisitive, preferring to let government agencies make their own determination as to when these requests are proper. This has led to cases like *United States v. Leonard,* where the government started out with no evidence of a crime, no evidence of a suspect, and only a vague idea that a mail cover might come up with something useful.

The Postal Service has run mail covers on about 4500 persons per year, picking up all the information that could be gleaned from the envelopes addressed to the individuals under surveillance. Many of these mail covers have been initiated by the Postal Service itself in an effort to combat mail fraud. But an almost equal number have been initiated by IRS, many of them based on a pretext as skimpy as in the Leonard case. Other big users of mail covers have been the Bureau of Customs, the Drug Enforcement Administration, the FBI, and local police and sheriff's offices.

Although the Postal Service has the last word on whether or not to allow the mail cover, it often defers to the agency requesting that a cover be placed on someone's mail. According to Chief Postal Inspector Cotter, "They suggest that a mail cover would be most desirable to see the extent of his contacts, and we would undoubtedly agree to that request." When pressed to justify the practice, Postal Service representatives like to talk about the mail-fraud cases that have been cracked through the use of mail covers. What they don't like to talk about is the number of innocent people who have been harmed by mail covers or who have been wrongly placed under surveillance simply because they corresponded with someone whose mail was being covered. Mostly, they don't like to talk about Lori Paton.

CONGRESSMAN ROBERT DRINAN (D-Mass.): Mr. Cotter, could the case of Lori Paton happen once again? This was a 16-year-old girl who wrote the Socialist Workers Party in New York City, asking for information. The FBI investigated her, her teachers and her family; and as you know, there is a lawsuit pending in the whole matter. Have you altered the regulations so that we can never have another case like Lori Paton?

MR. COTTER: No, Sir, but I hope we won't have another case like Lori Paton; that was human error. The mail cover was on the Socialist Workers Party. This young lady wrote a letter to the Socialist Labor Party, who are incidentally in the same building. The clerk got the mail mixed up and recorded her name on the list of mail going to the Socialist Workers Party, as I recall, and that's how the whole confused mixup started.

Mail covers are roughly analogous to government surveillance of telephone toll records or checking accounts. All three techniques stop short of eavesdropping on the actual correspondence or transaction itself but instead nip around the edges. A mail cover will not tell an investigator what was said, but it will tell him a great deal about the person by recording with whom he corresponds and how often. Not surprisingly, critics of government policy have contended that a search warrant should be required for mail covers because they involve a significant intrusion on the mail recipient's "reasonable expectation of privacy." Also not surprisingly, the Supreme Court has declined to uphold such an argument for the same reasons as with bank records and telephone toll records. Although the Postal Service has been under some pressure to tighten up its surveillance policies, any restraint it exhibits may be short-lived. Its legal authority to institute mail covers remains intact.

Mail covers are serious enough, but "mailtapping" is worse. Officially, it is illegal for government agents to open first-class mail and read it. However, Professor Mel Crain of San Diego State University told Congress that he was hired by the CIA to do just that. "It was with no little surprise," he testified, "that one day in 1958 I found myself extensively involved in mail-tapping of American citizens." His project was a joint operation of the Post Office and the CIA. "The letters were opened, reproduced, resealed, and sent on their way without interrupting mail flow or their opening in any way being detected," according to

Crain. The FBI had its own mail-opening projects during this period. Like the CIA projects, it was theoretically illegal. But both the CIA and FBI mail-opening projects continued well into the 1970s, when the Watergate scandals supposedly forced them to shut down.

Government mailtappers started from a "watch list" of about 600 names, most of them of political dissidents. About 25 percent of the letters opened were from persons on this list. But another 75 percent were opened randomly, according to the Center for National Security Studies. The Center quotes a former CIA agent who was a mail-opener in New York as stating that the choice of such letters was "according to individual taste . . . your own reading about current events." Most estimates put the total number of letters opened and photographed in the vicinity of 300,000. According to Robert Ellis Smith, editor of the *Privacy Journal,* the CIA took down the names of every person mentioned in such letters—a total of 1.5 million—and stored them in its files in McLean, Virginia. The CIA list supposedly includes John Steinbeck, Jane Fonda, and Senator Frank Church—whose mother made the mistake of writing him a letter while she was on a trip to the Soviet Union.

Officially, at least, mailtapping no longer occurs. Unofficially, no one can say for sure, since the CIA and others have developed techniques for reading a letter without opening the envelope. But even the official policy against reading other people's mail has its exceptions. The Postal Service claims the right to read anything that is not mailed first class. According to Chief Postal Inspector Cotter, when something is sent by second-, and third-, or fourth-class mail, this is "considered consent by the sender to examination of the mail contents since the sender is free to choose the greater privacy of first-class mail." Whether the sender knows that he has given such consent is another matter.

First-class mail cannot be opened legally without a search warrant, but even that has exceptions. In 1977 the U.S. Supreme Court upheld the practice of Postal Service inspectors in opening first-class mail from outside the United States based on their suspicion that the mail might contain contraband. Three dissenting justices argued to no avail that the Postal Service should be required to obtain a search warrant if they had sufficient evidence to suspect the illegal importation of items into the country. The end result appears to be that postal inspectors can open mail from overseas based on mere suspicion about its size, shape, or country of origin.

The technology of the near future is likely to make the problem of mail privacy worse. Robert Ellis Smith points out that the Postal Service is moving in the direction of eight-digit zip codes—a development that will reduce each addressee to a number instead of a street address. This augurs more than just the type of identity crisis that nostalgia buffs experienced with the advent of all-digit dialing. It suggests a distinct change in the way that mail is sorted and delivered—and scrutinized.

An expanded zip-code system means that the delivery of mail can be computerized and mechanized. Without human hands to slow it down, the whole mail-delivery system may move faster. The problem is that the mail surveillance system will probably move faster as well. As each addressee is computerized, it will not take much ingenuity to institute an electronic mail cover. The computer can simply be programmed to "read out" all correspondence to or from a particular addressee or postal meter. Surveillance of the mail currently requires substantial diversion of human labor from other tasks, and this acts as some restraint on the number of mail covers that are undertaken. It is hard to imagine much restraint at all when the same type of mail cover can be instituted with the flick of a switch.

But even computerized, zip-code mail delivery will soon be obsolete for many types of mail. The ultimate mail-delivery system is a facsimile machine, which reproduces letters that have been transmitted electronically. These systems, of course, are already in use by many businesses. In privacy terms, however, electronic mail delivery simply substitutes one potential form of surveillance for another. The mail of the future may be susceptible to the same forms of wiretapping and microwave interceptions as now plague telephone calls. The only unresolved issue may be whether the Postal Service or the telephone company will get the honor of monitoring the transmission.

Searches and Seizures

The right of the people to be secure in their persons, houses, papers, and effects, against unreasonable searches and seizures, shall not be violated, and no Warrants shall issue, but upon probable cause, supported by Oath or affirmation, and particularly describing the place to be searched, and the persons or things to be seized.

Fourth Amendment to the Constitution of the United States

We hold therefore that upon arresting petitioner for the offense of driving his automobile without a valid operator's license, and taking him into custody, the policeman was entitled to make a full search of petitioner's person. . . . Having in the course of his lawful search come upon the box of cigarettes, he was entitled to inspect it; and when his inspection revealed the homemade cigarettes which he believed to contain an unlawful substance, he was entitled to seize them as "fruits, instrumentalities or contraband" probative of criminal conduct.

Supreme Court Justice William Rehnquist,
Gustafson v. Illinois, 1973

The fifty-four words of the Fourth Amendment are the most important in the U.S. Constitution in matters of privacy. They set forth fundamental limitations on the power of the government to search private property, deprive people of their freedom, and engage in acts of surveillance. Words are fine, but they need institutions to give them force. The essential question is what these words mean in practice.

There have been times in our history when the words of the Fourth Amendment have seemingly meant very little. In the period culminating in the Watergate crisis government agents freely engaged in bugging, wiretapping, surveillance, "bag jobs," and other invasions of privacy in massive violation of the Fourth Amendment's guarantees. The irony is that this occurred at the same time that the Earl Warren majority on the Supreme Court was issuing important decisions expanding the protections of the Fourth Amendment. It was as if the government were operating on two parallel tracks, one official and one unofficial. Officially, privacy of individuals was being cared for by the rulings of the Supreme Court. Unofficially, the situation was a disaster.

In the post-Watergate era things have begun to reverse themselves. Increased public awareness has forced government agencies to cut back on the more heavy-handed techniques of surveillance. As far as anyone can tell, the FBI has stopped committing burglaries, the IRS is no longer stealing briefcases, intelligence agencies are getting warrants for their wiretaps, and government officials in general are playing by the rules. The problem now is with the rules. The Earl Warren Supreme Court has been replaced by the Warren Burger Supreme Court, and the new Court's attitude toward the protection of the Fourth Amendment has become increasingly hostile.

Persons concerned about their privacy probably have less to fear from illegal government intrusions into their lives than they did ten years ago. But that's only the good news. The part that is not so good is the government's expanded *legal* powers to engage in searches and surveillance. As a practical matter, the formal opinions of the Supreme Court are becoming more important in determining the status of individual privacy at the same time those opinions are beginning to allow more and more government encroachment. How far has the Supreme Court shifted? If Justice Rehnquist's decision in *Gustafson v. Illinois* is any indication, the movement has been drastic and may be getting worse. Privacy rights are in trouble when failure to carry a driver's license can justify a full body search to find a couple of joints.

The Fourth Amendment protects "persons, houses, papers, and effects" against government intrusion. The eighteenth-century phraseology of the amendment has proved remarkably flexible, but no one could have foreseen the strains that modern technology and society would place on it. A key question that has confronted the Supreme Court, therefore, has been whether it is willing to reinterpret the Fourth Amendment in terms of twentieth-century realities. In 1967, in *Katz v. United States,* the Warren Court marched forward to do just that. But most of the marching since then has been in the opposite direction.

In the *Katz* case government agents placed a microphone against the outside wall of a telephone booth in order to record a phone call placed by a suspected gambler. The government agents had no warrant, but they argued that they didn't need one. The phone booth was not the property of the suspect, they argued, and in any event they were not trespassing when they placed the microphone on the outside. The Supreme Court rejected that argument and struck out boldly to redefine the individual's rights: "The Fourth Amendment protects people, not places." It made no difference that the government agents hadn't committed a trespass, because they had "violated the privacy upon which [the user of the phone booth] ... justifiably relied."

In the *Katz* decision the Supreme Court came to grips with a basic reality: eavesdroppers no longer have to trespass on private property to carry out their work. A spike mike attached to the outside wall can be as effective as one placed in the room. A parabolic or directional microphone will pick up a conversation at a considerable distance from a person's home or office. Telephone wires can be spliced at the telephone pole as easily as in the house. By focusing on the snooper's conduct and the individual's need for privacy, the Supreme Court tried to ensure that electronic gadgetry would not outflank the Fourth Amendment the way it has walls and windows.

The Supreme Court under Warren Burger has not retreated significantly from the *Katz* decision in matters of electronic or mechanical surveillance, but that may be more a lack of opportunity than anything else. Key cases (such as the use of high-powered telescopes or cameras) have not yet been decided by the Court. Will the present Supreme Court members follow the precedent established by its immediate predecessors and rule that magnified pictures constitute a search for which a warrant is required? Or will they find some way to retreat from that position? The precedent of the *Katz* case is broad enough to extend to all types of surveillance, whether it is conducted from next door, down the block, or a satellite in orbit around the earth. The principal question should be whether the surveillance violates a person's "reasonable expectation of privacy." If it does, the logic of the prior Supreme Court decision would indicate that such surveillance cannot be done without a search warrant.

But logic may not count for much in Supreme Court-watching. Later decisions of the high court have not only declined to extend the mantle of Fourth Amendment protection to other situations where there has been a "reasonable expectation of privacy" but have also stood that doctrine on its head to defeat the claims of privacy. This crucial turnabout has come in matters that may be of greater practical importance to the average individual than physical surveillance: confidentiality in private papers. The Court has refused to find any privacy interest in bank-account records, accountant's workpapers, telephone toll records, mail covers on incoming mail, or any other documents held on an individual's behalf by a third party such as a bank or the telephone company. Surveillance in all these areas has been allowed by the Supreme Court without a search warrant.*

The Court's reasoning in *Smith v. Maryland* is typical of these cases. "It is too much to believe that telephone subscribers ... harbor any genuine expectation that the numbers they dial will remain secret." Under this view of things, it is all right for the government to seize such information without a warrant because no one really believes they wouldn't try to do it or that the third party wouldn't divulge it. By

---

* As the U.S. Supreme Court has retreated, some state courts have moved in to take up the slack. California—the most notable in this trend—has interpreted its *own* state constitution to prohibit state or local agents from seizing bank records, telephone records, and the like without a warrant. In cases that have not yet been ruled on by the Supreme Court, lower federal courts have been able to extend the protection of the U.S. Constitution into new areas. A federal district court in Hawaii, for example, has ruled that surveillance into an apartment with a telescope is unconstitutional. The exact status of the individual's rights against unwarranted surveillance depends on where he is and who is doing the peeking. It is a question that almost always requires the advice of a good lawyer.

lowering its level of conduct, the government can lower the expectation of individuals that anything will remain private or confidential. Using this approach, the Court has been able to turn around a constitutional doctrine designed to enhance privacy and use it to limit that same right. Smart people, so the argument goes, have no reasonable expectation that the privacy of such information will be maintained so therefore the courts are under no obligation to recognize any privacy rights in such documents. It is a circular argument that sounds a bit like "might makes right," but it is really that doctrine's second cousin: "cynicism makes acceptable."

For "persons, houses, papers, and effects" that *do* fall under Fourth Amendment protection the basic rule is that no search or surveillance will be permitted unless the government agent has a search warrant. Government investigators normally have to submit the proposed search to some prior scrutiny by a judge or magistrate and have that official sign a warrant. But, like everything else, there are exceptions to the search-warrant requirement. One of the principal battlegrounds within the shifting alliances on the Supreme Court has been whether the exceptions will gobble up the rule.

One exception is for searches conducted with a person's "consent." This is a seemingly harmless idea, since an individual can presumably withhold his consent whenever he wants to and tell the officer to go get a warrant. But it is not that simple. An individual's consent will be "implied" under a variety of circumstances. If, for example, a person voluntarily invites a policeman into his home to report a burglary, he has given his implied consent to the officer's observation of anything in view within the house. If he is cultivating a marijuana plant in the kitchen, the police may seize that as evidence of *his* crime despite the fact that they were invited into the house to investigate *someone else's* crime. This type of vignette happens often enough in the United States that crime statistics should probably include a new category: "crime unsolved but victim arrested."

How about a "consent" that is given by someone else? The Supreme Court opened up that little trap in 1974 when it held that a woman could consent to a warrantless search of the room in which she had been living with a man. This was allowed by the Court despite the fact that it was him—not her—that the police were investigating and she had not been advised that she could refuse the police request. This opens up all types of possibilities of "consent" searches and surveillance of persons sharing apartments, offices, lockers, and so on. If a person under investigation won't voluntarily allow his financial record to be copied or his conversations to be recorded, the investigators can contact his girlfriend, partner, or roommate and get one of them to consent to it. The police can simply approach the weakest link in the chain (the roommate least likely to say "no") and get consent to search everyone else.

How about the "consent" of the taxpayer who goes to the IRS offices at the request of an auditor to discuss his tax returns? Departmental regulations supposedly prohibited the IRS from making a surreptitious recording of the taxpayer's conversation with the IRS official. But that didn't stop the IRS from secretly recording a conversation with a taxpayer in the San Francisco regional office in 1974. Nor did it stop the Supreme Court in 1979 from upholding the taxpayer's conviction for bribery, based on the information in the tape recordings.

Consent can be implied in other ways. The fire department has an owner's implied consent to enter a building to put out a fire, and this consent extends to a fire investigator whose later search may turn up something having nothing to do with the fire itself. Closely akin to "consent" searches is the "plain view" doctrine. If an officer has a legitimate reason to look inside a doorway, through a car window, or the like, he can act on whatever he sees (or hears or smells, for that matter). A baggie of marijuana on the floor next to the driver may be sufficient justification for the cop to arrest the driver and search the rest of the car.

Another exception to the search-warrant requirement is a search "incident to" a lawful arrest. This sounds innocuous enough: nice people don't get themselves arrested, so why worry about what happens when it occurs? The problem is that a minor offense or no offense at all may trigger an arrest and result in consequences far out of proportion to the original infraction. The Supreme Court ruled that driving without your license is serious enough to justify a full body search after your car is stopped.

Traffic offenses are the source of all kinds of problems. Unpaid parking tickets, for example, may result in the issuance in some states of a bench warrant for the person's arrest. If a person is stopped in his automobile for any purpose, the policeman is likely to make a warrant check by feeding the vehicle license number over the police-car radio to a central computer. If the computer flashes back "bench warrant," the driver can be arrested and subjected to both a body search and a search of the vehicle.

A policeman may stop and "detain" individuals for a short period of time even though there is no grounds for arrest. This in itself is ordinarily not a serious invasion of privacy, but what follows may be. If the officer has sufficient grounds to stop an individual for questioning, the courts have reasoned that he also has sufficient grounds to search him for hidden weapons. Although such a frisk for weapons is not as extensive as a full body search, it can lead to the same thing. The criminal casebooks are full of situations in which a cop testifies that he felt a "bulge" or "object" he thought was a weapon but which, on further investigation, turned out to be a vial of cocaine or a lid of grass. Theoretically, the cop did not start out looking for such items, but in the end it still results in a bust.

The Fourth Amendment has been virtually repealed when it comes to automobiles. Arguing that automobiles can be quickly moved, the Supreme Court has been quick to rationalize that the police can search a vehicle without taking time to get a warrant. The problem with this argument is that many of these warrantless searches have occurred after the car has been impounded, when it is obvious that it is not going anywhere. Such searches have also been allowed where there is no reason to believe that there is anything suspicious about the vehicle. Donald Opperman, for example, left his car parked in a tow away zone in Vermillion, South Dakota, on December 10, 1973. The police towed the vehicle away, picked the lock on the door, and made a full "inventory " search of the interior. After the inevitable baggie of marijuana was found in the glove compartment, Opperman appealed his conviction to the Supreme Court. Chief Justice Warren Burger concluded that a person's "expectation of privacy" in his automobile is "significantly less" than in his home or office. Whatever Donald Opperman's expectations were, his conviction was allowed to stand.

Luggage fares better than other items in a car under the rules fashioned by the Supreme Court. On April 23, 1976, Lonnie James Sanders flew into Little Rock, Arkansas, carrying a suitcase that—according to an informant—contained marijuana. Sanders retrieved the suitcase from the baggage area of the airport under the dutiful eye of the police and placed it in a waiting taxicab. The police stopped the cab, opened up the suitcase, and confiscated the grass. But Sanders was lucky. The Supreme Court concluded that this type of search was unconstitutional. The Court made a distinction between luggage and parts of the car itself (marijuana in a suitcase is somehow different from the same substance in the glove compartment) and ruled that the luggage could not be opened without a search warrant.

But luggage and packages aren't always safe from inspection. Luggage is routinely checked for weapons before a passenger enters an airplane. If the inspector finds some other illegal item in the process, it can be seized and used as evidence. Likewise, travelers returning into the country are subject to routine searches of their luggage, and if any illegal substance is found—whether duty-free or not—it can be seized as evidence. It also makes some difference whether the individual carries it or sends it across an international border. Customs officials have the authority to open any package sent into the United States in which they have "reasonable cause to suspect there is merchandise which was imported contrary to law." The "reasonable requirement" acts as some restraint on the opening of packages, but no such restraint applies to customs officials inspecting a traveler's luggage.

Random stops of innocent-looking vehicles are probably not allowed except at the national border or its "functional equivalent" where immigration officials can stop cars in search of illegal aliens. But in the rest of the country the rules are supposed to be different. In 1979, the Supreme Court struck down a case from New Castle County, Delaware, in which a patrolman stopped a car on a spot check and arrested the driver after seeing marijuana on the floor of the vehicle. Since the cop had no reason to suspect the driver of any traffic or other violation, the Court ruled that his actions violated the Fourth Amendment. However, the Court went on to suggest how vehicles could be stopped in a way that would be constitutional. One of the suggestions by the justices was arguably worse than what they struck down: "Questioning of all incoming traffic at roadblock-type stops is one possible alternative."

Searches without a warrant present obvious possibilities of serious abuse. But searches *with* a warrant present serious privacy problems of their own, and those problems are sometimes worse. Warrantless searches are often quick, spur-of-the-moment actions by police officers that can be avoided with some prudence. But a search with a warrant is ordinarily a carefully preplanned operation against which there is virtually no defense. The fairness of the warrant procedure, therefore, is critical to personal privacy.

A search warrant requires at least one supposedly independent judge or magistrate to review the proposed actions of the government agents in advance. In theory, there must be some adequate evidence of a crime before a search warrant can be issued. Occasionally a warrant is turned down by a judge because there is insufficient "probable cause" to justify issuing it, and such refusal may prevent an unjustified search or surveillance.

But it is easy to exaggerate the protection afforded to personal privacy by this process. Warrants are often signed by judges after only a hasty review of the documents. The review process is not conducted in public, so it is difficult to tell how conscientious a judge is in any particular case. Moreover, prosecutors and police are not above "forum shopping"—looking around for the judge who is likely to ask the least number of questions. Even diligent judges are at the mercy of the information supplied to them by the government agents. At the time the warrant is being considered there is no defense attorney present to argue the other side of the case. Under these circumstances, it is not surprising that the government usually gets a search warrant whenever it wants one. Statistics on warrants for wiretapping, for example, show that between 1969 and 1976 only fifteen applications for warrants were denied out of 5563 applications. Most of these denials occurred in Connecticut, which has a particularly tough policy.

Some type of quick warrant procedure is essential to law enforcement. There are many cases involving serious crimes where the police have to move swiftly and quietly to get a search warrant in order to secure important evidence. But not all search warrants involve serious crimes. Many cases involve persons suspected of only minor criminality. And in still other cases, the person being searched is not suspected of anything at all. Search warrants have been used against big-time criminal suspects, but they have also been used against the lawyers and doctors of suspects and against reporters who were merely covering the case. The procedure for issuing a search warrant is generally the same in all these situations. But short cuts that might be tolerable when the police are hot on the trail of an important suspect become serious abuses when they are simply planning to go through all the files of someone who is not suspected of any wrongdoing.

A properly issued warrant can authorize virtually any kind of search or surveillance. With a search warrant a government agent can be authorized to tap a phone, open letters, wire a house, search a bedroom, or poke through every desk drawer in an office. Warrants are generally drafted by prosecuting attorneys in the broadest possible manner so that once the warrant is signed they will have wide discretion to conduct the search any way they want. The boilerplate language in a typical search warrant authorizes a search of all "rooms, lofts, attics, basements, desks, closets, filing cabinets, safes, vaults, and all parts thereof." Limitations on the method of search are generally imposed only if a judge strikes out the standard form language and writes in his or her restrictions. This type of restraint is rare.

There is no law requiring that the intrusiveness of the search match the seriousness of the matter being investigated. A small-time gambler can be searched or put under surveillance as thoroughly as a Mafia capo. Whether the home of a suspected pot grower will be searched as thoroughly as the home of a suspected mass murderer depends only on how the search warrant is drafted by the prosecutor. Once the warrant is issued, it's issued. The power of the government agent to conduct the search or surveillance derives from that document itself and is not related to the seriousness of the matter under investigation. The government can, if it wants, use a cannon to kill a flea.

Government agents make their own decisions about priorities, and they don't try to get a search warrant in every case. Serious surveillance and search techniques cost money and drain off valuable manpower, so one would expect that the most intrusive investigations would be reserved for the most serious crimes. In fact, the opposite seems to be true. Between 1968 and 1974, there were 4334 warrants issued for wiretapping telephones. Of that number 13 were for kidnapping cases, 186 for homicide and assault, and the remaining 3412 were for gambling, marijuana, and other drug cases.* The statistics on convictions of suspected criminals in federal court during the same period are even more revealing: there were *no* convictions in homicide, assault, or kidnapping cases in which wiretapping had been authorized. According to Professor Herman Schwartz, professor of law at the State University of New York at Buffalo, the rate of convictions based on wiretapping "has clearly been a disappointment, even to its proponents." Schwartz's study, *Taps, Bugs, and Fooling the People,* concludes that law-enforcement officials have confined their wiretapping efforts

---

* These figures are derived from the report of the National Commission for the Review of Federal and State Laws Relating to Electronic Surveillance prepared in 1976. The remaining 723 warrants authorizing wiretapping during this period were lumped together in the Commission's statistics as "other." The term *other,* however, did not include espionage and sabotage, because these categories were officially listed as "O."

to relatively minor crimes and haven't even tried to use it against big-time criminals.

Most battles over the Fourth Amendment have found civil libertarians favoring search warrants over a clearly less desirable alternative—government searches and surveillance *without* a warrant. That battle has been tough enough, and as a consequence comparatively little thought and energy has gone into the problems of searches conducted with a warrant. As an example of this, the courts and everyone else have generally ignored the requirement in the law that wiretapping should not be authorized by a warrant unless there is no other means of accomplishing the same thing. This and other fine points of the search-warrant process have drawn little public attention.

But the sanguine attitude of civil libertarians toward search warrants is historically true only in the recent past. In the longer view, it was the abuses of searches conducted by agents of the Crown *with* search warrants that aroused alarm in pre-Revolutionary America. Some of that alarm has returned as a result of the Supreme Court's unsettling decision in *Zurcher v. Stanford Daily.* If government agents can use a search warrant to search the offices of an innocent third party, much more attention must be given to the way in which such warrants are issued and enforced.

The California legislature has attempted to blunt the effects of search warrants in certain types of investigations by requiring that a "special master"—usually a volunteer attorney—accompany the police and act as an intermediary in the conduct of the search. Senator Charles Mathias has proposed federal legislation that would require a hearing with both sides represented before a judge could issue a search warrant against an innocent third party. The Minnesota Supreme Court has ruled that state agents can only demand that an attorney turn over documents through a subpoena rather than using a warrant to search his office. These ideas and more have surfaced as courts and legislatures have at last begun to focus on how search warrants (the government's most potent legal weapon) actually operate.

Private Security Cops

The structure of the [Law Enforcement Intelligence Unit] combines aspects of the professional association, the fraternal society, and the private country club. Membership ... is limited to local or state law enforcement agencies. ...

Perhaps the most sinister aspect of the [LEIU computer] system is the "no-hit" file, another coordination function it provides for its members. When a department requests information on "John Brown," for instance, and there is no information on John Brown contained in the active file, then that name and whatever identifying information the requester may possess is inserted into the "no-hit" file. Both the active file and the "no-hit" file are checked whenever a request is made. If subsequent requests on John Brown are received, then whatever bits of information the next requester has are also added to the file. Eventually the no-hit file can be converted to an active file.

From The Police Threat to Political Liberty, *published by the American Friends Service Committee, 1979*

Surveillance by government agencies is only half the problem. The other half is the collection of agencies that lie just outside the pale of government—the quasi-governmental, semiofficial world of security cops, intelligence agencies, and Old-Boy networks that make up what author George O'Toole calls the "private sector." It is a murky, ill-defined world with few laws governing its activities. Those in the business of "private security" consider themselves removed from the restrictions placed on government agents. Nevertheless much of the activities in this business are supported directly or indirectly by private funds. An individual being investigated by a semiprivate snooper may find it a more harrowing experience than dealing with a government agent. The investigator may not have the full weight of government behind him, but he is also a good deal less likely to be restrained by legal and constitutional niceties.

The Law Enforcement Intelligence Unit (LEIU) falls into this netherworld of semipublic, semiprivate agencies. In theory it is a private organization, but its members are all public agencies—the "intelligence squads" of approximately 250 state and local police agencies. Its purpose is to provide a private network of intelligence information for public agencies. The organization is entirely controlled by its members, without any regulation by a public agency. The public is, however, allowed to participate with tax money. Since 1971, the LEIU's intelligence network has been underwritten with public money provided by the federal Law Enforcement Assistance Administration, the state of California, and other public funds.

The LEIU maintains files on suspected criminals, suspected associates of criminals, and those suspected of nothing more than having been the subject of a prior LEIU inquiry. No actual proof of a crime is needed for a person to be indexed in the LEIU files. Any member agency can simply submit information about an individual's suspected criminal activity and it is added to the LEIU file. According to an American Friends Service Committee study of the matter, the categories of information in LEIU files go far beyond traditional crime categories and include people who merely travel extensively, have electronics capability, or are associates (friend, lawyer, or relative) of another crime target. In many cases an individual's LEIU "face card" will consist more of unpopular political beliefs than any criminal activity. And with a bow to the tactics of its predecessors, the LEIU has adopted one of the worst techniques of the black-list manipulators of the McCarthy era: adding someone's name to the suspect list merely because an agency has inquired about him.

The LEIU operates under the protective wing of the California Department of Justice in Sacramento. It is not an official state agency, but the California Attorney General provides the LEIU administrative staff support and materials. Other LEIU members remain in contact with the Sacramento office on a toll-free WATS line. But despite the network of public money and services that are interwired into LEIU operations, the agency remains effectively beyond the range of any governmental regulation. Neither the federal Privacy Act of 1974 nor the similar Fair Information Practices Act adopted by California apply to LEIU operations. An individual can neither examine his file, attempt to correct it, nor have any control over its distribution to other agencies.

The LEIU is not bound by any of the nettlesome restrictions of a governmental agency, which probably seems just fine for the government officials who make up this semiofficial organization. As an Old-Boy network, it is probably the most extensive—but it is hardly alone. Another group with even broader connections and less visibility is the 6600-or-so former FBI agents who make up the Society of Former Special Agents of the FBI. The ex-FBI agents in this organization maintain no formal files on suspects, but they have an even more important link-up—themselves. According to George O'Toole, the Exes who are members of this group hold senior executive positions in virtually every major private security department in America, ranging from General Motors to American Express and from Mobile Oil to Harvard University. Many have obtained senior positions in major metropolitan police forces, while others either own or have important positions with large private security firms such as the Wackenhut Corporation, Pinkerton, Burns, and Fidelifacts. The power of this society is a two-way street: former FBI agents get informal access to FBI files, and the FBI gets access to information from the outside.

The International Association of Chiefs of Police is another semiprivate network, but its members—unlike former FBI agents—are not nearly so prone to be part of an information-sharing network. Yet even an organization as seemingly benign as the IACP has participated in quasi-governmental activities that have had enormous implications both for personal privacy and American foreign policy. According to the American Friends Service Committee, the IACP helped establish the International Police Academy, which was involved in the training of such friendly folks as the Iranian SAVAK.

As one moves from the semipublic to the wholly private, the keeping of black lists becomes less restrained. The American Security Council, founded by a former FBI agent, reportedly has an index of approximately 6 million cards on individuals that it shares with the more than 3000 companies that subscribe to its services. Its subscribers are reported to include Sears, Roebuck and Co., Lockheed, Motorola, Allstate Insurance, Honeywell, U.S. Steel, and General Dynamics—all companies that have former FBI agents on their security staffs.

The Church League of America boasts "the largest and most comprehensive files on subversive activity, with the single exception of the FBI." It apparently picked up this worldly treasure as a donation from the Wackenhut Corporation, an investigative firm that still dips into the Church League files when it needs information for a background check. The Church League claims that it does more than just clip and index articles, since it sends "undercover operatives" to sit in on leftist meetings. An offshoot of the Church League has been the *Information Digest,* a newsletter about left-wing movements subscribed to by various police agencies around the country. Other groups, such as Research West, have sprung up to provide personal political information about individuals for various corporate clients. For example, Pacific Gas & Electric Co. in California is reputed to have given $90,000 to Research West to obtain background information about critics of its nuclear energy policies.

Viewed as a whole, it appears that private and semiprivate organizations have taken over many of the functions that have become a little too controversial for government agencies to handle. These organizations can act with a freer hand but still make information available whenever it is needed. What is this function? In the 1950s and 1960s it was called "strategic intelligence." A draftsman for the federal Omnibus Crime Bill of 1968 described strategic intelligence by comparing it with a normal criminal investigation. Ordinarily, he indicated, the investigation "moves from the known crime toward the unknown criminal." But strategic intelligence is used where you have "known criminals but unknown crimes." And strategic intelligence is what most of these groups are doing in compiling information on their enemies or suspected enemies. The purpose is rarely articulated. Most likely, however, they intend to turn the information in their dossiers over to the government when they feel it is time to round up the usual suspects.

More numerous than private black-list operators are private cops—the semiofficial security guards that have grown in a baby boom of badges and gray uniforms. There are an estimated 50,000 private guards in California as opposed to only 45,000 police. In New York City the private guards outnumber the police by about three to one. In 1975 there were more than a million private security guards in the United States, compared with 650,000 people in all the federal, state, and local law-enforcement agencies combined. The disparity would be even higher if one included as private security personnel the number of police officers who moonlight in private jobs. Not surprisingly, Americans pay more for private security than the combined budgets of the entire criminal justice system. Between 1958 and 1973, for example, the expenditures for private security jumped from $428 million to $1.92 billion—an increase of over 400 percent.

What do Americans get for this expenditure—more privacy or more invasions of privacy? It would appear that private cops are part of the problem, part of the solution, and sometimes both simultaneously.

A desire for greater privacy and personal security is one of the prime factors behind the tremendous growth in the number of private cops. Celebrities, politicians, and anyone else who feels insecure commonly have private guards to protect themselves. Hardly an apartment house is now built without a provision for security guards and various special locks, cameras, audio devices, and the like as part of the security system. The trend is not limited to apartment houses, since entire subdivisions are frequently designed with controlled access points, security guards, and electronic monitoring of visitors. Older neighborhoods that are not surrounded by walls have found their own solution—residential patrol services that cruise the neighborhood in search of anything suspicious. Approximately 20 percent of the private security dollar goes toward residential and institutional security—mainly an effort by homeowners to purchase privacy against unwanted visitors. According to the national Task Force on Private Security, "Traditionally, people's homes have been considered their castles, but many homes are now becoming fortresses."

All of this protects someone's privacy—but often at someone else's expense. The person inside the building or apartment may feel more secure in knowing that visitors are being constantly watched. But the situation may not be so comforting to the visitor under surveillance. Closed-circuit television sets have become standard equipment not only in apartment houses but also in clothing stores, public buildings, markets, lobbies, walkways, and all sorts of locales. Those buildings that do not have electronic equipment frequently have mirrors rigged to cover every corner of a room or building. There is virtually no law anywhere prohibiting this type of surveillance. Georgia law, for example, makes it illegal to photograph anyone surreptitiously, but only if done in a "private place and out of public view." Any public area—or area that is not strictly private—is fair game for anyone who wants to watch and observe. Whether a videotape is kept of such surveillance is strictly up to the user—no law prevents it. The security guard at his television monitor has become almost as common as the burglar-alarm tape on the store window.

Surveillance is often coupled with controlled access. While security guards at a public building may channel visitors through a metal detection device, guards at a private building may go much further. The Standard Oil Building in downtown San Francisco, for example, requires a visitor to show identification, sign a roster, and obtain an ID card before entry. For a visitor to that city's largest law firm, which is housed in the Standard Oil building, the security restrictions can be a considerable nuisance. The bathroom doors cannot be opened unless a member of the firm slides an electronically programmed card into a special locking mechanism.

Sometimes egress is as tightly controlled as entry. Many merchants use price tags that activate an electric eye unless removed. If a customer walks past the mechanism with the price tag still on the goods, he is likely to find the security guards chasing him down the block. Entry and exit surveillance are almost totally at the discretion of the owner or merchant. An overzealous security guard can land his employer in a false-imprisonment lawsuit if he actually detains someone, but there is not much limit on surveillance within the open areas of the building.

The use of private security guards has increased dramatically, but their pay and training have not. According to the Task Force on Private Security, "the security industry is plagued by a variety of problems, including low wages, poorly qualified and untrained personnel, abuse of authority, [and] lack of regulation." As of 1976, only two states* required any special training for unarmed security guards and only seven† required special training for *armed* guards. Eighteen states have virtually no regulation of any sort pertaining to private cops. A survey conducted by the RAND corporation showed that some major security firms put private guards out on the job with as little as three hours training.

The RAND study also showed that a large percentage of private security guards don't know what their legal powers are to arrest, search, or use force against a suspect. That's not surprising, since lawyers and judges aren't sure either. Private cops do *not* have the same authority as the regular police. In most cases, their only power is to make a "citizen's arrest"—a term that is virtually lost in popular misconception. Only thirty states have any statutory language clarifying the term, and those that do vary widely in what it means. In some states the citizen/private cop can detain a suspect for any "crime," while in others his authority is limited to a "breach of peace" or a "public offence" or a "felony." Some states say that the arresting party's knowledge must be based on "reasonable grounds," while others say that "immediate knowledge" or "knowledge in fact" is needed. All of this is supposed to be understood by a poorly trained, underpaid guard standing there with a gun in his hand.

The individual's problem is more practical than legal. He is under no legal obligation to provide any information to a private guard or to submit to any attempted arrest. The crime of "resisting arrest" does not apply to citizen's arrests. He may even have basis for a lawsuit if the guard gets too heavy-handed. But his ability to walk away from the

---

* Georgia and Ohio.
† California, Florida, Georgia, Illinois, Ohio, Pennsylvania, and Texas.

situation is somewhat tempered by the prospect of removing lead from the small of his back.

Although private cops have less legal authority to detain an individual, the practical consequences of such detention for individual privacy may be a good deal worse. Ironically, the Bill of Rights offers almost *no* protection against abuses by private cops. In most cases a private cop—without any kind of a warrant—can bug a room, open locked packages, extract a confession without a warning, and monitor a suspect's movements with electronic equipment. In short, he can do almost all of the things that old-timers on a police force thought were possible before the Supreme Court told them that they couldn't do it. Evidence seized by regular police using such methods would normally be thrown out of court in a criminal prosecution because the suspect's constitutional rights were violated, but the *same* evidence might very well be admitted when it is obtained by a private cop. The reason for this anomaly? The Bill of Rights only protects against government misconduct. Private cops—so the argument goes—are only private citizens, and the Constitution does not require that evidence seized by them be thrown out, no matter how high-handed their methods.

But the vast increase of private police forces in the last ten years suggests that the rules governing private cops are badly out of touch with reality. In Washington, D.C., house detectives at the Lord & Taylor department store have routinely peeked into dressing rooms through mirrors, louvers, and overhead peepholes in order to spot suspected shoplifters. This voyeurism led to the detention of one woman who had a blouse in her purse, despite her protests that she was only bringing it back to exchange it. In that case the store cops opened her purse and wallet, forced her to strip, subjected her to a body search, and then turned the matter over to the police. This proved too much for the jury in a civil case that ultimately awarded her $51,000 in damages in 1979. Equally important, however, the high-handed tactics of the store detectives persuaded a district court judge in the criminal case against her to throw out the only incriminating evidence—the blouse—on the grounds that it was illegally seized under the Fourth Amendment.

This ruling was quickly followed by a similar ruling from the California Supreme Court. In both cases the courts came to grips with the reality of the situation: that private cops were performing the functions of public law-enforcement officials. These two courts both concluded that the security guards should be held to the same standards as the police and that evidence should be thrown out if it was obtained by unconstitutional means. Are these cases the start of a trend? Perhaps. But there is a long way to go before private cops are brought under any kind of public control. The need is urgent, because the trend in both numbers and dollars suggests a continued expansion of private security agents. The next time you ask to see a badge, look closely. It may say *Burns* or *Pinkerton.*

Low-Profile Strategies

And if your lifestyle demands something more discreet . . .

CCS brochure

Just how discreet do you need to be? Total security against surveillance is an impossible dream; the only question is how much money and energy an individual wants to expend to reduce his or her level of exposure. The lifestyle of most people probably requires only simple precautions, but for others that is not enough. What may seem cautious to one person is likely to seem silly or overdone to another. The range of alternatives offers room for some highly individual decisions. But whether a person is acting out of prudence or paranoia is something each person will have to decide for himself.

- Beware of unfamiliar rooms. It is virtually impossible to detect a sophisticated bugging device that someone has installed on his own turf. You can pick up a phone to check whether an "infinity transmitter" has kept the line open, but that is only one possibility. A sophisticated "mike and wire" installation or radio transmitter cannot be detected without a very expensive—and very obvious—sweep by an audio-countermeasure expert.
- Pick a random spot for a conversation. A random location is even safer than your own home or office, since a bugging team won't have an opportunity to penetrate the premises. At a random location the main threat comes from a recording device carried by the other party. That, however, can usually be detected by a "bug alert" carried in your pocket.
- Think about how a tape-recorded conversation will sound. If the batteries on your bug alert are dead or if the whole idea of audio countermeasures strikes you as silly, you can still watch for mannerisms of the other person that may tip you off to a tape recording. Most obvious, perhaps, is the person who makes a lot of self-serving statements that recapitulate what has gone on before that

particular conversation. He is probably trying to come up with a self-contained tape that will make you sound as bad as possible and make him sound innocent. If you need an example, go back and reread the transcript of Richard Nixon trying to set up John Dean on April 16, 1973.

- Think about how you *want* a tape-recorded conversation to sound. It may be possible to control the tape. If you nod your head or shrug in answer to a key question, you'll probably drive the bugger nuts. Cluttering up a suspected tape with references to the other party's indiscretions or statements such as "I'm glad this isn't being taped" may also destroy the usefulness of the recording. Pointing to a written document without reading it will make the tape sound totally meaningless. If the bugger attempts to repeat audibly what you have only pointed to, that should be a tipoff that you are being recorded.
- When in doubt, use a pay phone. Home and office phones are too vulnerable to penetration for any kind of sensitive call. Office phones can be legally tapped by others in the office, just as home phones can be monitored by others in the household. This type of monitoring can be detected by a voltage-drop meter attached to the line, but installation of such a meter would arouse more than a few suspicions. Any phone can be monitored without detection by the government with a warrant and by the phone company without even an apology. Even if the call is not monitored, the date, time, and the number called probably will be. The answer? A pay phone—selected randomly.
- Use first-class mail. Any other class of mail can be legally opened by the Postal Service for almost any reason. If something is important enough, it is worth the extra postage.
- Consider a private mail drop. A street address or post office box can easily be placed under a mail cover in which all incoming mail is monitored. Having sensitive mail sent to another address may do some good, but it doesn't solve the problem. A sophisticated mail cover can be set up to check names—as well as addresses—and thus monitor a person's mail wherever it is delivered. Changing the address *and* the name may be enough in most cases, but even that isn't foolproof. If the government monitors all the mail from one source, such as a Swiss bank, it can then make inquiries at the other end to determine the true names and addresses of all mail recipients. Probably the closest thing to total privacy in the mails is a double number

system: an identifying number and address to be used by the sender, and another identifying number to be used at the mail drop for picking up the mail. For $4 *Loompanics Unlimited* (P.O. Box 264, Mason, Michigan 48854) will send you a list of over 800 "mail receiving companies" in North America, many of whom will allow you to establish a small drop without giving them any personal identification.

- Sensitive items should be kept out of a car. The protection against searches and seizures without a warrant is highly tenuous when a vehicle is involved. An item may seem just as secure when locked in the trunk as in a locked suitcase in the back seat. But the difference may be critical if a federal agent conducts an investigation: the trunk can be searched without a search warrant while the suitcase cannot. State investigations may turn on even more subtle distinctions: whether the glove compartment is locked or unlocked, whether the car was parked or moving, whether there are any unpaid parking tickets, and so on. The only sure rule is to keep anything out of a vehicle that you don't want examined.
- Don't invite in government agents, unless you don't care what they see. The homeowner may want to report a stolen television set, but the officer may be more interested in the homeowner's favorite marijuana plant than his Betamax. Inviting a cop into a home or office is a waiver of the warrant requirement, and he can act upon anything he sees within plain view.
- Stake out your own turf. If you share rooms or offices, be careful to delineate which part is yours and lock it if necessary. Not only will this deter casual snoopers, but it may also prevent a search by government agents. A roommate can consent to a search of the *entire* premises if the portions occupied by the different occupants are not carefully delineated. On the other hand, a locked closet, trunk, or room may force the police back to the courthouse for a search warrant. A similar problem of consent may arise with secretaries, housekeepers, and the like. It may be advisable to give them written instructions that they do not have authority to let anyone into the premises for any purpose. Such a document may come in handy if anyone later claims that such an individual consented to the search.
- Ask to see any search warrant. It is probably worth reading a warrant to find out if any limitations on the scope of the search have been written in by a judge or magistrate. If you have time, call your lawyer and have him or her come by and witness the

search. If you are holding documents for someone else, alert that person as quickly as possible.
- Be sure of a guard or officer's authority. A weapon gives a private cop a certain amount of clout, but his legal authority is no greater than anyone else's. An individual doesn't have to submit to an interrogation, detention, search, or anything else unless he is forced to do so. It is hard to imagine a set of circumstances where it would be advisable to hand this power over to a private cop voluntarily.

CHAPTER 9

"4,015,500,000 Files"

GOVERNMENT FILES AND COMPUTERS

Sec 2
(a) The Congress finds that—
- *the increasing use of computers and sophisticated information technology, while essential to the efficient operations of the Government, has greatly magnified the harm to individual privacy that can occur from any collection, maintenance use, or dissemination of personal information;*
- *the right of privacy is a personal and fundamental right protected by the Constitution of the United States; and*
- *In order to protect the privacy of individuals identified in information systems maintained by Federal agencies, it is necessary and proper for Congress to regulate the collection, maintenance, use and dissemination of information by such agencies.*

From the Privacy Act of 1974

The Privacy Act, it turns out, is no protection at all. You can drive a truck through the Privacy Act.

Robert R. Bellair, counsel to the National
Commission on the Confidentiality of Health Records

With the enactment of the Privacy Act of 1974 Congress attempted to do the impossible: bring the vast bulk of personal information in government files under some sort of control. The act has allowed individuals in some instances to get access to some of the federal files containing information about them, although this right has been fraught with exceptions and unresolved problems. But the Privacy Act has been far less successful in meeting its other objectives: controlling the flow of personal information into federal files, providing restrictions on disclosure of such information, and providing security against unauthorized access. Almost every effort to bring federal agencies into line with the act's requirements has been met with delays, evasions, and confusion by the myriads of people and agencies involved.

Even counting the files has proved almost impossible. The Privacy Act directs the government to publish an annual count of files containing personal information, but the number of files which are excluded because of an exemption, an arbitrary definition, the wrong index system, or because of faulty accounting far exceeds the official number of files. But even so, the official total is staggering. By the end of 1977 the official count was 4,015,500,000 files.

What the Privacy Act excludes is far more important than what it includes. If all excluded files with personal information were included in the government's calculations the resulting figure would make the 4-billion figure look puny by comparison. Files of nongovernmental businesses and organizations, for example, are excluded from the list, because the Privacy Act only regulates government record-keeping. But the distinction between public and private records is often not an easy one to draw. There is a constant flow of personal information about individuals going back and forth between government and private agencies, and any cut-off point has to be arbitrary. Government agencies obtain health information about individuals from hospitals and insurance companies, credit information from credit bureaus, personal information from investigative agencies, and so on. Likewise, government contractors have access to a great deal of personal information in government files. What is or is not in the government files at any moment is not as important as the information to which the government has ready access.

State and local government files present a similar problem. The information flow from the federal government to other government levels is even a busier two-way street. The IRS and state taxing agencies share income-tax information, the Department of Transportation and state motor vehicle agencies share licensing and driving information about individuals, the Department of Justice and local law-enforcement agencies share arrest and criminal justice information—the list is practically endless. For virtually every federal agency there are counterpart agencies at another level of government with whom the agency is likely to share personal information about individuals. Information in government records only makes it into the Privacy Act tally if it is included in a federal record system. If the same information has been duplicated and sent to fifty statehouses, those latter files will not appear in the totals.

The sharing of information between the federal government and state and local governments does more than just upset mathematics of the record count; it removes any limitations that the Privacy Act might otherwise impose on the dissemination of the information in the record. Records in the hands of state and local agencies are generally not governed by federal law. What restrictions exist are a matter of state law, and only a minority of states have enacted legislation similar to the Privacy Act.* When information has been distributed through several levels of government, the level with the weakest restrictions is the only one that counts. Federal restrictions on the misuse of Social Security numbers, for example, have been undercut by programs requiring the federal government to share such information with states that have no restrictions on Social-Security-number disclosure.

Information that the federal government shares with private organizations or other levels of government leaves wide holes in the Privacy Act coverage, but there are other exclusions within the federal record-keeping process that are just as significant. The Privacy Act only applies to a "system of records" indexed by some sort of "personal identifier." This means that desk files, informal files, or personal files kept by many government officials are not included—they are not considered part of a system. It also means that personal information in files that are not listed by the person's name or identifying numbers are not included, because they are not indexed by a "personal identifier."

Alan Smiertka, a former IRS agent, tried to examine an agency file containing derogatory information about himself, but Judge John Sirica ruled that he had no such right. The reason? With somewhat uncharacteristic formality for the man who seized the Watergate tapes, Judge Sirica ruled that the IRS didn't have to disclose the information because it was indexed under the name of the investigator rather than the name of the person being investigated: *"The requested items are not accessed by plaintiff's name or other personal identifier. Rather they are retrievable by someone else's identifier, in particular the name of the agency investigator who prepared them. It follows from this that these reports fall outside the scope of [the Privacy Act] and hence need not be disclosed."*

The personal information was in the file, but the person affected

---

* Arkansas, California, Connecticut, Indiana, Massachusetts, Minnesota, New Hampshire, Ohio, Utah, and Virginia. The statutes of Arkansas, Connecticut, Minnesota, Ohio, and Virginia also appear to apply to one degree or another to local governments within those states.

could not reach it. What was true in this instance is true in countless other cases—personal information in government files is free from the restrictions of the Privacy Act because of the way it is indexed. Not only is the information in such files exempt from regulation, but such files are not even included in the official count of government files.

To add further doubt to the government's figures on files with personal information, there is evidence to suggest that the files and the figures may have been misstated for political purposes. Dissident groups have contended that the FBI and other agencies have closed down certain files just as the affected individuals were on the verge of getting access to them. They claim, in effect, that the Privacy Act was being used to cover up past invasions of privacy. More recently, the government issued a report claiming that the total number of files had been reduced to 3.652 billion, based mainly on a reduction of the number of record systems in the Treasury Department, HEW, and the General Services Administration. Follow-up inquiries by the *Privacy Journal* discovered, however, that no reductions actually occurred. At the Treasury Department, for example, information that had been in fifty separate record systems had been combined into one system. There was no decrease in the amount of personal information maintained on individuals—only a decrease in the official number of files by about 218 million.

The basic reason, however, that the official count of government files is meaningless is because the concept of a file itself is becoming meaningless. Many people have in their mind's eye an image of an unflappable bureaucrat, sitting behind a gray metal desk, guarding a drawer full of manila folders. But like other large organizations, the government doesn't work that way anymore. The files are probably still around in cabinets somewhere, but the most important information is now in computers. At least one-third of all personal information in federal files is now computerized, and the amount continues to grow. As the quantity of computerized information increases, access to that information increases. The Internal Revenue Service, for example, is reputed to have approximately 4000 computer display terminals to which about 18,000 IRS employees have authorized access.

Computerized information is located anywhere and everywhere. With telephone hookups between computers, the actual physical location of any one piece of data is practically irrelevant. The use or misuse of computerized information is no longer limited to the willingness of one civil servant to open a drawer, pull out a file, and read it. The same information is available to him and all of his colleagues who have access to a computer terminal. For statistical purposes, the folder in the desk drawer and the personal data contained in the silicon chip both count as one file. But the latter situation can just as accurately be described as 4000 files—or even 18,000 files—if the information can be instantaneously reproduced at that number of desktop computer terminals throughout the country.

The ineffectiveness of the Privacy Act mainly derives from one fact: no one was put in charge of enforcing it. The closest thing to an overseer has been the Office of Management and Budget. But according to OMB's Leslie Greenspan, that agency has basically functioned as a "Jewish mother"—advising and cajoling other agencies to comply with the act but with no power to enforce its views. Congress directed each of the ninety-seven or so federal agencies to set up privacy programs themselves within their respective departments. Although the various agencies are obliged to disclose the existence of all their record systems, they have been left to themselves to determine which records to keep and how much personal information such records will contain.

The privacy statutes enacted by states have generally contained the same basic problem: the agencies have defined for themselves the record systems that they want to maintain. Some states, however, have created an independent agency with some authority to oversee the other departments. California, for example, has an Office of Information Practices empowered to assist individuals in securing records, to investigate complaints, develop guidelines for other agencies, mediate disputes, and so on. The Arkansas statute establishes an Information Practices Board with even greater powers to regulate any state files containing personal information. But the other states that have adopted laws similar to the Privacy Act have normally followed that act in allowing each agency to decide for itself what personal records it will keep.

Federal agencies not only decide for themselves what record systems they will maintain, but they also are given the power to determine which records they can exempt. The existence of an exempt system must be disclosed within the agency's regulations, but that is as far as it goes. The agency needn't disclose the details of an exempt system nor does it have to grant an individual access to his file within the system. Out of 6424 records systems that were in existence in 1977, 898 had been declared exempt by the various agencies involved.

The problem is not quantity but quality. The record systems that agencies have put into the exempt category are usually the ones an individual would most like to see. The IRS, for example, has declared exempt the files on "Taxpayers on whom an investigation has been initiated for purpose of securing information necessary for Federal Tax Administration." Likewise, the Justice Department has exempted the "File of names checked to determine if those individuals have been the subject of an electronic surveillance." An agency is supposed to follow certain standards in determining which systems can or cannot be exempted. The standards, however, are so broad as to be almost meaningless. A record system can be exempted if it contains "investigatory material compiled for law enforcement purposes." Each agency defines for itself the purpose of its investigative files, and quite naturally agencies in that situation have all taken the position that they are in the business of law enforcement.

Federal agencies have been left to themselves to determine what record systems to maintain and have given only loose guidelines as to which systems will be exempt. But the guidelines about what type of personal information can be maintained in any record system are even looser. One provision of the Privacy Act directs agencies to maintain in their files "only such information about an individual as is relevant and necessary to accomplish a purpose of the agency." Congress apparently felt that even this bland admonishment would be too difficult for federal agencies to follow in every instance, so it stated that this provision of the act would not apply to any record system that an agency declares exempt. As a consequence, the most secretive files are likely to have the most extraneous material.

The few specific rules in the Privacy Act against collecting certain types of personal information have not been heeded. The act prohibits any "Federal, State or local government agency" from denying anyone any right or benefit because of a refusal to disclose a Social Security number. But the Privacy Act then goes on to exempt any government agency that demanded such information as part of a system of records that existed before 1975. The result? The Privacy Commission found that the "practices associated with most agency systems remain unchanged." The Privacy Act similarly admonishes federal agencies not to maintain records about "how any individual exercises rights guaranteed by the First Amendment." But there is an exception for "authorized law enforcement activity." As a result, concludes the Privacy Commission, agencies that have collected information about political activity, group affiliation, and other activity protected under the

First Amendment continue to do so on the justification that they are involved in some sort of law enforcement.

Some agencies have claimed that as a result of the Privacy Act they have engaged in a housecleaning that has eliminated certain files or systems. There is no evidence to suggest, however, that this has in any way reduced the amount of personal information about individuals contained in the total record system or the access of others to that information. That situation seems just as bad as ever. Major Daniel Fannin, a computer and privacy expert in the Department of Defense, has called the changes brought about by the Privacy Act "superficial" and "cosmetic." He claims that many agencies have kept additional informal record systems in violation of the act and that you can still find files or tapes of personal data "lying around on clerks' desks." The one success of the Privacy Act—qualified as it may be—has been to allow greater access by individuals to their own files. The Privacy Act in most of its other aspects has been that most futile of all legislative endeavors: directing a bureaucracy to reform itself.

Getting Your Own File

Privacy Act Officer
Federal Bureau of Investigation
9th and Pennsylvania Avenue, N.W.
Washington, D.C. 20535

    Re: *Privacy Act Request*

Dear Sir:
    Under the provisions of the Privacy Act of 1974 . . . I hereby request a copy of all files maintained by your agency containing information about me.

William Petrocelli

    Re: *Request No. 70071*

Dear Mr. Petrocelli:
    In response to your Freedom of Information-Privacy Act request, a search of the indices to our central records system at FBI Headquarters revealed no information to indicate that you have been the subject of an investigation by the FBI.
    If you believe your name may have been recorded by the FBI incident to an investigation of other persons or some organization, please advise us of the details describing the specific incident or occurrence and time frame. There-

after, further effort will be made to locate, retrieve and process any such records.

Allen H. McCreight, Chief
Freedom of Information-Privacy Acts Branch
Records Management Division

Re: Request No. 70071

Dear Mr. McCreight:
Thank you for your response to my Privacy Act request letter.
You indicated that I would have to give you specific details about any connection with any other persons or organizations before you could determine if you have any information about me in some other files. This leaves me in somewhat of a dilemma. First, I don't know what other persons or organizations you might have investigated. Second, I would be somewhat reluctant to suggest a link between myself and such persons and organizations if none already existed in your files.
I would appreciate your assistance in resolving this problem.

William Petrocelli

A principal purpose of the Privacy Act of 1974 was to allow an individual to "gain access to his record or to any information pertaining to him which is contained in the system." A reasonable enough idea, but in actual practice it suggests a basic question: who's getting information from whom?

If the FBI responded to the 70,070 requests prior to this one in the same manner, the likelihood is that they took in a lot more information than they gave out. There is no guarantee that information submitted to the FBI in response to such a letter would not, in turn, become the subject of a new FBI file. Even more distressingly, the individual may give new information to the FBI and still not get the information he wanted. He might find that there is a file with his name in it, but that he can't get it. This is the same situation that faced Alan Smiertka: the IRS had a file with information about him, but he was unable to see it because it was not indexed under his "personal identifier." Anyone contemplating a demand to the federal government to see his file should at least consider that possible scenario: they get some new information about him while he comes up empty-handed.

A lot of people apparently think it's worth a try. In 1977, for example, 1,417,214 requests were received by federal agencies for disclosure of records under the Privacy Act. The bulk of these went to the Departments of Defense, Justice, and Transportation and to HEW and the Veterans Administration. According to the government, 1,355,515 of those requests were granted "in full or in part." Government reports do not show the precise reasons why different agencies refused to disclose the information that was requested—either "in full or in part"—but presumably the denials relate to one or more exempt categories in which the requested information was categorized.

A request for disclosure of records under the Privacy Act is initiated by a letter from the individual to the agency. The government tried to simplify this process in 1977 by publishing a guidebook designed for the person who wants to request his or her records.* The guidebook is a good place to start, but it's just that—a start. The book has nine pages listing the addresses of various agencies, but only some of them are the right ones to write to. Others are likely to respond, directing the individual to another address. In most cases, the individual would probably do just as well writing to the main office of the agency in Washington, D.C. Likewise the guidebook contains a sample request letter that can be sent to the various agencies. The letter is good as far as it goes, but most agencies will respond by asking for more information:

Sample request letter:

Agency Head or Privacy Act Officer
Title
Agency
Address of Agency
City, State, zip

    Re: Privacy Act Request.

Dear _____:

Under the provisions of the Privacy Act of 1974, 5 U.S.C. 522a, I hereby request a copy of (or: access to)_____(describe as accurately and specifically as possible the record or records you want, and provide all the relevant information you have concerning them).

If there are any fees for copying the records I am requesting, please inform me before you fill the request. (Or: . . . please supply the records without informing me if the fees do not exceed $____).

If all or any part of this request is denied, please cite the specific exemp-

---

* "A Citizen's Guide on How to Use the Freedom of Information Act and the Privacy Act in Requesting Government Documents" (Stock No. 057-071-00540-4). Available for $3 from The Superintendent of Documents, U.S. Government Printing Office, Washington, D.C. 20402, or in bookstores in regional federal offices.

tion(s) *which you think justifies your refusal to release the information. Also, please inform me of your agency's appeal procedure.*

In order to expedite consideration of my request, I am enclosing a copy of _____ (some document of identification).

Thank you for your prompt attention to this matter.

Sincerely,
Signature
Name
Address
City, State, zip.

The agency is supposed to respond either with the records that were requested or a good reason why not. Frequently, however, the first response neither agrees to the request nor denies it. Agencies all respond in different ways. The Privacy Officer in one agency, HUD, may even phone you from Washington. Almost always the agency wants more information. If the agency finally consents to the request, the individual is entitled either to see the records at the agency or to obtain copies of them. The agency can charge for any copying cost. A special rule pertains to medical records, allowing the agency to disclose them only to someone such as the individual's doctor where the agency determines that the direct disclosure of the records might have an "adverse effect" on the individual. But the agency may respond by saying the records are exempt and refuse disclosure. Or it may deny that there are any records at all if the only records in the files are not indexed under the individual's "personal identifier."

If the individual receives an excuse rather than his records, his next step is to file an appeal within the agency. Each agency has its own appeal process, and it is supposed to inform the individual how that process works at the time it denies him his records. If, instead of a denial, the individual gets a copy of records that contain incorrect information, he can write to the agency demanding a correction of any information that is not "accurate, relevant, timely, or complete." The agency is required to respond in ten days by either correcting the record or stating the reasons for its refusal. A refusal in this situation also leads to an appeal within the agency.

If an appeal within the agency is not successful, the next step is the federal courts. If the individual wants to pursue the matter, this may be his or her only alternative. The record on administrative appeals within the various agencies has not been good from the point of view of the individual. In 1977, for example, the CIA upheld the lower-echelon decision in 17 cases, partially sustained it in 28 cases, and reversed it not at all. The Department of Justice sustained such rulings in 444 cases, partially sustained them in 1067 cases, and reversed them in only 38 cases.

How far should the individual go in fighting the matter? Despite the odds against reversal, it may be worth fighting the government if it admits that there is a record but claims that it is exempt. In such a situation the individual has little to lose: the government agents already have the information, and all the individual is trying to do is to find out what they already know. But what about a record that the government claims does not exist or that is not in a system of records indexed by the requester's "personal identifier"? A challenge may ultimately result in the record being produced—but it may also result in a refiling of the record so that thereafter it *will* be indexed under the individual's name or other "identifier." In other words, if the individual pushes too hard, the record may end up indexed in such a way that it is capable of doing him more harm than it would otherwise do. In such case the person has to weigh his need to see the record and his chances of correcting it against the possibility that all of the attention given to that record might make it a hot item within the bureaucracy.

When you get access to your record, what are you likely to find? The files kept by many agencies may be pretty bland stuff, but that's not true of all of them. FBI files, as befits their reputation, are likely to contain fact, fiction, rumor, and scuttlebutt ranging from the outrageous to the ridiculous. John Kenneth Galbraith, for example, found frequent references to himself in FBI files as a follower of "Dr. Ware," who was reputed to be a rather sinister economist. A further check showed that "Dr. Ware" was a shortened form of "Doctorware," which in turn was an incorrect transcription of a remark attributed to an unknown professor, who claimed that he might be "doctrinaire" in his views. The FBI solemnly enshrined this garbled gobbledygook in forty years' worth of government records.

Galbraith, fortunately enough, could survive being labeled a follower of the "Ware" school of economics. But John Seigenthaler, former Administrative Assistant to the Attorney General, almost didn't survive the scurrilous accusation that the FBI hinted about him: "allegations of Seigenthaler having illicit relations with young girls, which information obtained from an unnamed source." Seigenthaler, who later became the publisher of the Nashville *Tennessean,* was finally able to get a copy of the FBI file containing this dirt, but only after a year of persistent effort. He then chose to meet these allegations head-on in his own newspaper in hopes that the truth would finally catch up with the lies. But, in his words, "It is personal. It is painful." And, if the FBI had exercised any proper control over its files, it should have been unnecessary.

The Galbraith and Seigenthaler cases show one common fact: the name of the informer was withheld. The FBI frequently included rumor in its files without bothering to identify the source. But where the source *is* identified, the FBI has used this as an excuse either to deny the individual his or her records in their entirety or to bowdlerize them to the point where they are unreadable. The Privacy Act allows an agency to withhold certain information given to it "in confidence" when the disclosure would "reveal the identity of a source." But the FBI has often carried this to the extreme of deleting entire pages from a file—or the file itself.

Sometimes the information that is provided is tantalizing to the point of being maddening. Seigenthaler was given pages of a memo that were addressed to "The Director" and from "Memphis" with everything in between blacked out. Others who have sought their files from the FBI have had the same experience. Jane Fonda was finally given a copy of an April 1971 memo from the FBI that said "For the information of the Bureau, the following sources are in a position to provide coverage regarding the activities of the subject." And then? And then, nothing—what appears to be fifteen names were blacked out from the memo. Accompanying this was a telegram that had twenty names deleted to the point where it was unintelligible.

Many agencies feel there is a legitimate need to be able to promise confidentiality to one individual in order to get information about another. Without that they could not get candid evaluations of employees, grant applicants, and so on. Unless they can promise confidentiality, they argue, no one will make any comments about anyone else for the record. There may be a legitimate need for some confidentiality, but the practice of some agencies has gone far beyond that.

In some cases a chopped-up record may be the best you can hope for. Nat Tarnopol sued the FBI to obtain access to the Bureau's records involving the monitoring of his phone calls. A federal court denied his request on the grounds that it would "constitute an unwarranted invasion of privacy" of "the agents responsible for preparing the reports" and "the individual who furnished the FBI with information from the records of the New York Telephone Co." The court ended up protecting somebody's privacy, but it was probably not exactly what the proponents of the Privacy Act had in mind.

Commercial Use of Records

[W]hile agencies of State and local government have extensive detailed public-record information about the property we own, the taxes we pay, our political affiliations, the composition of our households, the number of cars we own, and our driving histories, the physical manner in which these records have been distributed and organized has served to minimize their utility as vehicles for intruding into our private lives. As long as the user of the public records has had to search them manually, a fair amount of effort has been needed to construct a personal profile of any one individual.

Recently, however, many large public-record systems have been automated to allow agency uses of the records that would have been impractical when they existed only in manual form. . . .

Should the same policy, however, apply to any automated public record? Should a citizen be able to walk into a real property records office and obtain a copy of all records in its automated system on his neighbor John Smith?

The Privacy Commission

Gaining access to personal information in your government files is one-half of the problem. The other half is trying to keep others out. But this is not one problem so much as it is a series of related questions. The issues involved tend to vary, based on who is asking and for what purpose. Disclosure to the general public is the broadest form of disclosure and arguably the most dangerous from a privacy perspective. But it is limited somewhat by the privacy exemptions in the Freedom of Information Act and ameliorated by the fact that it is done openly rather than surreptitiously. The problem of public disclosure is really the same as that of press access to government files viewed from a different perspective. Conversely, the problem of disclosure of personal information in government files to other government agencies, although more limited in scope, may have more pernicious effects. There is less restraint in the type of information that can be disclosed and a good deal less accountability as to who gets the information and for what purpose.

Between the problems of public disclosure and disclosure within the government is another type of disclosure of personal information in government files with problems of its own: disclosure for commercial purposes. Government files have always had a certain value for commercial use, but computerization of such files gives them an added dimension and value. The entrepreneur looking for certain personal characteristics in a target group need only tell the computer "what" in order to determine "who." With their vast reservoirs of personal information, government files are a prime source of information for businesses that want a list of names and addresses of potential customers.

Government records about private individuals are the bread and butter of direct-mail solicitation firms, and neither federal nor state laws have done much to curtail this flow of information. City and county records will generally show all property owned by an individual; births, deaths, marriages, and divorces within the family; any businesses engaged in; amount of property taxes; and so on. State records are even a more fruitful source of information. For example, approximately thirty-six states permit private companies to obtain lists of all the registered owners of vehicles within the state. The vice president of R. L. Polk and Company, a major record compiler, told the Privacy Commission how this information is used to compile a basic mailing list:

> We compile from official State records . . . a car owner list of 43,800,000 names; a truck owner's list of 11,400,000; a motorcycle owner's list of 2,600,000; and a monthly list of new car buyers averaging about 480,000. The information contained in the motor vehicle list is: owner's name and address; year model, make, series, body style . . . and license plate number. . . .
> From this information, the following selection factors are developed: sex, inferred from the first name, type of dwelling, i.e. single or multiple . . . inferred [from] the number of surnames found at a given address; price class of car owned, based on year, model, make and series; current market value of the cars owned . . . multiple car ownership, based on two or more cars registered at the same name and address. . . .

The name of the game is "selection factors," and government agencies often hold lists with all the key ingredients. The federal government, for example, will provide the names, addresses, and frequencies of all persons holding CB radio licenses for anyone willing to pay the cost of the computer-based list. State and local government will also provide commercial entrepreneurs with information that has a high selectivity factor, such as persons with fishing or hunting licenses, homeowners, lists of persons with occupational licenses, such as accountants, barbers, and nurses. Each of these lists contains names and addresses of people with special needs and interests—the ones who are the best type of target for direct-mail campaigns.

There are few restrictions on commercial access to government files. Many state and local governments will compile and sell any lists of names that have a commercial value unless there is some law prohibiting it. The Privacy Act prohibits federal agencies from selling lists to business firms, but it in no way restricts businesses from getting copies of files and lists under the Freedom of Information Act. Businesses can get copies of information to the same extent as anyone else as long as their requests don't constitute a "clearly unwarranted invasion of personal privacy" in violation of the Freedom of Information Act. In interpreting that vague language in the FOIA some federal courts have inclined to be a little more protective of privacy when the request for information is for purely commercial purposes. One court, for example, refused to order the Bureau of Alcohol, Tobacco and Firearms to disclose to a commercial firm the list of all persons who had licenses to make wine for home consumption on the grounds that it would violate the licensees' privacy. But other cases suggest that business firms are likely to be more successful in getting such lists if they are not too explicit about the commercial purpose they have in mind.

The list doesn't have to be accurate down to the last name in order to be valuable to a commercial firm. The U.S. census does not provide specific information about any individual or household, but it does supply valuable data about areas as small as 275 housing units. The Reuben H. Donnelly Corporation, another large record compiler, matches the census data with its master list of names and addresses to make a close guess about the lifestyle of everyone on its list, including median income, educational level, occupational characteristics, number of children, and even down to the probable number of washing machines and other heavy appliances.

Lists provided by government agencies are only one factor in a direct-mail campaign but frequently the most important. Private firms share lists as well and will either sell or rent the list of names and addresses to other firms. Prescreening is an important factor, enabling direct-mailers to sharpen up the selectivity of their list with the aid of credit bureaus and others. The buyer's responsiveness is another key factor—a person who buys in response to a direct-mail campaign gets placed on a "hit list" of highly desirable prospects for future direct-mail campaigns. While these other elements provide the refinements, personal information from government records is often the base upon which a direct-mail campaign is built.

But junk mail can be thrown away, so why worry? The simple answer is that the particular piece of mail can be destroyed, but the computer list that spawned the mailing is practically immortal. Compilers of direct-mail lists now characterize individuals as being part of one or several "market universes." With the aid of computers, such firms now claim to have their target groups refined down to certain precise characteristics. But the more they claim to know about the people on the list, the more one wonders how that information can be misused. The *Privacy Journal* recently quoted the claims of one firm that compiles and sells mailing lists:

> Applying advanced computer techniques to a constantly growing data base, we've been able to develop more information about more families—and the individuals who live in them—than has ever been achieved before. Essentially we are offering researchers immediate access to over 35,000,000 consumer households which can be subselected to provide many of the market universes which up to now took many months and many dollars to find by pre-screening.

Here are the Market Universes that are available ...

Adults by name, and year of birth
Children by name, and year of birth
Family size
Family members' ages
Male headed households
Female headed households
Working women by age
Families by income
Families by religion
Pre-School Children (Under 5 years old)
Grade School Children (6 to 12 years old)
Families with 2 children
Apartment families with children
Adults (35 to 49 by years of birth)
Married females (by year of birth)

Individual by month of birth
High School Children (13 to 18 years old)
Families with 3 or more children
Homeowners with children
Senior Citizens (over 50 years of age by years of birth)
Telephone subscribers by year of birth
Young adults (19 to 21 years old)
Parents of children (by age of child)
Adults (22 to 34 by year of birth)
Single females (by age)
Married males (by year of birth)
New homeowners (3 months after move)

If they thought about it, they could probably come up with a list of persons who have read books about privacy....

Government Record Sharing

JOHN DEAN: Murray, seriously, I need some advice. The President wants me to turn the IRS loose on a shit-ass magazine called Scanlan's Monthly because it printed a bogus memo from the Vice-President's office about canceling the 'seventy-two election and repealing the Bill of Rights.

MURRAY CHOTINER: John, the President is the head of the executive branch of this damn government. If he wants his tax collectors to check into the affairs of anyone, it's his prerogative. I don't see anything illegal about it. It's the way the game is played.

John Dean, Blind Ambition

Murray's pal played the game a little too well, with the result that Congress finally changed the rules. The Privacy Act of 1974, the Tax Reform Act of 1976, and the Right to Financial Privacy Act of 1978 all have something to say about one government agency sharing private information about an individual with another agency. What these statutes say is that the bad old days of loose disclosure of personal information by government agencies are officially over. The IRS will no longer be known, as it was in the Nixon Administration, as "the lending library." It and other government agencies will be bound by rules as to when it can and cannot disclose such information.

The rules may have changed, but the game remains familiar. Information in government files is still subject to an inordinate amount of disclosure, and protection of personal privacy in such information is still as big a problem as it ever was. Disclosure may no longer be a matter of bureaucratic whim, but the actual and potential use of personal information in government files under the new system of rules presents a different—if less obvious—type of threat. Murray might have found the rules a little strange, but nothing he couldn't have gotten used to.

Disclosure of information by most federal agencies is limited only by the rather anemic provisions of the Privacy Act of 1974. Disclosures can be made to other agencies so long as they are for a "routine use," which the Privacy Act defines as the use of a record "for a purpose which is compatible with the purpose for which it is collected." How strictly is this compatibility test enforced? The answer is pretty much contained in the fact that each agency is left to itself to determine what is or is not a routine use.

At the urging of the Justice Department, many agencies have promulgated the broadest possible rules regarding routine uses of records. The purpose of this tactic is to give the agency wide discretion in deciding what to do with its files. Indeed, some of the routine uses listed by various agencies place virtually no restrictions at all on the disclosure of personal information in the agency files. The Privacy Commission describes the following standard language as typical of the routine uses that are listed for many federal records systems:

1. In the event that a record within this system of records ... indicates a violation or potential violation of law, whether civil, criminal or regulatory in nature ... the relevant records in the system of records may be referred to the appropriate agency, whether Federal, State, local or foreign....
2. A record from this system of records may be disclosed to a Federal, state, or local agency ... if necessary to obtain information relevant to an agency decision concerning the hearing or retention of an employee, the issuance of a security clearance, the letting of a contract, or the issuance of a license, grant, or other benefit.
3. A record from the system of records may be disclosed, as a routine use, to a Federal agency, in response to its request, in connection with the hiring or retention of an employee, the issuance of a security clearance, the reporting of an investigation of an employee, the letting of a contract, or the issuance of a license, grant, or other benefit....

In other words, one agency will open its files to another when the other agency requests it, when it doesn't request it, or when some good information can be picked up in a trade.

The disclosure rules for other federal records systems are not that broad, but many are so vague or technical that it is difficult to tell what they mean. The Privacy Act requires each agency to disclose on the form in which it seeks information from an individual a statement of the principal purpose of the information and all of the routine uses to which such information can be put. This could be informative and useful, or, on the other hand, it could be like the kind of statement found in the fine print on a passport application:

> The information is made available as a routine use on a need-to-know basis to personnel at the Department of State and other government agencies having statutory or other lawful authority to maintain such information in the performance of their official duties; pursuant to a sub-

poena or court order; and, as set forth in Part 6a, Title 22 of Federal Regulations. . . .

To a layman (and to a lawyer as well) this seems to say that the agency is legally required to give the information to anyone to whom it is legally required to give the information.

The statements of principal purpose and routine uses are as varied as the agencies that formulated the regulations. The Justice Department has announced broadly that certain records may be disseminated to "federal, state, local, foreign, or international law enforcement agencies" to assist in "general civil matters." The Civil Service Commission, on the other hand, has listed twenty-two seemingly specific uses for certain records it maintains. While this appears to be more precise, the Commission's list of uses includes a catch-all provision allowing disclosures to any "Federal, State, or local agency responsible for investigating, prosecuting, enforcing, or implementing a statute, rule, regulation, or order where there is an indication of a violation or potential violation of civil or criminal law or regulation."

Although not written into the Privacy Act, a key rule seems to be "I'll show you mine, if you'll show me yours." The Privacy Commission noted the strong possibility that agencies were "trading" routine uses. When one agency wants information from another, ". . . it asks the agency holding the information to publish a routine use allowing the information to be disclosed to it, and the holding agency agrees so long as the requesting agency in turn publishes a reciprocal routine use allowing information in its records to flow the other way."

At the very least agencies have made sure that business will be carried on as usual, and have defined as routine those disclosures that they wanted to continue to make. According to the Privacy Commission, many agencies have "merely continue[d] disclosures, regardless of compatibility, that an agency habitually made prior to passage of the Privacy Act." Similar to this is an agency rule that merely shifts the question of compatibility to the agency making the request for the information. Both the Justice and the Treasury departments have record systems that allow, with minor variations, a disclosure "to the extent that the information relates to the requesting agency's decision on the matter."

Some personal information doesn't even get the weak protection provided by the routine-use provisions. Transfer of records within a single agency are not covered. In an agency as large, for example, as the Department of Health and Welfare, a great deal of shuffling about of personal records can occur without coming under the Privacy Act.

Records that have been transferred from one agency to another are in a virtual no-man's-land within the second agency. In many cases they will not fall within a "system of records" within the second agency, so that their further disclosure may not have to be accounted for. Records transferred to state, local, or even international agencies are outside the scope of the Privacy Act altogether, and further disclosure is limited—if at all—by whatever rules such other government agency has. Finally, there is the problem of government contractors. Federal agencies are supposed to make sure that private firms with access to personal information in government files maintain the security of such information. According to Major Daniel Fannin, a Defense Department expert, government agencies have done virtually nothing to insure compliance other than to insert boilerplate language in their contracts. There is no inspection of methods, no follow-up, and such contractors "really haven't changed their methods."

The thin string that holds the whole system together is the requirement that each agency keep an "accurate accounting" of the "date, nature, and purpose of each disclosure." This information is supposed to be made available to the individual at the time he requests copies of his records, along with the name and address of the person or agency to whom it was disclosed. Federal agencies have cried the loudest about this requirement, claiming that it cost more than $10 million within the first two years.* As with the rest of the Privacy Act enforcement, however, each agency is on its own to devise its own accounting system. All of the gaps within the Privacy Act—records not indexed by a "personal identifier," intraagency uses of records, exempt records systems—become even bigger loopholes here. Consequently, the agency's list of persons to whom the information has been disclosed is by no means complete. The individual seeking copies of his records should look at this accounting to get some clue as to how the government has handled sensitive information in its files, but he or she should realize that it is just a clue—not the whole story.

Two types of records within the federal bureaucracy get a somewhat special treatment superimposed over the general requirements of the

---

* That may sound high, but it amounts to less than $1500 per record system—supposedly to keep track of all disclosures of personal information. The annual cost for of "controls and security" on such information is approximately $200 per record system, another bargain. The simple fact is that these figures represent *too much* of a bargain. It means that many agencies are simply going through the motions and not keeping good track of anything. The sad fact is that the federal bureaucracy has become so entrenched in the record-keeping business that it may take *more* money to guarantee *less* intrusion.

Privacy Act. The Right to Financial Privacy Act of 1978 applies to records obtained from or "known to have been derived from" any bank or other financial institution. If one agency has such information and another agency wants it, the requirements of the Financial Privacy Act must be met. Those requirements, however, are not any more strict than the routine-use requirements of the Privacy Act. The requesting agency must simply state in writing that "there is reason to believe" that the financial records are "relevant to a legitimate law enforcement inquiry" within its agency. If it is willing to stick its bureaucratic neck out that far, it can get any financial records it wants.

The agency transferring the records is supposed to give the individual notice of that fact. But this is a wave-goodbye type of right. The individual is informed about the transfer, but he has no right to stop it. And if he wants to witness the send-off of his bank statements, he'll have to move fast. Notice need not be given until fourteen days *after* the transfer has occurred and can be delayed even longer for various reasons. Still in all, this situation is better than the rules that apply to most personal information held in government records. Under the Privacy Act the individual must demand a copy of his or her records in order to get an accounting of the transfers of those records that have been made between agencies. Under the Right to Financial Privacy Act the government is required—however belatedly—to take the initiative and inform the individual that the transfer has occurred.

The Tax Reform Act of 1976, following the general pattern, doesn't require the IRS to give the taxpayer notice of when information in his tax return is transferred to another agency. But, fortunately for the taxpayer, the rules on when such information can be disclosed are somewhat tougher. If a government agency conducting an investigation *unrelated* to tax liability wants to obtain a copy of the taxpayer's income-tax return, the agency must get a court order. But this protection for the taxpayer is weakened considerably by the fact that he would not necessarily be informed of the court proceeding. The debate in front of the federal judge over the confidentiality of the individual's tax return is likely to be conducted solely by the IRS and the other agency seeking the records.

The IRS is also allowed to disclose other income-tax information *without* a court order. This exception applies if the information came from some third-party source and was not taxpayer-return information. The Privacy Commission was critical of this exception, claiming that in many cases the information the IRS could disclose was information that the taxpayer "has no choice but to have that other party maintain, such as bank and credit card records." It is not normally "independent" information, the Commission argued, but information from "a surrogate without whom the taxpayer could not participate in contemporary society." Somewhat surprisingly, criticism has come at the IRS from the opposite angle. Senator Sam Nunn (D-Ga.) has been leading a fight in Congress to weaken the restrictions on IRS disclosure to other agencies. Nunn and others claim that the IRS has, in effect, bought the argument of the Privacy Commission and is withholding information from other agencies about taxpayers that it digs up on its own. The memories of these latter critics seems to go back to the days when the IRS could be enlisted in the fight against an Al Capone or a Frank Costello. But one wonders whether they may have not have forgotten the more recent days when the IRS was drafted into the not-so-glorious fight against the White House enemies list.

Computer Matches

Rather than attempting to organize and conduct a face-to-face mass registration, Selective Service could rely on existing computerized lists to form a registration data base. For example, it appears technically feasible to merge Social Security and IRS taxpayer files to produce a current address list for up to 85 percent of all 20-year-old males. The Social Security Administration and Internal Revenue Service already have a major tape exchange program in effect, and they estimate it would take about three to five days to merge the files to obtain a registrant list with the necessary personal data, such as birthdate and sex, from the Social Security Administration and current addresses from IRS.

"The Selective Service System:
Mobilization Capabilities and Options
for Improvement,"
Congressional Budget Office (1978)

When President Carter signed the legislation on July 2, 1980, restoring draft registration, he needn't have bothered. The information he wanted was stored in government computers and could have been available within a few days if the computers were properly programmed. The list of draft-eligible males didn't appear in any compilation of files, any "system of records," any list of "personal identifiers," or anywhere else. Officially, it didn't exist. But as a practical matter, it was available to government officials almost as if it had been stored in a cabinet in the White House basement.

The IRS has a list of all taxpayers. But it has no official list of all taxpayers who are Democrats or Republicans, who traveled outside the U.S. within the last two years, who were exposed to nuclear wastes in their employment, who own automobiles, who received unemployment checks, or who were arrested within the last year. Each of these subgroupings could, however, probably be converted into a "system of records" within a few days, given the information in government files and the processing capabilities of government computers. In precomputer days the absence of a file on a particular subject meant that the information could not be obtained without a laborious cross-referencing of information. Even if the information was somewhere in a government file, it would not be useful unless properly indexed. But now computer programs can be merged and the computers themselves "interfaced." The result of this is new files and new systems. For every actual file, there is a virtually infinite number of potential files that are lying in the computer waiting to be born.

This process of computer intercourse is known as a "match," and the offspring of such a relationship are called "hits." A hit is a name that appears on both lists—someone with the combined characteristics that the government agent is looking for. The Office of Management and Budget issued guidelines on March 30, 1979, that aptly describe matching programs. Although the OMB guidelines purport to regulate all matching programs, they in fact only affect a small part of them. The matching process of computers are far too ingrained in government procedures to be under anyone's control.

The IRS engages in matching programs all the time, but it doesn't call them that. According to Paul Strassels, a former IRS official, the IRS subscribes to certain mailing lists or trade lists of doctors, dentists, pilots, entertainers, independent contractors, and similar groups of targeted professionals and matches that computerized list with its list of taxpayers to generate a potential audit list. It also programs its computers to read out lists of "tax protesters"—anyone who has scribbled a nasty note along with his return—for an audit. The IRS also has a computerized list of tax preparers and accountants that it suspects of improper practices for one reason or another. The list is called the Problem Preparer's List, but through a matching program the IRS turns the preparer's problem into a taxpayer's problem. The computer provides the IRS with a list of all taxpayers who have used such accountants or tax preparers, and such a list becomes the basis for an audit.*

The most thorough use of a computer by the IRS, however, matches taxpayers not against another list of names but against a list of hypothetical characteristics. The program is called Discriminant Functions System or DIF, and a match between taxpayers and DIF produces the prime list of candidates for an IRS audit. Although the DIF measures the taxpayer against a hypothetical person, behind those composite characteristics stand a very real group of 40,000 to 42,000 individuals who have previously been put through the IRS equivalent of the third degree: the Taxpayer Compliance and Measurement Program or TCMP. A TCMP audit is a thing of pure horror for the taxpayer who must go through it. *Every* item on the tax return must be verified: canceled checks for every deduction, deposit slips for every receipt—even a marriage license to prove you are entitled to file a joint return.

The entire process of DIF and TCMP is built up through computer-matched statistics. The computer selects persons to go through the TCMP ordeal by matching them with a statistical profile. Information squeezed out of the TCMP group is then adjusted by the computer for various occupational groups, regional cost-of-living differences, and so on. The composite results form the DIF that is then computer-matched against the returns of other taxpayers.

The IRS is not the only agency in the computer-matching game. The Parent Locator Service within HEW has broad access to IRS files and other government files in order to locate absent parents and enforce child-support orders. The PLS uses its computer capabilities to match the list of people it is looking for against names, addresses, and other information in files maintained by the IRS, Social Security Administration, the Defense Department, and others in their computers. The PLS not only gets names and addresses from the IRS but also picks up financial information that it can use against the individuals.

In California and New York City the welfare departments match their lists with computerized lists of motor vehicle registrations and marriage licenses in order to detect possible welfare fraud. In Michigan the welfare departments match their lists with the lists of employees of

---

* They'll get you going the other way too. The IRS is likely to audit a complex tax return that the taxpayer prepares himself without professional assistance.

automobile manufacturers for the same purpose. The federal Office of Education matches its list of students who have defaulted on loans with the list of federal government employees in the hope that the computer will come up with a few hits that they can lean on for payment.

All of this is done with little fanfare and even less regulation. The prevailing attitude, according to one OMB official, is that "the computer is a part of our lives, so why not use it?" The OMB guidelines have taken aim at the problem, but they have fallen far short of the mark. These guidelines apply only to matching programs *between* federal agencies. They have no effect whatsoever on the continual matching of lists by agencies at the state and local level and no effect on the internal matching and rematching of lists within agencies such as the IRS. Given these limitations, it is not surprising that only a handful of official matching programs have been reported to OMB.

The OMB guidelines are interesting, however, not because of their effectiveness but because of the potential problems they have highlighted. The guidelines have broken matching programs into two categories: antifraud programs and all others. The "all others" category, however, receives almost no attention within the guidelines; any two agencies wishing to undertake a match that doesn't fall into the antifraud category are simply asked to report that fact to OMB without too much detail. OMB officials admit that they haven't given too much thought to restrictions on matching programs other than those in the antifraud category.

Antifraud matches, OMB suggests, should only be undertaken when a "demonstrable financial benefit can be realized which significantly outweighs the costs of the match and any potential harm to individuals." How do you weigh financial benefit to the government against loss of privacy to the individual? You can't, and government officials who have prepared matching programs have admitted as much. Once an agency goes forward with a matching program, it is required to prepare an "analysis of benefits, costs, and potential harm." This analysis—sort of the privacy equivalent of an environmental impact statement—is supposed to answer certain questions about the matching program. How long will the program run? Will it be a one-time match or will it be continuing? Will new hit lists that are generated be compared against old ones? Will the new lists that are generated become themselves a new "system of records" that will be accounted for? Which agencies or outside contractors will conduct the match and how will the new and old tapes be safeguarded? And—perhaps most importantly—will the existence of such a matching program "discourage individuals from exercising their rights"?

Matching programs are the method by which the government generates new information and new lists out of existing computerized files. But, in addition to the official programs, unscrupulous government employees and contractors are in a position to make a few matches of their own. The General Accounting Office has reported at least one instance in which the manager of a computer processing center was able to steal certain data about individuals from computerized government files and sell it to outsiders. Persons with access to computers are not any more dishonest than anyone else, but the computerization of government records has greatly increased the prospects of successful crime by anyone wanting to penetrate the system. According to Richard Thornburgh, former Assistant Attorney General in charge of the Criminal Division, computer crime is a low-visibility proposition: "There are no smoking pistols—no blood-stained victims; often the crime is detected by sheer accident."

Computerization of records has increased the threat to privacy from two directions that are seemingly the direct opposite of each other. Computerization has enhanced the ability of government to develop information about individuals by matching strands of information held in different computer systems. But at the same time it has aided the loner or the saboteur who wants to penetrate the system to either learn what information is in government files or alter that information. Computer crime has been growing at an alarming rate, and law-enforcement officials have found it to be extremely difficult either to catch computer criminals at their task or to obtain a conviction. The computer criminal and the overzealous bureaucrat share the same modus operandi—the ability to sift and sort computerized information from electronic terminals that may be far from the location of the actual file itself. In the hands of either one it is a power with few limitations.

Most attention has been paid to computer crimes that result in embezzlement of funds, but computer crime presents an even greater threat to privacy. If a criminal programs a computer to nibble small amounts out of various bank accounts, he may be able to get by with it for a long period of time before someone notices the discrepancy. But what about a computer programmed to alter records? If certain key words or numbers in a tax return, medical report, or other computerized document are altered, there will be almost no one in a position to detect an alteration. There would normally be no funds missing, no accounts that don't balance—nothing to indicate that a computer criminal has been at work. Government agencies would continue to act on the incorrect information printed out by the computer until someone—probably only the affected individual himself—went back and scrutinized the actual text of the altered document. But catching a computer alteration is easy compared to catching a computer snooper. If the person making an unauthorized access into the computer system simply reads the information (rather than altering it) there is virtually no way that this can be detected. The operation is noiseless, painless, and doesn't leave a trace.

Can this happen? The federal government has made strenuous efforts to try to improve computer security. The IRS in particular was directed by the Tax Reform Act of 1976 to take strict measures to ensure that only authorized persons have access to its records. With 4000 computer terminals nationwide, this would seem to be a major task. Yet if any agency was in a position to guarantee computer security, the IRS should be it. Nevertheless, one year after the Tax Reform Act was enacted the U.S. General Accounting Office had this to say about the security surrounding taxpayer information in the IRS computers:

> Its security safeguards could easily be penetrated—especially by I.R.S. employees and others having access to the facilities. Such individuals could obtain access to tax returns or income tax data on a large, random number of taxpayers with little chance of detection. Employees, depending on the position occupied, could make unauthorized access to tax data on preselected taxpayers. . . .
>
> Computer programmers could easily run an unauthorized program or make an unauthorized program change without detection. Magnetic tapes, each containing tax data on as many as 5000 taxpayers, were not properly controlled and some could not be accounted for. Computer printed products also were not controlled so that I.R.S. could be sure that they were received only by authorized persons.

Low-Profile Strategies

Computers don't discard information, unless they are ordered to. They don't forget it. They amass it. They retain it. And they spew it forth indiscriminately at the touch of a button. Any sort of information, in any quantity, can be flashed from city to city, and from country to country, without the subject knowing anything about it.

Senator Charles Mathias, Jr.

The Privacy Act may not provide much defense against government computers, but in most cases that act is all that the individual has to work with. Short of keeping information out of government files, the next best thing is to use the Privacy Act as best you can to find out what's in them.

- Read the notices on government forms. The federal government is required to list the principal purpose and any routine uses on forms seeking any personal information. If the form doesn't have it, ask to see the circular or regulation that the agency is required to publish. Usually these are stated in general terms, but occasionally they will say something useful. Most importantly, such notices will often indicate that some of the requested information is only "voluntary" and doesn't have to be given to the agency.
- Write in language limiting further disclosures. Occasionally an agency will restrict further disclosure of information if the individual requests it. The Interstate Commerce Commission, for example, will restrict disclosure from its complaint file if the complainant wishes "to remain anonymous." The California Information Practices Act allows the individual to delete his or her name from agency mailing lists that are presumably open to the public. A request that the agency not divulge your name won't always be honored, but it never hurts to make it.
- A demand for a copy of records should be made under both the Privacy Act and the Freedom of Information Act. The Privacy Act gives access to records that might otherwise be denied under the FOIA because they involve an "invasion of privacy" of someone—yourself. The FOIA, on the other hand, allows for fewer technical exemptions based on the way the records are indexed, information from confidential sources, and the like. Together they may get you what you want.
- A request for records should ask for an accounting of all disclosures that have been made. The agency is supposed to give the individual the name and address of each agency or person to whom a disclosure was made, the date of the disclosure, and the nature and purpose of the disclosure. This accounting won't be given unless the individual

requests it. The agency is not required to keep an accounting of disclosures within the agency, so the list will not be complete.
- Ask for additional information not in the agency's accounting. Theoretically, all disclosures outside the agency should be listed in the agency's accounting for disclosures, but as a practical matter they may not be. It may be necessary to ask for a list of other persons and agencies with whom the agency shares that *type* of record so that further inquiries can be made directly. These would include agencies with which it has a matching program and state, local, and government contractors with whom it shares the information. Ask if the information is computerized or not. The agency is not strictly obligated to provide that information, but a letter of inquiry might produce some useful results.
- Don't give more information than you get. Most agencies will respond to an initial letter by requesting further information for identification purposes. Information provided to an agency in this manner can be used to augment an old file or establish a linkage with a system of records where none existed previously. It might be useful with any information that is provided to specify in writing that the information is for "identification purposes only and is given with the understanding that it will not be maintained in any file or system of records."
- If the agency denies all access to records, try for partial access. Federal agencies may occasionally claim that an entire system of records is exempt in situations where the individual should be allowed access to most of the information. "Investigatory material compiled for law enforcement purposes" is normally exempt from disclosure, but the individual is nevertheless entitled to access if he or she has been "denied any right, privilege or benefit" because of such information. It may take a bit of arguing to convince the agency on the latter point. Similarly, an agency can withhold investigatory material if it would "reveal the identity of a source" who provided the information to the government under a promise of confidentiality. The agency may have to be pressured to reveal the information with the informant's name deleted rather than holding back the whole file. These types of cases, however, may ultimately require the filing of a lawsuit against the agency.
- Get a promise of confidentiality in writing. If you are on the opposite side of the fence and being asked to provide information to the government on someone else, make sure that the promise of confi-

dentiality is in writing. The law only protects express promises of confidentiality for information given after 1974. Also, if there is anything else in the information other than your name by which you could be identified, make sure that the government expressly agrees to withhold that as well.

- Word any correction carefully. An individual has the right to make a correction to any federal government record that is not "accurate, relevant, timely, or complete." But some care should be given to the wording of the correction so that it does not reveal more private information—albeit correct information—than the record that is being changed. There is usually no good reason to provide any more details than you have to. If the agency does not accept your correction, you have the right to have a statement of disagreement placed in the file along with the record, but the government can counter that with its own statement as to why it disagrees with your statement. Sometimes this procedure is a good idea when the agency won't change the record, but you should exercise some caution. The question is whether the uncorrected information in the file will ultimately do more harm than the attention that may be drawn to such information by the presence of such statements.
- Be sure that the corrections reach all copies of the records. If the government agrees to your corrections (or if a court orders it to accept them), the corrections must be made in any subsequent disclosure of the records. But the government does *not* have to go back and correct all copies that may have previously been disclosed. The only solution is to couple your demand for a correction with a demand for an accounting of all disclosures, and then contact each agency on your own to make sure it corrects the record. It's a long, cumbersome process, but in the end there is no substitute for doing it yourself.

POSTSCRIPT

The people of the United States may someday have to thank Mr. Nixon. This expression of gratitude would not be for anything he set out to do or thought he accomplished—it would be for what he did in spite of himself. What he did was give us breathing room.

The machinations and blunderings of the Watergate episode caught the attention of the American public about as dramatically as any event has been able to do. One of the principal themes of this modern morality play was the retribution visited upon those who would invade the privacy of others. Bugging devices, enemies lists, abuse of tax records, and virtually all the techniques that were available to privacy-invaders served as props in this docudrama. And the actors obligingly put them through their paces—demonstrating better than a hundred texts by political prophets just how dangerous our governmental and social institutions can be when they are used to intrude upon personal privacy.

The timing of this drama was fortuitous. It came early enough in the drift toward Big Brotherism to give us the opportunity to reverse the trend if we have the strength and the will to do so. Watergate left behind it a legacy of public concern and a sense among politicians that something must be done. Some things have been done. The Privacy Commission has studied the situation and issued its report. Several congressional committees have done likewise. The CIA, the FBI, and the IRS have all promised to behave, and various charters with provisions that would control arbitrary action by government investigators have been studied and debated. The Administration has proposed legislation, as have all sorts of other people. Some federal laws have been enacted, and many state legislatures have done likewise.

But none of this has been enough. We are in serious danger of wasting the breathing room we have been granted. The legislative and administrative changes that have been made have not gotten to the root of the problem, and respect for personal privacy is not firmly enough ingrained in government procedures to withstand the next wave of public apathy and governmental abuse.

And when the next wave hits it will be far worse. Technology continues to be the ally of the snooper. Future privacy-invaders will not only be more efficient in getting what they want, they will be much better able to cover their tracks. Informational systems used to have built-in limitations; the very bulk of the material maintained in the system imposed practical limitations on what an individual snooper could glean from the files. But the computer is rapidly depriving us of that protection. At the same time we are increasing the personal information in public and private data banks, we are expanding geometrically the accessibility of that information to those who are bent upon misusing it.

The confluence of advancing technology with a recurring round of government immorality could be fatal to personal privacy. If the political system misses this opportunity, it may not get another. Individuals in the meantime must try to protect themselves the best they can and not rely on a night watchman or a couple of reporters to come to their rescue again.

APPENDIX

The following is a list of important federal and state laws on privacy. More complete lists are contained in Appendix 1 of the Privacy Commission Report (*Privacy Law in the States*), in a publication of the National Commission on Confidentiality of Health Records (*Health Records Confidentiality Law in the States*), and in a *Compilation of State and Federal Privacy Laws* prepared by the *Privacy Journal.*

Federal Laws

> *The Privacy Act of 1974* (Public Law 93–579) Title 5 U.S.C. §522a
> *The Fair Credit Reporting Act* (Public Law 91–508) Title 15 U.S.C. §§1681 et seq.
> *The Right to Financial Privacy Act of 1978* (Public Law 95–630) Title 12 U.S.C. §§3401 et seq.
> *The Tax Reform Act of 1976* (Public Law 94–455) Title 26 U.S.C. §7609
> *Family Educational Rights and Privacy Act of 1974* (Public Law 93–380 and 93–568) Title 20 U.S. §1232g.

State Laws

> *Alaska*
> bank records: *Alaska Statutes* §06.30.120
> secret tape recordings: *Alaska Statutes* §11.60.290
> *Arizona*
> credit reports: *Arizona Rev. Statutes* §44–1693(A) (4)
> *Arkansas*
> government data banks: *Arkansas Statutes Ann.* §16–801
> *California*
> bank records: *Government Code* §7460
> credit reports: *Civil Code* §§1785.1 et seq. and §§1786 et seq.

medical records: *Civil Code* §§56 et seq.
secret tape recordings: *Penal Code* §§630 et seq.
government data banks: *Civil Code* §§1798 et seq.

Connecticut
credit reports: *Connecticut General Statutes Ann.* §36–432(b)
Connecticut General Statutes Ann. §4–190

Illinois
medical records: *Illinois Revised Statutes,* ch. 91½, §§801 et seq.

Indiana
government data banks: *Indiana Statutes Ann.* IC 4-1-6-1

Kansas
credit reports: *Kansas Statutes,* §50–720

Maine
credit reports: *Maine Rev. Statutes,* §1311

Maryland
bank records: *Maryland Ann. Code,* art 11, sec 225
credit reports: *Maryland Com. Law Code Ann.,* §14–1201 et seq.

Massachusetts
credit reports: *Mass. Gen. Laws, Ann.,* ch. 93, §50 et seq.
government data banks: *Mass. Gen. Laws, Ann.,* ch. 66A, §§1 et seq.

Michigan
employment records: *Michigan Statutes Ann.,* §§17.62(1) et seq.

Minnesota
government data banks: *Minnesota Statutes Ann.,* §§15.162 et seq.

Montana
credit reports: *Montana Rev. Codes Ann.,* §18–501 et seq.

New Hampshire
credit reports: *N.H. Revised Statutes Ann.,* §359–B:1–21

New Mexico
credit reports: *N. M. Statutes Ann.,* §50-18-1

New York
credit reports: *General Business Law,* §370, 380

Ohio
government data banks: *Ohio Revised Code.,* §§1347.01 et seq.

Pennsylvania
secret tape reordings: 18 *Pa Cons. Statutes Ann.* §5701

Utah
government data banks: *Utah Code Ann.* §63-50-1

Virginia
government data banks: *Va. Code* §§2.1–377 et seq.

SELECTED BIBLIOGRAPHY

Books

American Friends Service Committee. *The Police Threat to Political Liberty.* Philadelphia, Pa.: AFSC, 1979.

Annual Report of the President, First Report. *Federal Personal Data Systems Subject to the Privacy Act of 1974.* Washington, D.C.: U.S. Government Printing Office. Stock No. 041-001-00127-1. 1976.

Annual Report of the President, Second Report. *Federal Personal Data Systems Subject to the Privacy Act of 1974.* Washington, D.C.: U.S. Government Printing Office. Stock No. 041-001-00154-9. 1977.

Annual Report of the President, Third Report. *Federal Personal Data Systems Subject to the Privacy Act of 1974.* Washington, D.C.: U.S. Government Printing Office. Stock No. 041-001-00170-1. 1978.

Annual Report of the President, Fourth Report. *Federal Personal Data Systems Subject to the Privacy Act of 1974.* Washington, D.C.: U.S. Government Printing Office. Stock No. 041-001-00190-5. 1979.

Harris, Louis, and Associates. *The Dimensions of Privacy* (The Harris Poll). Stevens Point, Wis.: Sentry Insurance Company, 1979.

Miller, Arthur R. *The Assault on Privacy.* Ann Arbor, Mich.: University of Michigan Press, 1971.

Murphy, Harry J. *Where's What: Sources of Information for Federal Investigators.* New York: Warner Books, 1979.

O'Toole, George. *The Private Sector.* New York: W. W. Norton & Co., 1978.

Privacy Protection Study Commission. *Personal Privacy in an Information Society.* (The "Privacy Commission Report.") Washington, D.C.: U.S. Government Printing Office. Stock No. 052-003-00395-3. 1977.

Appendices to the Privacy Commission Report:
No. 1. *Privacy Law in the States* (Stock No. 052-003-00421-6)
No. 2. *The Citizen As Taxpayer* (Stock No. 052-003-00422-4)
No. 3. *Employment Records* (Stock No. 052-003-00423-2)
No. 4. *The Privacy Act of 1974: an Assessment.* (Stock No. 052-003-00424-1)
No. 5. *Technology and Privacy* (Stock No. 052-003-00425-9)

SELECTED BIBLIOGRAPHY 247

Report of the Task Force on Private Security. *Private Security.* Washington, D.C.: U.S. Government Printing Office, 1976.
Rowan, Ford. *Technospies.* New York: G. P. Putnam's Sons, 1978.
Schnepper, Jeff A. *Inside IRS.* New York: Stein & Day, 1978.
Schwartz, Herman. *Taps, Bugs, and Fooling the People.* New York: Field Foundation, 1977.
Skousen, Mark. *Mark Skousen's Complete Guide to Financial Privacy.* Alexandria, Va.: Alexandria House, 1979.
Smith, Robert Ellis. *Privacy: How to Protect What's Left of It.* Garden City, N.Y.: Anchor Press/Doubleday, 1979.
Strassels, Paul N. *All You Need to Know about the IRS.* New York: Random House, 1979.
United States House of Representatives Committee on the Judiciary, Subcommittee on courts, civil liberties, and the administration of justice. *Surveillance* (2 vols.) Washington, D.C.: U.S. Government Printing Office, 1975.
United States Senate Committee on the Judiciary, Subcommittee on the Constitution. *Polygraph Control and Civil Liberties Protection Act.* Washington, D.C.: U.S. Government Printing Office. Stock No. 052-070-04772-1. 1978.
Wagner, Charles R. *The CPA and Computer Fraud.* New York: Lexington Books, 1979.
Westin, Alan F., and Stephan Salisbury (eds.). *Individual Rights in the Corporation.* New York: Pantheon Books, 1980.
Westin, Alan F. *Computers, Health Records, and Citizens' Rights.* Washington, D.C.: U.S. Government Printing Office. Stock No. 003-003-01681-1. 1976.
Wheeler, Stanton (ed.). *On Record: Files and Dossiers in American Life.* New Brunswick, N.J.: Transaction Books, 1969.
Whiteside, Thomas. *Computer Capers: Tales of Electronic Thievery, Embezzlement and Fraud.* New York: Thomas Y. Crowell, 1978.
Wise, David. *The American Police State.* New York: Vintage Books/Random House, 1976.

Periodicals

The News Media and the Law, The Reporters' Committee for Freedom of the Press, 1125 - 15th Street, N.W., #403, Washington, D.C. 20005.
Privacy Journal, P.O. Box 8844, Washington, D.C. 20003.
R_x *(Confidentially),* National Commission on the Confidentiality of Health Records, 1211 Connecticut Avenue, N.W. #504, Washington, D.C. 20036.

ACKNOWLEDGMENTS

When you borrow from one person, that's stealing. When you borrow from everyone, that's research.

> Tommy Prothro,
> former football coach

There are many people whose time and help I borrowed. Any list is bound to have a few inadvertent omissions, but some of those that I would like to thank are: John Allen, Burt Beck, Leon Brillant, Congressman John Burton, Arthur Bushkin, Mark Davis, Kevin Faley, Jerome Falk, Jackie Fielding, Robert Geddes, April Gray, Leslie Greenspan, Hon. Paul Halvonik, Mel Honowitz, James Howard, Jeffrey Howard, Professor Edgar A. Jones, Jr., Mike Klipper, Jack Landau, Bruce Lehman, Professor David Linowes, Hal Lipset, Loretta McDonnell, John Metelski, Harold Mortimer, Anna Navarro, Richard Neustad, David Nord, John Olmsted, Neal Petersen, Robert F. Phillips, Mark Rosenbaum, John Shattuck, Natalie Davis Spingarn, and Steve Verdier, and George Zannis.

I want to give a special thanks to Birgitta Garde for her yeomanlike work on the manuscript.

And since I cannot resist a good quote, I would add that I now fully appreciate a statement I heard from Barbara Tuchman a few years ago: "Research is endlessly beguiling, but writing is hard work."

INDEX

Abortions, 78, 160–161
Accountants' workpapers, 128, 135–137, 193
Ackerman, John E., 143
ACLU (*see* American Civil Liberties Union)
Aetna Life and Casualty Company, 92, 106, 109–110
Agnew, Spiro T., 152
Alabama Supreme Court, 166
Albuquerque *Journal* and *Tribune*, 167–168
American Bar Association, Canon of Ethics, 131
American Civil Liberties Union (ACLU), 11, 24, 103, 104, 105
American Friends Service Committee, 201, 202, 203
American Medical Association, 84
American Medical Records Association, 84
American Medical Society on Alcoholism, 71
American Opinion (magazine—John Birch Society), 163–164
American Polygraph Association, 99, 102, 106
American Psychiatric Association, 71
American Psychiatric Society, 84
American Security Council, 107, 203
American Service Bureau, 61, 79
American Telephone and Telegraph (AT&T), 106, 107, 150, 185
  monitoring phone lines, 178–181, 183
Anderson, Jack, 151, 155*n*
Answering machines, 6, 183
"Aptitude" tests, 96–97
Arkansas Information Practices Board, 216

Arrest records, 161–163, 166
Ashley, James, 184
Associated Credit Services, Inc., 43
AT&T (*see* American Telephone and Telegraph)
Attorney General, U.S., 141, 222

Bailey, F. Lee, 115, 116, 131
Bailey, William O., 12*n*, 92
Bank Secrecy Act of 1970, 23–25, 26, 31, 39, 39*n*
Banks, bank records, 11, 14, 18, 19–41, 71, 84, 85, 99, 105, 137, 139, 141–142, 188, 193, 232–233
  and credit cards, 20–21, 22, 30–34, 35, 38, 47
  and government access, 23–30
  record-keeping requirements, 24–25, 26, 31
  and low-profile strategies, 38–41
  and sense of discretion, 22–23
  check truncation, 35
  checking accounts, 20–21, 22, 25, 35, 38–41
  checks, odd-colored, 38–39
  electronic fund transfers, 32, 34–38, 40
  privacy officers, 30
  Swiss banks and accounts, 16, 186–187, 209
Barefoot, J. Kirk, 102, 103
Bayh, Birch, 11, 103, 106, 146
Bell, Alexander Graham, 7
Bell, Griffin, 183
Bellair, Robert R., 212
Bergne, Louis, 142–143
Berkowitz, David, 132

251

INDEX

Bilandic, Michael, 101–102
Bill of Rights, 6–8, 140, 207, 228
Black Panthers, 156
Blewes, Don M., 104
Blue Cross, 75
Blume, Sheila, 71
Boyd, Robert, 151
Bradlee, Ben, 146
Brandeis, Louis, 8, 152, 153
Branzburg, Paul, 155
Branzburg v. Hayes (Supreme Court decision), 156, 157
Brennan, William, 10
Bryant, Bear, 163
Bulletin, The (newspaper, Catholic), 160
Burden of Proof: The Case of Juan Corona (Cray), 132
Bureau of Alcohol, Tobacco and Firearms, 226
Bureau of Customs, 187
Burger, Warren, 140, 191, 193, 196
Burton, John, 141
Butts, Wally, 163
Byrne, Jane, 101–102
Byrne, Matthew, Jr., 77

Caesar, George, 72, 115
Caldwell, Earl, 156
California Attorney General, 145, 202
California Bankers Association, 24
California Confidentiality of Medical Information Act, 85–86
California Department of Justice, 202
California Information Practices Act, 239
California Office of Information Practices, 216
California Public Utilities Commission, 185
California Supreme Court, 184, 207
Cameras, 193
Capone, Al, 233
Carter, President Jimmy; Carter Administration, 11, 12, 13, 84, 85, 146, 233
Cashless society, 34–38
CBS, 157, 166, 167
CCS Communication Control (*see* Counterspy Shop)

Center for National Security Studies, 189
Central Intelligence Agency (CIA), 7, 28, 90, 159, 160, 172, 178, 185, 188–189, 221–222, 242
Charleston (W. Va.) *Gazette* and *Daily Mail*, 151, 162–163
Checks, checking accounts (*see* Banks, bank records)
Chesapeake and Potomac Telephone Company, 184–185
Chilton Corporation, 43
Chotiner, Murray, 228
Church, Frank, 189
Church League of America, 203
CIA (*see* Central Intelligence Agency)
Civil Rights Act, 94n
Civil Service Commission, 230
COINTELPRO (FBI), 46
Commercial use of government records, 224–228
Complete Guide to Financial Privacy (Skousen), 39n
Computer crime, 36–38, 237–238
Computers, 3, 7, 9–10, 15, 91, 107, 152n, 238–239, 243
  and bank records, 21, 22, 33, 34–38
  and government files, 212, 215–216, 225, 227–228
  and low-profile strategies, 238–241
  and prospects of crime, 237
  computer matches, 233–238
  and IRS, 215
  and LEIU, 201
  and mail delivery, 190
  and plucking telephone calls, 182
  and press access to files, 160–161
  credit bureaus, 43–45, 47, 53
  medical records, 52, 53, 67–68
Congressional Budget Office, 233
Constitution, the, 6–7, 191, 193n, 207
  (*See also* Fifth, First and Fourth Amendments)
Consumer reports, investigative, 54–56, 60, 61–62
Coors Brewery, 89–90, 99, 107
Corona, Juan, 132
Corporate programs to protect privacy, 106–112
Costello, Frank, 233
Cotter, William J., 187, 188, 189

INDEX 253

Couch, Lillian; Couch v. United States (Supreme Court decision), 135–136
Counterspy Shop (CCS Communication Control), 172–174, 176–177, 180–181, 208
Countersurveillance equipment and strategies, 172–178
County Seat Digest, San Rafael, California, 117–118
Courts and lawyers, 115–149
  accident cases, 117, 121, 122, 123, 135, 149
  and low-profile strategies, 147–149
  confidential disclosures, 126–132, 133, 148
  commercial exploitation of secrets, 132
  state and federal, 128–129
  contested matters, 120–121
  divorce, 117, 118, 119–120, 149
  "fishing" and "discovery," 122–124
  inheritance, 118
  jurors, 123–124
  privacy suits, 124–126, 127, 165, 166–167
  probate, 118, 120, 149
  public records and disclosure, 115–119
  (See also Search warrants; Subpoenas)
Credit bureaus, 2, 12, 20, 21, 22, 30–31, 32, 43–48, 49, 52, 56–59, 61, 71, 84, 98, 112, 113, 153, 213, 226
  and low-profile strategies, 59–63
  computer confusion, 43–45
  Credit Bureau, Inc. (CBI), 43, 61
  "gatekeepers," 45
  Pocatello, 42
  Rochester, 59
  (See also Fair Credit Reporting Act)
Credit cards, 2, 3, 5, 7, 25, 30–31, 38–41, 233
  authorization services, 32, 33–34
  bank-affiliated, 20–21, 22, 31–34, 38, 47
Credit reports, 7, 11, 13, 14, 18, 20, 42–43, 49, 56, 105, 126, 133
  (See also Investigative bureaus and reports)
Cummins Engine Company, 92, 106, 108, 109, 110

DASH *(see* Database Acquisition for Student Health)
Database Acquisition for Student Health (DASH), 65
Dean, John, 209
Blind Ambition, 228
Death in Canaan, 101
Defamation of character, 165, 170–171
Department of Defense, 218, 219, 231, 235
Department of Health, Education and Welfare (HEW), 7, 65, 98, 215, 219, 230, 235
Department of Housing and Urban Development (HUD), 7, 138, 221
Department of Justice *(see* Justice Department)
Department of Transportation, 213, 219
Des Moines *Register and Tribune,* 155, 166
Detroit *Free Press,* 151
Deukmejian, George, 143–144
Dianetics, 64
Dickinson, William B., 12*n*
"Dimensions of Privacy, The" (Sentry Insurance Company), 3*n*
Direct-mail solicitation, 47–48, 63, 225–228
"Dr. Ware," 222
Donnelly, Reuben H., Corporation, 226
Douglas, William O., 8, 19, 137, 147
Drinan, Robert, 188
Drug Enforcement Administration, 187
Dudman, Richard, 151
Dun & Bradstreet, 52, 54, 56–57
Dymally, Mervyn, 143

Educational records, 13, 14
EFTS *(see* Electronic fund transfers)
Electronic devices, 3, 5–6, 7, 8, 90, 151, 191, 198, 207, 217, 242
  and low-profile strategies, 208–209
  bugs and counterbugs, 172–178
  microphones, 192–193, 208
  pen registers, 186
  (See also Computers; Wiretapping)
Electronic fund transfers, 32, 34–38, 40
Electronic Funds Transfer Act of 1978, 38

INDEX

Employee files, 89–114
 and equal-employment opportunity, 93
 and investigative firms, 97–99, 109, 111, 113
 and low-profile strategies, 112–114
 and polygraphs, 99–106, 111, 112
 corporate programs, 106–112
 disparities and differences, 91–95
 and government regulations, 92–93, 95
 psychological tests, 96–97
 questions asked, 94–95
Equifax, 2, 42, 43, 48, 49, 50, 52–54, 56, 60n, 61, 79, 80, 97, 98
Erikson, Kai T., 74, 84
Ervin, Sam, 101, 105

Factual Service Bureau, 79
Fair Credit Reporting Act of 1970 (FCRA), 13, 14, 47, 54–63, 84, 88
Fair Information Practices Act (California), 202
Falk, Jerome, 145
Family Educational Rights and Privacy Act of 1974 (FERPA), 13, 14
Fannin, Daniel, 218, 231
Farber, Myron; Farber case, 154, 156–157
Fast food chains, 99–100, 112
FBI (*see* Federal Bureau of Investigation)
FCRA (*see* Fair Credit Reporting Act)
Federal Bureau of Investigation (FBI), 7, 15, 16, 17, 19–20, 23, 46, 141, 143, 155n, 160, 178, 180, 185, 187, 188, 189, 191, 202–203, 215, 218–219, 222–224, 242
Federal Communications Commission (FCC), 138
Federal Reserve system, 37, 139
Federal Trade Commission, 52
FERPA (*see* Family Educational Rights and Privacy Act)
Fifth Amendment, 7, 140
Files and dossiers, 2, 7, 33, 43, 48, 49, 52, 68, 80, 84, 108, 109–110, 123–124, 141, 154, 160, 201
 (*See also* Employee; Government)

Financial privacy, 11–12, 232–233
 (*See also* Bank records; Credit bureaus and reports; Right to Financial Privacy Act)
Financial Privacy Act (*see* Right to Financial Privacy Act)
Financial statements, multiple, 40–41
Firestone, Mary, 164
First Amendment, 155, 156, 164, 167, 217–218
Fisher v. United States (Supreme Court decision), 136–137, 145n
FOIA (*see* Freedom of Information Act)
Fonda, Jane, 189
 surveillance by FBI, 19–20, 23, 155n, 160, 223
Ford, Gerald Rudolph, 125
Fortune list of companies, 93, 95, 107
Fourth Amendment, 7, 24–25, 82, 190, 191–200, 207
Freedom of Information Act (FOIA), 159–160, 218–219, 220, 224, 226, 239

Galbraith, John Kenneth, 222, 223
General Accounting Office, 237, 238
General Services Administration, 215
Genetic counseling, 81–82
Gertz v. Welch (Supreme Court decision), 163–164
Gilbertson, Daniel E., 74, 84
Goffman, Erving, 74
Goldwater, Barry, Jr., 12
Government files, 212–241
 and confidential source, 223–224, 240
 and low-profile strategies, 238–241
 commercial use of records, 224–228
 computerized, 215–216, 225, 227–228
 computer matches, 233–238
 count, official and unofficial, 213, 215
 duplication and sharing, 213–216, 218, 228–233, 240
 FBI vagaries, 222–224
 financial, 232–233
 individual access, 212, 214–215, 216–224, 239
  exempt category, 216–217, 220–222, 231, 240

INDEX

meaningless concept, 215, 234
public disclosure, 224
Grand jury, power of, 140–142
Greenspan, Leslie, 216
Grossman, Maurice, 71–72
Grumman Aerospace, 89, 90, 107
Gustafson v. Illinois (Supreme Court decision), 190–191, 192

Half-truth and misinformation, 4–5
Hammarley, John, 154
Handwriting analysis, 2
Hansen, George, 42–43, 58
Hansen, Orval, 42–43
Harley, Hugh, 99
Harris, Louis (Lou); Harris poll, 3–4, 10, 18, 60, 91, 92, 92n, 95, 152, 158, 179
Harvard Law Review, 152
Hawk, Richard E., 132
Hayden, Trudy, 103
Health Care Financing Administration, 77, 80
Health and employment, 80–84
Hearst, Patricia, 115
Henry, Betty, 57, 58
Herald-Tribune, International, 5
Herbert, Anthony, 167
Herbert v. Lando (Supreme Court decision), 150, 167
Herod Agrippa, 147
HEW (*see* Department of Health, Education and Welfare)
Hiss, Alger; Hiss case, 159
Hooper-Holmes bureau, 49, 61, 79
Hoover, J. Edgar, 3, 29
House Committee on Government Operations, 106
House Republican Task Force, 26
HUD (*see* Department of Housing and Urban Development)
Hufstedler, Shirley, 73
Hughes, Howard, 16
Hunt, Howard, 182
Hunter, Harry C., 103–104
Hutchinson, Ronald, 164

IBM (*see* International Business Machines)

ICC (*see* Interstate Commerce Commission)
ICS (*see* International Credit System)
Illinois Mental Health and Developmental Disabilities Confidentiality Act, 85–86
Individual and society, 6, 10, 178
Industrial Foundation of America, 49
INET (*see* Interbank Network for Electronic Transfer)
Information Digest, 203
Information-gathering bureaus, 7
Informational conglomerates, 50–52
Infosystems, 34
Inks and checks, 39n
Inn-Guard, Inc. 49
Inner-Facts, 79
Insurance claims, medical, 74–80, 87–88
  and Gresham's Law, 76
  and group plans, 76–77, 83, 87
  and patient's consent, 78–79, 86, 88
Insurance investigations, 49, 51, 65, 69–70, 73, 79–80, 88, 125, 127, 213
Intelligence agencies (*see* Investigative bureaus; Private security police)
Interbank Network for Electronic Transfer (INET), 32–38
Internal Revenue Code, 137
Internal Revenue Service (IRS), 3, 7, 14, 20, 26–27, 28, 37, 39, 40, 86, 98, 128, 135–137, 138, 139, 185, 186–187, 191, 195, 213, 214, 215, 217, 219, 228, 232–236, 238, 242
  computer matching and audits, 234–235
International Association of Chiefs of Police, 203
International Business Machines (IBM), 92, 106, 107, 108, 109, 110, 112
International Credit System (ICS), 32
International Police Academy, 203
Interstate Commerce Commission (ICC), 7, 138, 239
Investigative bureaus and reports, 2, 48–59, 61, 88, 97–99, 109, 111, 113, 133, 141, 153, 201–202, 213
  computerization, 43–45
  consumer reports, 54–56, 59, 60, 61–62

INDEX

Investigative bureaus and reports (*Cont.*)
  economics of the industry, 51
  fictitious reports, 50–51
  (*See also* Credit bureaus and reports; Equifax)
IRS (*see* Internal Revenue Service)

Javits, Jacob, 84
Jobs (*see* Employee files; Medical records)
John Birch Society, 163–164
Jones, Edgar A., 101
Junk mail (*see* Direct-mail solicitation)
Justice Department, 12, 37, 98, 213, 217, 219, 222, 229, 230

Kahn, Andrew, 91–92, 102
KAKE-TV, 154
Kaplan, Livingston, Goodwin, Berkowitz and Selvin, 144
Kastenmeier, Robert W., 187
Katz v. United States (Supreme Court decision), 192–193
Knight-Ridder bureau, 151
KOB, Station (Albuquerque), 155
Koch, Edward, 12
Kraft, Joseph, 151

Landau, Jack, 150
Lando, Barry, 167
Larkin, Kenneth, 47
Law Enforcement Assistance Administration (LEAA), 162, 201
Law Enforcement Intelligence Unit (LEIU), 3, 200–202
Lawyers (*see* Courts)
LEIU (*see* Law Enforcement Intelligence Unit)
Lewiston (Maine) *Morning Tribune,* 154
Ley, Richard G., 58
Liberty Graphics, 38, 39*n*
Liddy, G. Gordon, 182
Lie detectors (*see* Polygraphs)
Liebholz, Stephen W., 37
Lifshutz, Joseph E., 72, 115
Linowes, David, 12*n*, 21, 30, 107
Lipset, Hal, 177

Loompanics Unlimited, 210
Lord & Taylor's ladies' dressing rooms, 124–125, 207
Los Angeles *Star,* 143
Louisville *Courier Journal,* 155
Low-profile strategies (*see* Strategy of prevention)
Lykken, David, 100

Mail privacy, 186–190
  and classes of mail, 189, 209
  and increasing mechanization, 190
  and low-profile strategies, 209–210
  covers, 186–188, 190, 193, 209
  tapping, 188–189, 198
"Market universes," 227
Marshall v. Barlow (Supreme Court decision), 82–83
Marston, Theodore, 106
Marvin, Lee and Michele, 120*n*
Maryland Court of Appeals, 165–166
Mason, E. J., 136
Masry, Edward, 115, 142, 143–144
Mathias, Charles, 7, 146, 200, 239
Mazzochi, Anthony, 80, 81, 82
McCarthy era, 202
McKinney, Stewart B., 29
Medicaid, 3, 16, 65, 72, 77, 78, 86, 87, 144, 158, 160–161
Medical Datamation, 65
Medical Information Bureau (MIB), 2, 7, 80
Medical insurance claims (*see* Insurance)
Medical records, 11, 13, 49, 55, 64–70, 108, 109, 110, 112, 126, 128, 129, 133, 135, 145–146, 148, 149, 160–161, 213, 221, 238
  and abortions, 78
  and computers, 52, 53, 67–68
  and "defensive medicine," 68–69
  and employment, 80–84, 91, 92
  and insurance, 70
  and legal requirements, 69, 72, 81, 86
  and low-profile strategies, 86–88
  and payment of doctors, 69–70
  and pharmacist, 86
  industrial medicine, 83, 87
  laws and proposals, 84–85
  state laws, 85–86

INDEX

psychiatric, importance of confidentiality, 70–74, 76–77, 85, 87, 122
Medicare, 65, 77, 78, 87, 158
Menninger, Karl, 96
Merit Protective Service, 97, 105
Merritt, James, 20
MIB (see Medical Information Bureau)
Michigan Employee Right to Know Act, 92, 110–111
Miller, Mitchell, 24
Miller, Frederick W., 84
Millstone, James C., 48–49
Minnesota State Crime Bureau, 101
Minnesota Supreme Court, 78, 146–147, 160–161, 200
Misinformation and half-truths, 4–5
Mitre Research Corporation, 182
Monsanto Company, 109, 110
Moore, Sara Jane, 125
Morgan Guaranty Trust, 19, 23
Morgan, Melvin, 42
Mortimer, Harold, 29
Motor vehicle registration, 225, 235

Nashville *Tennessean*, 223
National Association of Chain Drug Stores, 100
National Association of Convenience Stores, 93, 103
National Association of Criminal Defense Lawyers, 143
National Center for Health Statistics, 84
National Commission for the Review of Federal and State Laws Relating to Electronic Surveillance, 199n
National Commission on the Confidentiality of Health Records, 70, 71, 84, 212
National Commission on Electronic Funds Transfer, 36
National Data, 30–31, 32, 33
National Labor Relations Board (NLRB), 138
National Law Journal, 142
National Seminar on Individual Rights in the Corporation, 106
Nazi methods, 144, 146

New York State Controlled Substances Act, 69
New York Times, The, 81, 146, 151, 154, 156–157, 163
New York Times v. Sullivan (Supreme Court decision), 163
Newtonian physics, 15
Nitto v. Credit Bureau of Rochester (New York Supreme Court decision), 59
Nixon, Richard Milhous; Nixon years, 159, 177, 182, 228
 social contribution, 242
 Watergate tapes, 99, 160, 209
Nunn, Sam, 233

Oakland *Tribune,* 164n
Occupational Health Association, 109
Occupational licenses, 168–169
Occupational Safety and Health Administration (OSHA), 80–83
O'Connor, David, 115, 143, 147
Office of Education (federal), 236
Office of Management and Budget (OMB), 216, 234, 236
O'Hanlon Reports, Inc., 48–49, 59, 61, 79
Oil, Chemical and Atomic Workers Union, 80, 81, 83
Old-Boy networks, 201, 202–203
OMB (see Office of Management and Budget)
Omnibus Crime Bill of 1968, 204
On Record: Files and Dossiers in American Life (Erikson and Gilbertson), 84
Onassis, Jackie, 154
Opperman, Donald, 196
Orwell, George: *1984,* 3–4
Orwellian logic, 144–145
OSHA (see Occupational Safety and Health Administration)
O'Toole, George, 172, 179, 201, 202

Pacht, Perry, 144
Pacific Gas & Electric Company, 203
Pacific Telephone Company, 184, 185
Pappas, Paul, 155–156
Parent Locator Service (HEW), 235

Paton, Lori, 188
Peckham, Robert F., 144
Pennington, Joe, 154
Perry's Drug Stores, 93
"Personal Privacy in an Information Society" (Privacy Commission), 12
Personnel Security Corporation, 96, 103
Philadelphia Police Department, 125
Playboy magazine, 102*n*
Police Threat to Political Liberty, The (American Friends Service Committee), 201
Polk, James, 151
Polk, R. L., and Company, 225
Polygraphs, 11, 89, 90, 91–92, 97, 99–106, 111, 112, 114
  bill to outlaw, 103, 106
  incompetent operators, 101
  unreliability, 100–103
  unscrupulous and uncontrollable, 103–105, 114
Postal Service, 186–190, 209
Powell, Lewis, 136, 140–141
Prescreening, 47–48, 52, 226, 227
Press, freedom of, 150–171, 243
  ambiguous position, 150–154, 155, 158
  and low-profile strategies, 169–171
  and public figures, 163–169
  and public records, 158–163
    arrest records, 161–163, 166
  drawing the line, 158–59
  protection of sources, 154–158, 170
  public reaction, 152–153, 158
  (*See also* Zurcher v. Stanford Daily)
Prevention (*see* Strategy)
Preyer, Richardson, 84
Privacy:
  and cover-up (*see* Press, freedom of)
  corporate programs to protect, 106–112
  legislation on, 10–15, 18, 84–86, 92
  right of, 8–9, 13, 152
Privacy Act of 1974, 13, 14, 77, 88, 124, 125, 202, 223, 224, 226, 228, 239
  guide to use, 220
  limitations, 212–220, 228–232
  similar state laws, 214, 216
Privacy Commission (*see* Privacy Protection Study Commission)

Privacy Journal, 18*n*, 49, 102*n*, 189, 215, 227
Privacy of Medical Information Act, 13, 84
Privacy Protection Study Commission, 12–13, 21, 22–23, 34, 36, 37, 42, 43, 45, 50, 57, 79, 92, 98, 106, 107, 133, 141, 142, 224, 225, 229, 230, 232–233, 242
Private papers (*see* Courts and lawyers)
Private Sector, The (O'Toole), 172, 179
Private security agencies, police and guards, 200–208, 243
  powers and responsibilities, 206–207, 211
Privileged communications, 126–132, 145, 148
  (*See also* Subpoenas)
Professional Exchange Service Ltd., 49
Professional Standards Review Organizations, 77
Proxmire, William, 164
PSE (*see* Psychological stress evaluator)
Psychiatric records (*see* Medical)
Psychological information, studies and profiles, 7, 65, 71
Psychological stress evaluator (PSE), 100–101, 103, 106, 111
Public figures, 163–169
  gradations of exposure, 168–169
Public opinion, American, on personal privacy, 3–4, 10, 18, 91, 92, 92*n*, 95
  and freedom of the press, 152–153, 158
  suspicion of wiretapping, 179
Public Records, 158–163

RAND corporation, 206
Rather, Dan, 151
Rehnquist, William, 191, 192
Reporters' Committee for Freedom of the Press, 150, 151, 185
Research West, 203
Reston, James, 146
Retail Clerks Union, 11, 100, 104, 105
Retail Credit Company, 58–59
Retailers Commercial Credit Agency, 58
Ribicoff, Abraham, 84
Rice, Robert, 89

INDEX

Right to Financial Privacy Act of 1978, 11–12, 13, 14, 24, 26, 27, 29–30, 31, 37, 84, 124, 125, 138, 141–142, 228, 232
Rockefeller, Nelson, 179
Rosenbaum, David, 151
Rosenberg spy case, 159–160
Rowan, Ford, 182

Sackler, David, 89–90
Sacramento *Union,* 154
St. Louis *Post-Dispatch,* 151
St. Petersburg *Times,* 166
San Francisco *Chronicle,* 115
San Francisco *Examiner,* 112
Sanders, Lonnie James, 196–197
Santa Clara County Narcotics Bureau, 157
Scanlan's Monthly, 228
School records, 13, 14
Schwartz, Herman, 199
Scientology, 64
Search warrants, 127, 142–147, 183, 188, 189, 190, 193, 210–211
  and exceptions to law, 194–195
  and privileged material, 145–146, 147
  procedures, 197–200
Search with "consent," 194–195, 210
Searches and seizures, 190–200
  and low-profit strategies, 210–211
  automobiles, taxis, 196–197, 210
  luggage, 210
  traffic offenses, 190–191, 195–196, 210
  warrant procedures, 197–200
  without a warrant, 190–191, 194–197, 200
SEC (*see* Securities and Exchange Commission)
Secret Service, 28
Securities and Exchange Commission (SEC), 7, 28, 98, 130, 138
Security police, and guards, private (*see* Private security agencies)
Seigenthaler, John, 222–223
Selective Service, 233
Sentry Insurance Company, 3n, 92
Shakespeare, William: *Twelfth Night,* 163
Shattuck, John, 104

Shelledy, Jay, 154
Sinatra, Frank, 152
Sirica, John, 214
60 Minutes, 157, 167
"Skid Row Stabber," 132
Skousen, Mark, 39n
Small Business Administration (SBA), 138
Smiertka, Alan, 214, 219
Smith, Hedrick, 151
Smith, Howard K., 146
Smith, Robert Ellis, 18n, 102n, 189, 190
Smith v. Maryland (Supreme Court decision), 186, 193–194
Social Security Administration, 233, 235
Socialist Labor Party, 188
Socialist Workers' Party, 160, 188
Society and the individual, 6, 10, 178
Society of Former Special Agents of the FBI, 202–203
"Son of Sam," 132
Southwestern Bell, 184
Spingarn, Natalie Davis, 70, 71
Stanford Daily, 142–143, 144–145, 146–147, 150, 151
Stanford University Medical Center, Psychiatry Clinic, 143
Stark, Fortney H., 23, 26
Steinbeck, John, 189
Stevens, J. P., and Company, 89, 90, 107
Stevens, John Paul, 9–10
Stewart, Potter, 139–140, 146
Stillman, Jeanne M., 81
Stop & Shop Companies, Inc., 34
Store detectives, 124–125, 205–206, 207
Strassels, Paul, 234
Strategy of prevention, 15–17
  banks and credit cards, 38–41
  courts, lawyers and private papers, 147–149
  credit bureaus, 59–63
  employee files, 112–114
  government files and computers, 238–241
  medical records, 86–88
  press exposure, 169–171
  surveillance, 208–211
Stress Reduction Center, 64
Student loans, 236

INDEX

Subpoenas, 127, 132–142, 145, 148–149, 151
  administrative, 138–140
  and tax documents, 135–138
  and toll-call records, 185
  grand jury, 140–142, 147, 185
  issuing, 133–135, 138–140
  John Doe summons, 14, 27–28, 139–140
  traditional and extended use, 133, 136, 138
Supreme Court, U.S., 8–10, 207
  and arrest records, 162–163
  and defamation of character, 165
  and Farber case, 154
  and freedom of the press, 155–156, 159, 167–168
  and mail surveillance, 188, 189
  and public figures, 163–164, 165
  and search and seizure, 190–197
  and Shelledy case, 154
  and subpoena power, 139–141
  and tax documents, 136–138
  and wiretapping, 185–186
Supreme Court decisions:
  Branzburg v. Hayes, 156, 157
  California Bankers Association v. Schultz, 24
  Couch v. United States, 135–136
  Fisher v. United States, 136–137, 145n
  Gertz v. Welch, 163–164
  Gustafson v. Illinois, 190–191, 192
  Herbert v. Lando, 150, 167
  Katz v. United States, 192–193
  Marshall v. Barlow, 82–83
  New York Times v. Sullivan, 163
  Smith v. Maryland, 186, 193–194
  United States v. Bisceglia, 139–140
  United States v. Miller, 22–25, 26
  Whalen v. Roe, 9–10
  Zurcher v. Stanford Daily, 143, 144–145, 146–147, 150, 151, 200
Surveillance, 192–194, 217
  (*See also* Electronic devices; Mail; Private security police; Searches and seizures; Wiretapping)
Swiss banks and accounts, 16, 186–187, 209

Taps, Bugs, and Fooling the People (Schwartz), 199–200

Tarnopol, Nat, 223–224
Task Force on Private Security, 205, 206
Tax documents, 135–138
  (*See also* Internal Revenue Service)
Tax Reform Act of 1976, 13, 14, 24, 26–27, 138, 139, 228, 232, 238
Taxpayer Compliance and Measurement Program, 235
Technospies (Rowan), 182
Telecredit, Inc., 38
Telephones, 7, 150, 151
  and electronic bugs, 174–175
  (*See also* Wiretapping)
Telescopes, 193, 193n
Television, 153
  closed-circuit, 2, 7, 97, 124, 205
Telident, 49
Tennessen, Robert J., 12n
Textile Workers Union, 90
Thornburgh, Richard, 237
Topeka *Daily Capital,* 151
Trans Union Systems, 43
Treasury Department, 11, 23, 24, 25, 39, 141, 215, 230
TRW Credit Data, 43, 46, 56, 61, 106, 107
Twin Falls *Times-News,* 155

United Electrical Workers, 99, 104
United States Circuit Court of Appeals, 186–187
United States Court of Appeals, San Francisco, 144
United States v. Bisceglia (Supreme Court decision), 139–140
United States v. Leonard (Circuit Court), 186, 187
United States v. Miller (Supreme Court decision), 23–25, 26
U.S. census, 226
U.S. National Security Agency, 181–182

Validata, 33
Veterans Administration, 20
Voice stress analyzers, 1–2, 100, 101, 173–174
Voiceprints, 7, 182

INDEX

Wackenhut Corporation, 203
Walker, Edwin, 163
Wall Street Journal, 63
Wallace, Mike, 167
Ware, Willis H., 12*n*
Warren, Earl, 19, 192
Warren, Samuel D., 152
Washington *Post,* 101, 146
Washington *Star,* 151, 165
Watergate, 99, 146, 154, 155*n*, 160, 173, 182, 189, 191, 209, 214, 228, 242–243
Welch, Robert, 163–164
Welfare departments, 235–236
Westin, Alan F., 3*n*, 74, 93, 107, 110
Whalen v. Roe (Supreme Court decision), 9–10
White, Byron, 136–137, 144–145, 156, 167
White House enemies list, 233, 242
Wilson, Louis D., 37
Wilson, Phillip and Elsa, 117
Winn, William H., 100
Wiretapping, 172, 178–186, 190, 191, 223–224
  and federal law, 185
  and low-profile strategies, 208–209
  and major crimes, 199–200
  and microwave interception, 181–182, 190
  and Supreme Court, 185–186
  and warrants, 198, 199, 200
  by consent, 182–183
  by phone companies, 178–181, 183–185
    Phone Phreaks, 179–180
  by police, 184–185
  techniques, 179–181, 192
  toll-call records, 185–186, 188, 193
WJAR-TV (Providence, R.I.), 143
Wolston, Ilya, 164
Wood, Glen, 30–31, 32, 34
Wood v. Holiday Inns (U.S. Circuit Court), 30–31
Woodward and Bernstein, 154
WSB-TV, 162

Zenger, Peter, 153
Zimmer, George, 126
Zurcher, James, 142
Zurcher v. Stanford Daily (Supreme Court decision), 143, 144–145, 146–147, 150, 151, 200

JC
596.2
.U5
P47

JC
596.2
.U5
P47